Ferrari
308, 328 and 348

The Complete Story

Robert Foskett

THE CROWOOD PRESS

First published in 2015 by
The Crowood Press Ltd
Ramsbury, Marlborough
Wiltshire SN8 2HR

www.crowood.com

© Robert Foskett 2015

All rights reserved. No part of this publication may be reproduced or transmitted in any form or by any means, electronic or mechanical, including photocopy, recording, or any information storage and retrieval system, without permission in writing from the publishers.

British Library Cataloguing-in-Publication Data
A catalogue record for this book is available from the British Library.

ISBN 978 1 84797 885 1

Typeset and designed by Shane O'Dwyer,
Swindon, Wiltshire

Printed and bound in India by Replika Press Pvt Ltd

ACKNOWLEDGEMENTS

My thanks go to everyone who has assisted in the production of this book: the many Ferrari enthusiasts who have been so generous with their time and their knowledge, and not least for their agreement to allow me to publish their superb photographs. In particular I must express my appreciation to those who extended courtesy and hospitality as they took time to educate me about their own specialist subjects, and for their invaluable knowledge, so freely shared. I must thank in particular Tony Worswick, Andy Garrett, Bryan Sherwin and Richard Davis.

My appreciation goes also to Paul Gough for his unflinching efforts in cleansing the text of so many errors, and to John Dickens, for invaluable editorial input, super photographic content, and his eloquent owner's insight. Grateful thanks to Letizia Benzi, for her kind assistance in securing support from Italian sources. Thank you to my family and friends for their support, especially those press-ganged into interminable visits to Italian car events at showery Brooklands or windswept Silverstone: I am most grateful for your encouragement and tolerance! And of course to my children Olivia and Joseph, who offer inspiration and encouragement in everything I do.

Hot Wheels and associated trademarks and trade dress are owned by, and used under license from Mattel, Inc. © 2013 Mattel, Inc. All Rights Reserved. Mattel makes no representation as to the authenticity of the materials contained herein. All opinions are those of the author and not of Mattel.

All Hot Wheels images and art are owned by Mattel, Inc. © 2013 Mattel, Inc. All Rights Reserved.

CONTENTS

	Introduction	5
CHAPTER 1	A BRIEF HISTORY OF FERRARI	9
CHAPTER 2	THE MID-ENGINE REVOLUTION	13
CHAPTER 3	THE 308GT4	25
CHAPTER 4	THE 308GTB AND 308GTS	43
CHAPTER 5	THE FUEL-INJECTED 308	63
CHAPTER 6	THE 2-LITRE AND TURBOCHARGED RELATIVES	75
CHAPTER 7	THE 4-VALVES	88
CHAPTER 8	THE 348	109
CHAPTER 9	SUCCESSORS	135
CHAPTER 10	MARKETING AND SALES	142
CHAPTER 11	ON TRACK	150
CHAPTER 12	ACCESSORIES AND MODIFICATIONS	165
CHAPTER 13	BUYING AND OWNERSHIP	179
	Index	191

INTRODUCTION

More words must have been written about legendary Italian sports- and race-car constructor Ferrari than any other maker – indeed perhaps more than every other marque combined. Enthusiasts voraciously devour information about the capable, beautiful, exceptional cars that hail from that tiny factory in Maranello, many hoarding anything and everything related to the marque, absorbing every fact and any rumour or myth, better to understand the object of their affection – and sometimes their obsession. Even sports-car fans who proclaim indifference to Maranello's mystique can usually be made, grudgingly, to accept that Ferraris are far from ordinary, and are certainly worthy of respect.

Part of the reason for holding Ferrari in this elevated level of esteem must be the near-legendary history of the marque. It was created by upstart race driver and ex-racing team manager Enzo Ferrari who, having learned his craft at dominant Alfa Romeo, turned against them in the area of Grand Prix racing, eventually to best his former employer with cars bearing his own name. And the iconic drivers who raced Ferrari's wonderful machines sometimes gloried in their superiority, as others laboured heroically to overcome inferior – yet usually still magnificent – machinery their creator would never accept could possibly be second best on the track. Even today, Ferrari cultivates mystery, giving little away about who or what or why

OPPOSITE PAGE:
328GTS.
PAWEŁ SKRZYPCZYŃSKI

THIS PAGE:
Three generations of Ferrari's two-seat V8s at Brooklands Museum.
JOHN DICKENS

INTRODUCTION

308GT4: note the driving lamps hidden beneath the car's front grille.

with respect to the design and development of their cars or their racing: strategic decisions and exceptional deeds were shrouded in intrigue and secrecy worthy of a cold-war thriller.

The road cars draw by association glamour and a hint of mystery, each a desirable piece of mobile sculpture, sometimes outlandish, sometimes classical, but always impressive. No wonder drivers of Ferraris soon discover that their cars can cause a minor sensation, strangers striking up spontaneous conversations, asking for photographs, or even to sit and dream in the driver's seat. This is no surprise: each new model Ferrari in turn represents to many enthusiasts the pinnacle of sports car design and engineering, and the relative rarity imposed by the process of careful, labour-intensive construction, and as an outcome the elevated price tag, serves only to reinforce the cars' desirability. No wonder that attaining ownership represents for many the ultimate dream, a symbol of achievement, of taste, of success.

Happily, older Ferrari models in general buck the typical automotive trends as they age by remaining eminently desirable. They usually assume instant classic car status, rather than falling into the inevitable unpopularity of more mainstream motors, enthusiasts appreciating them with the gusto – and often the florid language – of art lovers. Designs are soon considered influential, even iconic, and while the cars fall short of the outright pace of their modern equivalents, they remain exciting to drive, challenging and rewarding, each a true thoroughbred despite its advanced years.

So while older Ferraris are still fully capable of attracting an audience and fulfilling an owner's enthusiasm, happily many models can be had for a fraction of the cost of a brand new equivalent. If chosen carefully, they can be surprisingly cost effective to own and run. The subjects of this book, the earliest series of V8 sports cars, are some of the best examples of just such Ferrari models. Quite affordable – in comparison to other Ferrari models, at least – yet eminently capable of delivering all the fun that the best of Maranello's models can offer, today they are attainable Ferraris, a dream that can be achieved without breaking the bank.

The families of cars in this book differ in their aesthetics, in their role, and in their level of performance, and while outwardly there is little to link the earliest Dino 308GT4 with the final 348, nevertheless they share many similarities – not least the V8 engine, recognizably the same basic design, albeit having benefitted from continuous evolution. But just as important is a characteristic that connects the tube-framed cars with the semi-monocoque models: that of a relatively

INTRODUCTION

ABOVE: **1989 328GTS.**
STEVE BAMBER

RIGHT: **Inviting 348ts interior.**

INTRODUCTION

non-technical approach to their design and construction – an approach that eschews active suspension or advanced aerodynamics, that avoids 5-valve heads or complex electro-hydraulic gearbox technology, even power steering – a design ethos that embraces relative simplicity.

This is the key that defines the experience of ownership of all these cars, from the 308, through its 328 evolution and on to the polished 348. Each model is capable of being understood, maintained and repaired by a technically literate motor enthusiast, and without the backing of a substantial bank balance. There is no magic in the engineering, and whether an owner chooses to dirty their hands or not, that simplicity permeates other aspects of ownership. It is a characteristic that shines through not only in the workshop, but also on the road, giving an 'analogue' driving experience, a simplicity that connects the driver with the engineering, and if mastered, allows the driver really to feel 'at one' with their car.

So here are four models that share so much, but are visually so distinct: first the GT4 with its curiously dated edginess, courtesy of space-age specialists Bertone, which after a period in the desirability doldrums has more recently been reappraised as a masterclass in 1970 modernism. Then the classically elegant 308 by Pininfarina, with its instantly familiar sculptural styling and often cited as the most beautiful Ferrari ever. Its successor, the 328, is a 308 'plus', with more performance, more refinement, more dependability and more usability. Finally the 348, an efficient, competent Ferrari that could be used every day, blending all the benefits of Fiat Group influence in construction with even greater performance than any previous small Ferrari.

As different as they are, many characteristics bring these four together: each is a desirable ownership prospect, affordable to buy and relatively straightforward to maintain, courtesy of that unsophisticated engineering. All of them are capable of dynamic excitement of the highest order, whether on road or track, and eminently capable of satisfying even the most demanding performance driver. This is a fabulous selection of cars, each model absolutely a true Ferrari: the 308, 328 and 348.

308GTB Quattrovalvole.
JOHN DICKENS

CHAPTER ONE

A BRIEF HISTORY OF FERRARI

Scuderia Ferrari came into existence on 1 December 1929, to operate as Alfa Romeo's factory-sanctioned racing team. This small but highly professional ensemble was entrusted with the honour of preparing Alfa Romeo's P2 Grand Prix cars and a selection of 6C cars, in 1500 and 1750cc guises. It was also perfectly placed as the trusted factory partner to race prepare Alfa Romeos for wealthy private clients. In those early days, Enzo Ferrari quite literally lived over the shop, his race-preparation premises featuring an upper floor with a large balcony, where he set up home with his wife Laura.

The birth of his son Alfredo in 1932 was a momentous occasion, an event that would impact profoundly on the future of this ambitious racing driver, and would have equally dramatic repercussions on the factory that bore his name. New-found responsibility for his beloved son Alfredo – nicknamed Alfredino, thereafter often shortened to Dino – caused Ferrari to retire completely from the dangers of his now sporadic competition driving assignments, and to focus instead, with absolute intensity, on the management of his Modena-based fledgling racing stable.

Having himself been a racer, first for minor Italian manufacturer, CMN, then from 1920 with his beloved Alfa Romeo, Enzo Ferrari had learned how to motivate and manipulate the racing drivers in his team. But his influence extended far beyond driver coaching: Ferrari had a valuable knack for enticing the most capable people to collaborate with him – for example, while at Alfa Romeo, he had persuaded legendary engineer, Vittorio Jano, to defect from Lancia, a managerial feat rewarded richly with the many successes accrued by the dominant Alfa Romeo P2 Grand Prix car that Jano went on to create. Success followed success as Ferrari managed Alfa Romeo's factory team: wins in Grands Prix, on the arduous Mille Miglia and breakneck Targa Florio races made the 'cavallino rampante' ('prancing horse') emblem synonymous with Alfa Romeo's victorious racers.

But with war looming again, Alfa Romeo decided to bring their racing efforts in-house, and Ferrari soon found his new

The iconic Ferrari script, barely altered since 1946.
JOHN DICKENS

■ A BRIEF HISTORY OF FERRARI

appointment as Director of Alfa Corse constricting. In 1939 he left Alfa Romeo to retake control of his own destiny, famously explaining 'I'm keeping my bad habits and going back to my home town' as he returned from bustling Milan to Modena, determined to make a new start.

Despite his new-found independence, Ferrari was not free in every sense, in that his settlement with Alfa Romeo prevented the eponymous naming of any cars he might devise for a period of four years. Even so, his automotive creativity would not be denied, and within a few months he had created a new car, and named it the Auto Avio Costruzione 815. Pragmatically constructed, the touring-bodied 815 was based on a cleverly re-engineered Fiat chassis powered by a 1.5-litre straight-8 motor, imaginatively borne out of a pair of recycled Fiat 4-cylinder engines. However, development of this promising new car was curtailed as World War II broke out: Allied

From small beginnings: Ferrari's first solo foray into sports-car construction, the Auto Avio.
JONATHAN TREMLETT

Ferrari 166 Inter. Ferrari's first road and race cars powered by the V12 engine design. Initially of 1.5 litres, capacity was soon increased to 2.0 litres, making sense of this model's designation.
JONATHAN TREMLETT

bombing raids motivated a move to Maranello – a sleepy village that was home to just 600 people – and Ferrari's factory then spent the hostilities engaged in building aeroplane engines and engineering equipment. Ferrari's facilities by no means survived the war unscathed: his new factory was bombed twice before Italy surrendered to the Allies, but it remained viable and operational as hostilities concluded.

The First Ferraris

Business soon flourished as Italy set to the task of rebuilding itself. Ferrari's machine tools were much in demand, but thoughts of racing cars never left Ferrari's fertile imagination. Alfa Romeo's edict preventing Ferrari from fielding racers bearing his own name had expired as war raged, and now Scuderia Ferrari could be reborn: this time the cars that this famous stable would use to compete on the world's stage would be unambiguously badged as Ferraris. Lofty ambition meant that this time, recycled Fiat components were unfitting, and Ferrari's post-war efforts would be centred on a brand new engine, created by ex-Alfa Romeo engineer, Gioacchino Colombo. A V12, no less, would be installed in the first true Ferrari racer, the 1500cc 125 of 1947, a magnificent little machine that would prove victorious in only its second race.

Ferrari's upstart would go on to win seven of the fourteen races in which it was entered that year, and the following year the engine received a stretch to 2000cc to power Ferrari's evolution racer, the 166. This car won the Mille Miglia in 1948, and the following year grabbed the international limelight for the fledgling manufacturer by winning both Le Mans and Spa 24-hour races, astonishing successes at the highest sporting level for a marque barely two years old. The Scuderia's first victory in Formula 1 arrived the following year, as Gonzales took the chequered flag at the British Grand Prix.

Road Cars

While the factory racers aspired to victory at the highest level, so ambitions grew for the road-going models Enzo Ferrari often suggested existed only to fund his team's racetrack endeavours. Hand built in tiny volumes, the 166 and its successor the 195 would barely reach a production run of sixty cars in four years, but they whetted the appetite of the resurgent sports-car market for further Ferraris. Factory output doubled with the introduction of the 212 Inter, with eighty made in two years, but it would not be until 1955, with the introduction of the 250 Europa GT, that Ferrari at last would make road cars in meaningful numbers. While by no means mass produced, the Pininfarina-styled coupé could finally be offered to more discerning customers, and Ferrari's reputation as the purveyor of performance cars for the road would approach that of the racing team.

One of the most beautiful of Pininfarina's collaborations with Ferrari, the 250GT Lusso.
STEFAN KOSCHMINDER

■ A BRIEF HISTORY OF FERRARI

This early collaboration with Pininfarina would be the start of a long and fruitful partnership, as the famous carrozzeria gradually came to dominate road-car design at Maranello for almost two decades. The image-building 250 models would continue into the early 1960s, variations of essentially the same elements – engines, chassis and even bodywork – being adapted with success to both road and competition use. Many of the most famous Maranello racers could be ordered in street trim: the 250GT SWB (short-wheelbase) could be had with either lightweight aluminium alloy bodywork for the track or more durable steel for the rigours of road use. A selection of power outputs was also available for its 3-litre V12 motor.

As the early 1960s progressed it became clear that road-based race cars could no longer dominate on track, and more specialized machinery would be required if Ferrari were to continue to compete at the uppermost level, certainly in sports-car racing at such illustrious venues as Le Mans or Daytona. And so Ferrari's road cars began to diverge from their competition-focused stablemates. Fast, comfortable, front-engined grand tourers became the order of the day, built in ever greater numbers – by 1965 the factory was producing 600 cars each year. Maranello's road cars may still have shared a factory, a name and an evocative emblem with the Scuderia's racers, but they now had relatively little in common with the mid-engined projectiles the competitions division fielded in the pursuit of glory. But the link between race and road car was not permanently broken: as the 1970s drew near, so road car designers, eager to provide enthusiast drivers with the most dynamic performance possible, began to look to the track for fresh mechanical inspiration.

FERRARI NUMBERING – DECIPHERING THE DIGITS

With a handful of exceptions, including the Lancia-derived Grand Prix designs campaigned between 1955 and 1957, few of Ferrari's cars – either competition or road-going models – have been formally named, most being referred to by model number only. While some of the numbers selected as designations may appear random, they are generally descriptive and decipherable.

In the early days cars tended to be numbered in recognition of the cubic centimetre capacity of a single cylinder: a 250GT V12 motor therefore of 3 litres total capacity, and a 500 Testa Rossa from 1956 featuring a 4-cylinder 2-litre motor. From 1957, with the arrival of the Dino Formula Two racer, a new numbering scheme would come into effect, whereby the capacity of the engine in litres would prefix a number representing the count of its cylinders. So the 246 F1 Grand Prix car used by Mike Hawthorn to win the World Driver's Championship in 1958 was propelled by a 2.4-litre V6 unit.

Confusingly, both numbering schemes ran in parallel for some time, the latter gradually gaining favour through the 1960s and 1970s. In 1981, with the turbocharged 126 Formula 1 racer, the competition cars abandoned the traditional numbering convention for good. Through the course of this decade, some of the road cars began to acquire names rather than numbers: Mondial and Testarossa were two early

Three-point 2 litres and 8 cylinders, indicated by Ferrari's descriptive numbering scheme.
PAWEŁ SKRZYPCZYŃSKI

examples, and the F40 was christened in celebration of the fortieth anniversary of the company's foundation.

More recently, numbering has become less standardized. Both 360 Modena and F430 model designations explain their respective 3.6- and 4.3-litre capacities but not cylinder count, while the earlier F355 was more meaningfully – if not consistently – numbered in recognition both of a 3.5-litre capacity and in the number of valves per cylinder its motor design featured. And the recent 612 Scaglietti may be a 12-cylinder car, but its capacity is 5.7 rather than 6 litres.

CHAPTER TWO

THE MID-ENGINE REVOLUTION

Ferrari was by no means the only iconic motor-racing constructor to write the opening chapter of its legend in 1946. In the same year that Colombo was hard at work creating Ferrari's magnificent V12 engine, a small garage in Surbiton, Surrey, became the somewhat unlikely base from which Charles Cooper and his son John began work on a diminutive racing car, its small size belying its importance in terms of the future of Grand Prix racing. Cooper's tiny 500cc JAP motorcycle-engined racer was mid-engined.

Mounting the powerplant behind the driver was certainly not a new idea: Porsche had chosen this layout for the mighty Nazi-backed AutoUnion Grand Prix cars of the 1930s, but it was a tricky layout to make work well with primitive tyres and unsophisticated suspension. Nevertheless, Cooper found a way to make it work, and work beautifully, in a series of successful Formula 3 and Formula 2 racers, as the concept of small racing cars featuring mid-mounted engines became synonymous with Cooper Cars. And when the same formula was tried in a Grand Prix racer, the results were startling.

Winning two races in 1958 against resolutely front-engined competition, Cooper proved the concept was viable in the modern era, and in the following year, Jack Brabham would become the first Formula 1 World Champion to win the title driving a mid-engined Grand Prix car. The far-sighted team

Ferrari's future, as imagined by Marcello Gandini.
BERTONE HISTORICAL ARCHIVE

■ THE MID-ENGINE REVOLUTION

1958 Ferrari Dino 246 Grand Prix car.
SIMON HODSON

proved that the feat was no fluke when they repeated their successes the following year. But not everyone was enamoured of the mid-engined revolution: Enzo Ferrari disliked the concept and shunned Cooper's lead wholeheartedly until 1961. By then it was inevitable that all teams would emulate Cooper's efficient concept, and since 1959, every Formula 1 World Champion has preceded his engine across the finish line.

Conveniently, the Scuderia's scramble to emulate Cooper's racers was greatly simplified by the ready availability of a compact motor design ideal for the mid-engined template. Ferrari's Grand Prix cars had been powered by the dependable V6 Dino engine since the retirement at the end of 1957 of the Lancia-Ferrari D50s, entrusted to Ferrari by Lancia's race team on their withdrawal from competition. The Dino engine, and the cars into which it would be installed, were named in honour of Ferrari's son who had died in 1956, a tribute that would continue in the naming of every V6-powered Ferrari until the advent in the 1980s of new, turbocharged Grand Prix engines of the same configuration.

Dino Ferrari was said to have participated in design work for the engine alongside Ferrari engineering stalwarts Massimino and Jano, the three collaborating to devise an engine bound at first for Formula 2 racing, but with the potential to be developed into a whole dynasty of smaller capacity Ferrari motors. The Dino motor would soon see service in Formula cars, sports racers and even an extended family of road cars, the first iteration ready for use in a 1957 Formula 2 Ferrari. This much admired motor would subsequently serve to excellent effect in the Scuderia's Grand Prix racers from 1958 to 1963, initially installed ahead of the driver, though later switched to a modern mid-mounted location. The motor saw mid-mounted service in numerous Ferrari sports racers, including the 1962 Dino 246SP and the smaller, 2-litre capacity 196SP.

Often overshadowed by the larger sports cars of the day, including Ferrari's own 330P3, the Dino racers were nevertheless highly successful in competition, particularly at circuit events such as the Monza 1,000km, on the roads that comprised the Targa Florio route, and even in international hill-climbing events.

By the mid-1960s, the mid-engined revolution was in full effect at Ferrari. Not only were the Grand Prix cars now by default constructed in this layout, the Scuderia's big sports racers were also cast in the same mould. The Testarossa was replaced in 1963 by the accomplished 250P, a 3-litre V12-powered prototype, which won at Le Mans and twice more to take three out of four of that season's world sports-car races. The cars fielded in the GT racing class soon followed suit, though not without some delays in homologation caused by the 250GT LM's lack of similarity to the 250GT on which it was supposedly based – rather the mid-engined GT was far closer in design to the dominant 250P. Later cars featured a bigger 3.3-litre engine, the 275 LM in 1965 giving Ferrari their most recent Le Mans win to date. In lesser race series, Dino lineage continued through 1965, with 1.6- and 2-litre models, the 166P and 206P followed by the 206S, all of them sharing similarity in appearance – if not in specific line or detailing – to the Dino road cars already in development at Maranello.

A Race Car for the Road

The Lamborghini Miura

While Ferrari presented race cars and concepts featuring mid-mounted motors, rival manufacturer Lamborghini determined to raise the stakes on the road. At Turin in 1965, Ferrari's rival presented a nearly production-ready bare chassis of such ambition that all current high-performance road cars were instantly rendered obsolete. The Miura's monocoque substructure, designed by Gianpaolo Dallara and Paolo Stanzani, proudly carried its engine behind the cockpit: the lengthy but narrow transverse-mounted 4-litre V12 nestled hard against the bulkhead, enabling Lamborghini to package a 1,090mm (42.9in) long motor within a compact 2,504mm (98.6in) wheelbase.

Its installation was beautifully conceived: the gearbox sat beneath the motor, and validating Issigoni's innovative packaging for the Austin Mini, the engine and gearbox shared oil.

THE GRAND PRIX DINO

Ferrari first began experimenting with a mid-engined layout for the Grand Prix cars during the 1960 season, when a prototype 246 Dino appeared alongside conventional front-engined racers at Monaco that year. The mid-engined Ferrari was immediately on the pace, finishing a creditable sixth on its first outing. Nevertheless, the team chose to focus their efforts on the front-engined cars for the remainder of the season, and work to develop the mid-engined Grand Prix concept would instead centre on a new design aligned with the incoming 1961 season's 1.5-litre formula.

Ferrari's beautiful 156 Dino, often referred to as 'Sharknose' in reference to distinctive twin-nostril air intakes feeding the front-mounted radiator, would represent Ferrari in the World Championship throughout 1961. Meeting new regulations, a new engine design of 1.5-litre capacity was fitted. As with previous Dino Grand Prix cars, it was a V6, heavily based on the preceding 246 Dino motor. Curiously, two versions of the motor were produced for use in the 156, each featuring a different V angle: some cars raced with a 65-degree variant, others were propelled by a 120-degree low-line version. The 156 Dino achieved fame as the car that Phil Hill piloted to the Formula 1 World Driver's Championship in 1961, and notoriety in the same year, as the car in which Wolfgang von Tripps crashed and perished at Monza, killing fourteen spectators in a horrific accident.

Despite the tragedy of Von Tripps' death, tolerated at the time as an inevitable, almost intrinsic feature of motor racing, Ferrari should have been ready to follow up the

Chris Rea in a 156 'Sharknose' Grand Prix car, Goodwood Festival of Speed 1995.
ANTHONY FOSH

World Championship with repeat success in 1962. But it was not to be. Following a dispute that saw many of Ferrari's most senior managers leave the team, the Scuderia suffered perhaps their most disastrous racing year of all time, withdrawing before the end of the season. Nevertheless, they regrouped around a new car design for 1963. Though different in many details, with a new simple oval radiator intake, six-speed gearbox and revised body, the 156 was still recognizably a descendant of the successful 1961 car, even wearing the same wire-spoked wheels – the last Grand Prix Ferrari to do so. Results were similarly reminiscent of the earlier cars, the revitalized Dino delivering wins for John Surtees in a successful, if not World Driver's Championship-winning season.

An early Ferrari attempt at a mid-engined sports car, the 250GT LM.
JULIAN BOWDIDGE

■ THE MID-ENGINE REVOLUTION

Lamborghini's groundbreaking, beautiful Miura, first of the mid-engined road-going supercars.
JONATHAN TREMLETT

Even the differential unit was located to the rear of the same casting, perfectly positioned at the car's centreline, so the driveshafts could be equal in length.

The bodywork fitted to Lamborghini's clever chassis was no less startling: twenty-five year old Marcello Gandini's stunning design for Carrozzeria Bertone receiving a rapturous reception when unveiled at Geneva in March 1966. Somewhat reminiscent of contemporary mid-engined racers of the period, especially the GT40, the Miura was sculptural – low and lithe, and elegantly detailed. Perhaps most importantly, the car's relatively short nose and balanced proportions emphasized its radical mid-engined configuration.

The effortlessly stylish appearance and apparent simplicity of the Miura belied frantic engineering turmoil in the factory as Lamborghini's designers slaved to solve problem after problem and make their ground-breaking supercar viable. There were vibration problems to overcome as various solutions were tried for feeding power into the gearbox – in the end an idler gear between crank and gearbox provided the solution, though it necessitated a minor redesign of the engine so the crank would spin in the opposite direction and thereafter turn the driveshafts the correct way. Achieving an acceptable and reliable gearshift forced a redesign of the crankcase, so the shift could pass right through it just beneath the crankshaft. Heat build-up in the engine bay meant a polycarbonate rear window had to give way to the slats that are now a core element of the Miura's iconic design.

The end result certainly justified the effort. The mid-engined Miura was a revolutionary – and headline-grabbing – re-imagining of the ultimate sports car for the road. Here was a new template for the modern high performance car, one that even conservative Enzo Ferrari would be forced to adopt – this despite his wariness at the prospect of inexperienced and under-skilled drivers being let loose in really high performance cars that featured challenging mid-engined handling characteristics, such dangerous territory previously the preserve of the professional racing driver.

The Ferrari Prototypes

While Lamborghini laboured to make the Miura a practical production prospect, Ferrari and Pininfarina were hard at work together, shaping a similar concept, albeit on a slightly more modest scale. One of Ferrari's tiny 206P race cars was selected for a makeover and given a swoopy new berlinetta (coupé) body to become the Dino Berlinetta Speciale. This influential Ferrari, introduced to the public at the Paris Salon in 1965, would give motoring enthusiasts their first glimpse of a possible mid-engined road car from Maranello. While the Speciale was clearly the forerunner of Ferrari's Dino production cars, this first iteration was far from production ready. Details including the impractically low-slung roofline and vulnerably low-set headlamps would give way, in a second

THE MID-ENGINE REVOLUTION

prototype shown at the Turin Show in 1966, to a more production-feasible shape, the second car's bodywork subtly shifted to achieve more practical proportions.

Ferrari's Dino prototypes were not the only mid-engined musings emanating from the Maranello factory at that time: a big GT, the 365P 1966 three-seater Berlinetta, also appeared at the Turin show, this 'full-size' Ferrari body shape very much hinting at the design of the soon-to-arrive production Dino. While the standout feature of the car was its unusual three-seat cabin, with the driver seated centrally, there were many other details to signpost the direction Ferrari would be taking as the mid-engined road-car revolution gathered pace. Its unadorned haunch air intake in particular was very close to that featured in the finalized Dino design, lacking as it did the aluminium strip that bisected this vent on both iterations of the smaller prototype.

The 365P also wore a most remarkable set of alloy wheels of a modern and minimalist stylized five-pointed star-shaped design, the edges of each spoke framed with a squared-off raised border. While the 365P proved to be a design cul-de-sac in terms of future V12 model designs, those wheels would be adopted across the range, becoming a motif synonymous with Ferrari design through the next two decades.

Ferrari customers would have to wait until 1968, a full three years from the introduction of the Dino prototype, until a mid-engined road car could actually be bought from the factory. True, a 250 LM in road trim had been shown at Geneva in 1965, but that was a disguised racer and not a car purpose-designed for highway use. Finalized for Turin in 1967, the space frame and alloy-bodied masterpiece, designed by Pininfarina and constructed at Scaglietti, would begin to trickle out of the factory the following year, and while the 206GT Dino was certainly a close relative of the cars that had adorned Ferrari's show stands in the past three years, there were significant differences. Unlike the previous design studies, the production car would carry its V6 motor transversely, like Lamborghini's Miura, the engine attached to a new transmission design whereby a single casting formed the gearbox case and engine sump. Although road-going Dino engines would grow in capacity and cylinder count in the coming years, this mechanical layout would persist as the definitive template for smaller Ferrari models for more than twenty years.

Just 152 cars would be built before the Dino design received a comprehensive overhaul, partly in response to the strong performance available from Porsche's competing 911S, but also to facilitate larger-scale production of the largely hand-built

Dino prototype by Pininfarina, permanently displayed at the Le Mans 24 Hours Museum.
PAUL AND KELLY GERRARD

THE MID-ENGINE REVOLUTION

Tribute to a lost son: Ferrari's Dino GT.

car. At Geneva in 1969 Ferrari unveiled the 246GT, visually near-identical to its predecessor, but similarity belying a radical refactoring. Longer in both wheelbase and length, and wearing bodywork of steel not aluminium alloy, at 1,080kg (2,381lb) the new Dino was heavier by a full 180kg (397lb) than the earlier car, though greater power would compensate for the beefier build. The 246GT would receive a new variant of the Dino motor, designed to work as well in a Fiat as in a Ferrari. The revised unit was no longer of all-alloy construction, but now based on an iron block, specified in the interest of larger-scale production. It was enlarged to 2419cc, achieved through use of larger bores and longer stroke, for a worthwhile increase in power to 195bhp, and perhaps more importantly for driver satisfaction, a good deal more torque.

The 246GTS

The popular Dino GT was soon joined by an open-topped car. Arriving at the 1972 Geneva Show, the 246GTS, as it would be designated, was not a full spider design, instead featuring a lift-out roof panel, very similar to the arrangement installed in the Dino GTS's arch rival, the targa-topped 911. Thereafter, and until the advent of the 348 Spider more than twenty years later, the smaller-engined two-seat Ferraris would mirror the Dino model range, each successive model offered first as a berlinetta and then as a GTS equivalent, featuring a lift-out roof panel.

While collaboration with Fiat had made the Dino project a viable proposition for Ferrari, also facilitating its engine's use in Formula 2 racing, even greater dependence on Fiat was on the horizon. Motivated to ensure a future for the company that bore his name, Enzo Ferrari entertained the possibility of a Ford takeover in the early 1960s. Though he subsequently had a change of heart, the idea of finding a safe haven for his beloved marque persisted, and in 1969 the tiny, race-obsessed firm was subsumed into the Fiat Group, though Ferrari himself retained a significant shareholding, and critically retained absolute control over the competition division.

Under Fiat Group stewardship, Ferrari completed the transition to mid-mounting of engines in the range's highest performing cars, with the arrival of the 365GT4 Berlinetta Boxer. This flat 12-powered supercar, first shown at Turin in 1971, was a belated response to Lamborghini's Miura, its showroom arrival tactically delayed until 1973 as a result of the outgoing Daytona's continued sales success. The Berlinetta Boxer was clearly an evolution of Pininfarina's earlier work on the Dino, more modern in its detailing and almost complete lack of chrome work, radiator grill apart. Here was a car that was truly contemporary and looked it, a genuine mid-engined supercar and a really modern Ferrari.

THE DINO FAMILY

Entry to the 1967 Formula 2 race series was dependent on the use of an engine limited to 1.6 litres capacity, and based on a volume-produced design. These regulations had been designed to encourage the use of adapted road-car engines instead of expensively engineered, all-out race designs. Although Ferrari clearly had the expertise to create such a motor for its team, it was by no means certain that the factory could series-produce them in the required volume, and so an expedient deal was struck with Fiat: Ferrari would develop the engine in two formats, a 1.6-litre design for the track, and a 2-litre unit for the road, to be installed in flagship Fiats as well as Ferrari's own offerings.

The magnificent new motor was designed by Franco Rocchi, and tweaked for production by engine design legend Aurelio Lampredi, the man responsible for the V12 design that replaced Colombo's original unit, in Ferrari's esteemed 250GT range. The newest Dino motor would share the same 65-degree V6 of earlier designs, this unusual angle selected to allow sufficient space within the V for nrestricted intake breathing. Unlike the previous Dino engines that had been reserved for the racetrack, a 2-litre version of this mechanical masterpiece would soon become more widely available than any Ferrari motor had been before. Formula 2 regulations dictated that at least 500 enthusiasts per year must have the opportunity to own a Ferrari-engined car, and so the motor began to feature in a selection of Fiat Group offerings.

Fiat couldn't wait to show their Ferrari-powered sports cars. At Turin in 1966 they presented both the elegant Bertone coupé and the sporty Pininfarina spider. Both models used adapted Ferrari engines, achieving a claimed 160bhp rather than the 180bhp of the same unit installed in the Ferrari Dino. In reality, the only differences between Fiat and Ferrari motors were in carburettor jetting and exhaust pipework; perhaps the more modest Fiat claim was a courtesy to uphold Ferrari's honour. The Dino V6 was mounted up front and longitudinally ahead of a five-speed gearbox in both Fiat models.

Both cars were underpinned by an adapted Fiat 125 platform, the two-seat spider on a compact 2,280mm (90in) wheelbase, the plus-two coupé a longer 2,540mm (100in). Promising double-wishbone front suspension was partially undermined by an archaic semi-elliptic leaf-sprung rear set-up, though contemporary road-testers found the road-holding of these early Fiat Dinos very satisfactory. In step with Ferrari's Dino, both Fiats received the larger 2.4-litre motor in 1969, the so-called 2400 Dino models now quoted as achieving 180bhp against Ferrari's 195bhp, and sporting improved semi-trailing arm independent rear suspension.

ABOVE: **Fiat's pretty Dino Spider.** PETER KABEL

RIGHT: **Bertone-designed Fiat coupé.**

Continued overleaf

■ THE MID-ENGINE REVOLUTION

Continued from previous page

THE DINO FAMILY

Sadly, despite the cachet of its Ferrari motor, fewer than 8,000 of Fiat's excellent Dinos would be built, and the range was quietly discontinued in 1973.

But that was by no means the end of Ferrari's inter-marque collaboration, because an innovative, audacious new home had been found for Ferrari's compact motor. Originally conceived as a theatrical, Fulvia-based show car, the Lancia Stratos concept had been reworked at the insistence of Lancia's competition manager Cesare Fiorio, to replace the ageing Fulvia as Lancia's next rally weapon. By now Lancia was an autonomous element within the Fiat Group, and as Fiorio surveyed the Group for a suitable motor he spied the Dino V6, an ideal choice. Despite wrangles within the Fiat Group, the motor was eventually approved for use in the Lancia in 1972, though it took a dalliance with Maserati around potential use of their Bora V8 to unblock Ferrari's resistance to the idea.

With breathtakingly taut, angular bodywork designed by Gandini for Bertone, the Stratos was incredibly compact: its wheelbase was just 2,180mm (85.8in), and the entire car an astounding 480mm (18.9in) shorter than the dainty Dino 246GT. Initially campaigned as a prototype, the Stratos was soon winning for Lancia, scoring its first victory in the 1973 Firestone Spanish Rally. Once the Stratos was homologated in October 1974, somewhat dubiously by including part-completed cars in the count of the required 400 units, the Stratos was soon established as a rally sensation. This unfeasibly rapid wedge enabled Lancia to secure three back-to-back world championships between 1974 and 1976, after which Lancia withdrew from front-line rallying.

But despite its advancing years and lack of direct factory support, the Stratos continued to win. In 1978 Markku Alén

Lancia Stratos.
JOHN DICKENS

won the Giro d'Italia in a turbocharged Group 5 Stratos, the third time the car had won this challenging road race, and the Stratos took its last World Rally Championship victory in 1981, with its fifth win of the Tour de Corse. But in spite of its competition success, the Stratos road car was a slow seller, and it could still be purchased 'new' several years after production had ceased in 1975.

Ferrari and the V8

While placement of power-plant would have a most dramatic effect on the architecture and design of Ferrari's road cars, the challenge of building contemporary sports cars suited to the design-savvy 1970s market, and capable of meeting an inrush of safety and environmental regulations, meant that the marque could not rest on its laurels. New motor designs, cleaner and more powerful, would be needed to propel a new generation of more accessible and relevant Italian sports cars in the coming decade. Like so many US-based manufacturers facing the very same challenges, Ferrari opted to develop a new V8.

Popular myth has it that Enzo Ferrari felt that only V12 power was appropriate for a car bearing his name. While there

THE MID-ENGINE REVOLUTION

are many documented quotations to confirm his enthusiasm for the configuration, especially in the earliest days of his firm, Ferrari was ambitious and pragmatic enough to accept race victories, irrespective of cylinder count. Indeed, in its sixty-plus year history Ferrari has fielded cars with a wide variety of mechanical architectures, from straight 4s to boxer 12s. The very first Ferrari road car, albeit not one bearing the Ferrari name – the Auto Avio Costruzione of 1940 – was fitted with a 1.5-litre, straight 8-cylinder engine.

The Ferrari factory's first V8 experience would not be with a Maranello design at all. Following their withdrawal from competition after driver Alberto Ascari's death in 1955, Lancia entrusted their innovative pannier-tank D50 Grand Prix cars to the Scuderia. Six of these Jano-designed beauties arrived at Maranello in July 1955, and with them an obligation to uphold Italy's racing honour at the highest level. Ferrari would contest Grands Prix with their inherited V8-powered machinery until they were superseded by newer, Dino-engined Grand Prix cars as the 1957 racing season drew to a close.

Just a few short years later, in 1962, Ferrari would unveil its own V8 racing motor, a unit designed by Carlo Chiti for a proposed 248GT, a car that would never materialize. But the V8 was put to use on the race track, making its debut with the NART team at Sebring in the 248SP sports racer. In its initial guise, with a capacity of 2458cc, the V8 generated 250bhp at 7,400rpm, an output that proved inadequate on track, leading to a lengthening of stroke by 5mm to 71mm. The bore at 77mm remained as before. With its new capacity of 2644cc the motor provided 260bhp, at 7,500rpm. However, despite some promise, only three were built, and the design was not extensively campaigned.

Nevertheless it would be just two years before another Ferrari V8 arrived in the pits: a new 1.5-litre motor was devised by designer Angelo Bellei in line with contemporary Grand Prix rules. The Tipo 158 was a 90-degree V8, featuring twin camshafts for each cylinder bank, and with 64 × 57.8mm bore and stroke for a capacity of 1487cc. Output was an excellent 205bhp at a heady 10,500rpm, enough to buzz John Surtees to the 1964 World Championship, and bring a fifth constructor's title home to Maranello. Ferrari's radical V8-powered monocoque car was a great success, but although its competition career continued into 1965, Enzo's beloved V12 configuration would return during the course of the season, and the victorious V8 would be permanently retired for 1966.

ABOVE: **Lancia D50, the first V8-powered Grand Prix car to be campaigned by the Scuderia.**
ROBERT KNIGHT

RIGHT: **Dino 248SP.**
JOHN DICKENS

■ THE MID-ENGINE REVOLUTION

LEFT: **Surtees reunited with the V8 Tipo 158 at the Goodwood Festival of Speed, 2010.** GRAHAM KEEN

BELOW: **Tipo 158 1.5-litre V8 Grand Prix engine.** PHIL MARKHAM

A V8 for the Dino

Ambitions for the next generation of smaller Ferrari models, designed to replace the much loved 246 Dino range, would render the excellent V6 engine design obsolete. The challenge from larger capacity models from Porsche and others would define the new engine: it would emulate the charisma of the outgoing V6, but was bigger and could therefore provide more power – and power that was more readily accessible – for a user-friendly experience, resulting in broader appeal. Ferrari no doubt reviewed the experience gained with various V8 racing powerplants through the 1960s, as they plotted the specification for a bigger, more practical and usable Dino, better suited to the 1970s international marketplace. Thus the next in the line of compact, mid-engined cars conceived to honour Ferrari's lost son would be powered by an all-new V8, boasting a worthwhile capacity increase to 3 litres.

In his own inimitably eloquent style, Enzo Ferrari once expounded that 'engines are like sons: one settles down and studies, and another signs cheques and is dissolute'. Well, the 90-degree V8 designed for the larger Dino would be a motor in the studious mould, hard working and high achieving, the first example of a design configuration that would cause a realignment of the marque's entire model line-up. Indeed since its introduction, the Ferrari range has never been without a V8-powered model, and it would not be long before the V8 range would represent Maranello's most popular and accessible line.

While chassis and body construction for the new Dino would be outsourced, in accordance with Enzo Ferrari's often repeated personal view that the engine was the most important element of any car bearing his name, the new Dino V8's crankcase and heads would be cast, machined and assembled in house. Cast entirely in aluminium alloy, initially using the traditional sand-casting method, the factory soon switched to the more robust die-casting process as production was ramped up to meet growing demand. Perhaps in order to perpetuate Ferrari's legendary air of creative mystery, no engine designer was ever confirmed, though work is usually attributed to Franco Rocchi, assisted by Angelo Bellei.

THE MID-ENGINE REVOLUTION

Excellent picture of the Ferrari V8 engine on display at Malaga Motor Museum, taken by Belfast journalist Gary Fennelly: an early carburettor-equipped motor featuring twin distributors. The unit attached to the nearer of the cambelt covers is the belt-driven air-conditioning compressor.
GARY FENNELLY

Removable liners of cast iron were shrunk into the crankcase, which was of a flat-plane design with five main bearings. Crankshaft throws were set at 180 degrees, and the pistons and connecting rods were carefully matched and graded for weight. Ferrari's favoured thin-wall bearings were used. Bore and stroke of the skirted pistons with four rings were set at 81 × 71mm, the same dimensions used in the Daytona's V12. The firing order would be 1-5-3-7-4-8-2-6.

The cylinder heads were of a relatively conventional design, with a hemispherical combustion chamber and with 2 valves per cylinder, set in cast-iron inserts at an angle of 46 degrees. Oil vapours from the cylinder heads were drawn into the air-filter housing via an oil separator designed to return condensed oil to the sump. The valves featured inverted thimble-type tappets and concentric helical return springs, and were operated by twinned camshafts, the pair on each bank driven via a separate toothed rubber belt.

The new V8 would be only the second Ferrari engine to feature belt-driven camshafts, this feature making its debut on the expansive 365 Berlinetta Boxer engine. Thus the maintenance chore of routine chain adjustment that faced owners of the outgoing Dino 246 would be a thing of the past for small Ferrari owners, albeit at the cost of periodic cambelt replacement – the 308GT4 workshop manual specified 60,000km (37,300 miles) as the appropriate replacement interval, though it advised careful inspection every 15–20,000km (9–12,000 miles).

The toothed rubber cambelt for each cylinder bank was driven by a separate drive-gear, and was tensioned by its own idler. Valve clearances were adjusted by shims, though in a token effort to ease at least one aspect of maintenance, the camshafts and their covers bore alignment marks. Spark-plug replacement interval was set at 10,000km (6,200 miles).

An oil radiator was mounted at the transmission end of the engine, working to cool the engine in partnership with a substantial water radiator to be installed in the car's nose, pressurized to 0.9kg/cm^2 and force-fed air by thermostatically controlled twin electric fans. A water pump shared its rubber drive belt with the car's alternator.

At first, each engine was assembled by a single engine builder, though this process was discontinued in the 1980s in favour of production-line style working, whereby each operative specialized in a specific part of the overall motor construction; single operative assembly was thereafter reserved only for special units such as the F40's turbocharged powerplant.

THE MID-ENGINE REVOLUTION

RIGHT: **First home for Ferrari's new 3-litre V8, Bertone's 308GT4.**

BELOW: **Engine bay detail.**

Like the preceding Dino V6 design, the sump and gearbox housing was cast by Ferrari as a single unit, its interior partitioned to separate the oils from the motor and gearbox. It was a more satisfactory solution than the compromises imposed on Lamborghini's Miura, in which engine and gearbox were required to share oils. The deep sump gave a generous engine oil capacity of 9ltr (2gal) and a gearbox capacity of 4ltr (0.9gal), oil pressure maintained by a geared pump at around 6kg/cm^2 using oil of the recommended 10–50w type. Acknowledging the degradation inherent in engine oil formulations of the period, Ferrari recommended an engine oil change after every 5,000km (3,100 miles) travelled, or at six-month intervals, whichever arrived first.

One somewhat unhappy aspect of the transmission design was that the clutch was mounted rather high up, on the end of the crankshaft, a train of three gears conveying drive to the gearbox beneath – the idler gear slightly increasing the drive by a ratio of 27:30. The result was a rather higher than ideal centre of gravity, a drawback that would remain inherent in V8 Ferrari design until the revised 3.4-litre powerpack arrived with the Mondial T and 348.

The gearbox itself was also built in house, an aluminium alloy-cased, five-speed design, all forward gears being synchromeshed, and the solid-rod shift mechanism featuring a dog-leg first gear selection. First gear was at the rear left of the gate opposite the reverse slot, and the further four gears arranged in a conventional 'H' pattern. Inadvertent selection of reverse gear was prevented by a detent overcome by downward gearstick pressure. A dry single-plate diaphragm clutch was fitted.

The sump and gearbox casting also housed the rear axle assembly, containing four limited slip clutch plates of molybdenum-coated steel to each side, passing power to solid Lobro-type axle shafts fitted with Birfield-Rzeppa constant velocity joints, the inboard ones of sliding type.

CHAPTER THREE

THE 308GT4

The first car to receive this excellent new V8 powerplant would be a two plus two-seat berlinetta unveiled at the Paris Motor Show in 1973. Once again christened Dino in honour of Ferrari's lost son, and therefore successor to the popular V6 Dino range, the new car had quite some reputation to live up to. Its full given name was Dino 308GT4 in recognition of its 3-litre capacity, 8 cylinders and four seats. Not only would this be Ferrari's first road-going production V8 model, it also represented a new direction in terms of styling. It would be the first Ferrari not designed by Pininfarina for two decades, a strikingly angular, wedge-shaped coupé of compact dimensions. Extremely – perhaps excessively – similar in overall style to Lamborghini's equivalent V8-powered Urraco, another Bertone design, here was a car that, while undeniably dramatic and exotic in appearance, by no means conformed to the populist view of how a Ferrari was expected to look.

So why was the commission for this new model design entrusted to Bertone? As always, the factory's decision-making process has been veiled in mystery. While details are hard to confirm, it seems Pininfarina was enjoying a comparatively busy period, and so Fiat suggested Bertone as a worthy alternative for the commission, perhaps motivated to keep the vying carrozzerie on their toes in pursuit of future Fiat Group projects. No doubt the Ferrari factory had recent, first-hand experience of Bertone's undoubted competence and capability following their joint involvement in the Fiat Dino project. Bertone had first designed the Dino GT, and later taken over its construction. But while Bertone was entrusted with the honour of penning its design, the role of builder for this new Ferrari's bodywork would be reserved for Maranello-based Scaglietti, who assumed body construction duties for the new berlinetta on completion of the first example by Bertone.

Design

Bertone's design team was led by legendary designer Marcello Gandini, the genius behind Lamborghini's stunning Muira, the outrageous Countach, and Lancia's purposefully compact Stratos, among many automotive gems. Work progressed efficiently on the two-plus-two seat Ferrari, and the car's essential lines settled quickly, the production car bearing a close resemblance to the earliest design sketches. Surprisingly compact for a two-plus-two, the 308GT4 sat on a 2,550mm (100.4in) wheelbase, a scant 210mm (8.3in) longer than the preceding Dino 246GT. At just 4,300mm (169.3in) long, the car was efficiently packaged within a purposeful and taut design scheme strongly in tune with the modernist aesthetic of the decade.

Like many of Bertone's other works of the period, the car was strongly wedge-shaped in profile, and while it was far from razor-edged, it did boast a crisp, somewhat angular appearance, with large and relatively unadorned flat surfaces, and minimal curves in evidence. Indeed the scheme featured many straight, or almost straight, edges, particularly around the rear buttresses and rear windscreen, though it avoided the excessively angular appearance of cars such as Bertone's own Alfa Romeo

FOLLOWING PAGES:
P.26: **308GT4.**

P.27:
TOP: **Styling model under construction at Bertone; note the Uracco-like radiator air outlet on the front bonnet.**
BOTTOM: **Fussy air-intake treatment behind the rear side window, and twinned engine cooling vents are evident on Bertone's part-completed styling model.**
BERTONE HISTORICAL ARCHIVE

THE 308GT4

THE 308GT4

■ THE 308GT4

Carabo show car. The tapered tail was pinched inwards from just aft of the rear wheel arches, giving the final fifth of the car a striking resemblance to Gandini's earlier Lancia Stratos, particularly in profile. Even in its detailing, the new Dino departed from Ferrari tradition, Bertone ignoring Pininfarina's round tail-lamp motif in favour of trapezoidal-shaped rear lamps, though triple circular lamps were inset within each cluster.

Design Details

While the car's overall appearance was quickly confirmed, the detailing evolved as the design scheme took shape in full scale. Various details were tried and discarded on the full-size clay model, including heavily slatted twin radiator outlet grilles for the front luggage-bay lid on an otherwise remarkably flat front, reminiscent of Gandini's work on the similarly configured Lamborghini Urraco. A pair of air outlets was trialled on the engine cover, in a layout that predicted the one that would appear on Pininfarina's 308GTB. Rear wing-mounted air intakes were reworked before being finalized too – a dog-leg-shaped grouping of meshed holes shadowing the trailing edge of the rear side window was rejected, before the Bertone team settled on the simple and elegant boomerang-shaped funnel that passed air discreetly into the engine bay, the left side intake feeding cooling air to the oil radiator, and the right side ducted to meet the airbox.

One design detail that was a constant throughout the car's development was the rear window treatment. Befitting its angular, flat-planed design motif, the preceding Dino's curved

Styling sketches: the 308GT4 silhouette is unmistakable despite the differences in much of the detailing. BERTONE HISTORICAL ARCHIVE

rear screen gave way to a completely flat, bolt-upright glass pane nestled in a tunnel projecting into the cabin area between stark, geometric buttresses. The body sides were tapered strongly inwards from a belt-line pressed into the sheet metal that extended between the wheel arches, the sill panels themselves mounted almost at 45 degrees when viewed from front or rear of the car, as they met an updated version of the original Dino chassis.

While certain contemporary design sketches from Bertone rather overstated the interior accommodation – one side-profile sketch showing an adult comfortably seated behind the driver – the 308GT4 was a very effectively packaged car.

BERTONE

Perhaps Bertone's most famous creation, Lamborghini's astounding Countach. This car shares garage space with a 1979 308GTB.
EMILIO PALTRINIERI

Carrozzeria Bertone came into existence in 1912, founded by Giovanni Bertone as a constructor of horse-drawn carriages, though operations were soon extended to offer bespoke automotive bodywork, mainly for Italian marques including Fiat and Lancia. Nuccio Bertone would join his father's company in 1933, taking the reins single-handed after World War II. As Italian industries began the painstaking process of recovery in an environment of post-war austerity, so clever, design-led new products became the country's stock-in-trade. Many revolutionary ideas were realized in metal, from Innocenti's Lambretta motor scooter, to Fiat's brilliantly simple 500. Bertone would be part of this movement, its reputation as an innovative creator of modern cars confirmed with such standout designs as the Alfa Romeo Giulietta Sprint, its successor the Giulia GT, and aerodynamic coupé studies also for Alfa Romeo, the outlandish BAT (Berlinetta Aerodinamica Tecnica) series.

Bertone went from strength to strength. Through the latter part of the 1960s, chief designer Marcello Gandini was Bertone's resident genius, and his audacious designs amazed motor-show visitors year after year. The breathtaking Miura was followed by the Marzal concept, which would evolve into the wild Espada four-seat supercar as Gandini made constant innovations on behalf of supercar constructor, Lamborghini.

Into the 1970s, more angular designs featuring powerful wedge themes began to dominate Bertone's output: the Alfa Romeo Carabo and Lancia Stratos Zero concepts previewed forms and detailing that would subsequently find their way into showrooms with Lamborghini's Urraco and Countach, the production version of Lancia's Stratos, and Fiat's miniaturized mid-engined supercar, the X1/9. Commentators speculated that Bertone was at last entrusted with a project for Ferrari due to the firm's good performance working on the conservative, Ferrari-engined Fiat Dino Coupe. But it would be the edgy and angular forms explored on the more outrageous concepts and Lamborghini road cars which would inspire the Grugliasco-based company's design for Ferrari.

Through the 1980s and 1990s, in line with rival Pininfarina, the company's emphasis shifted away from outlandish design towards construction arrangements with major manufacturers. The now iconic Bertone gothic 'b' badge adorned the flanks of more prosaic machinery, including Fiat's Ritmo and Punto cabriolets, and Opel's Astra coupés and convertibles, constructed in volume in Bertone's own factories.

With the passing of Nuccio Bertone in 1997, the Carrozzeria struggled with change within the automotive industry, culminating in the forced sale of its manufacturing capability to Fiat; this left a much reduced if more single-mindedly focused Bertone free to concentrate on innovation in design.

THE 308GT4

An early 308GT4, resplendent in so-called Boxer paintwork.
PHOTO © FERRARIBYNEILLBRUCE.CO.UK

Although legroom was very limited, the deeply scooped and rather upright rear seating was certainly usable by adults for shorter journeys, although front seat occupants would have to sacrifice some legroom to free sufficient space to accommodate two people in the cabin's cosy rear.

Penned by an Italian design genius, well packaged and practical (for its type at least), and powered by that superb new V8 motor, the 308GT4 Dino must have seemed a certainty for instant success. Unfortunately that purposeful Gandini styling proved controversial, and from the start, reports about the new car hinted, or in some cases clearly stated, that the car did not look like a Ferrari should. British *Car* magazine, in characteristically forthright style, opined in a November 1974 test of the GT4 that as well as being strongly similar in appearance to the Lamborghini Urraco, its rear aspect in particular was poorly conceived: '...fiddly and unattractive, rather like a woman with a narrow pinched backside.'

While the public may not have agreed with this specific criticism, clearly there was a lack of attraction to the model. While the 308GT4 was by no means the slowest of sellers Maranello had ever fielded, the orders were disappointing for such an innovative, practical and – on paper at least – most marketable model. A disappointing total of 2,826 cars would be constructed between 1973 and 1980, fewer than half the sales the two-seat 308 would achieve by 1980, despite its introduction a full two years later than the GT4.

Ferrari Badging

It cannot have helped matters that the new V8 car at launch lacked the cachet of Ferrari branding. While 'Dino' badging was in evidence everywhere, the evocative 'cavallino rampante' emblem and Ferrari script were harder to spot, though they were present on Maranello-produced engine and gearbox castings. The factory finally recognized the marketing benefit of appending the Ferrari name to the model, and in 1977 additional badging began to be fitted to clarify the car's parentage. US market dealers had an even tougher time, because the discontinuation of the popular 246GT and GTS in 1974 meant that the Dino 308GT4 – less appealing as a Dino than the outgoing car, and lacking any Ferrari badging – was the only model available in their showrooms from its January 1975 introduction; the contemporary 365GT4 Berlinetta Boxer and 365GT4 two-plus-two were not homologated for US sale.

The factory recognized the US dealers' plight, and in mid-1975 sent them instructions to retrofit Ferrari badges to existing stock – one of a series of image-building modifications conceived to improve showroom appeal. Each successive US-bound car would thereafter wear Ferrari badges on leaving the factory gates, though the name 'Dino' would remain on the boot-lid script badge through to the end of production.

US market cars were further hampered by mandatory performance-sapping emissions equipment. However, disappointed American owners soon discovered that certain unofficial modifications would restore lost power, one of which was the straightforward disabling of the air pumps by removing the drive-belts: this reclaimed around ten of the motor's missing bhp. Unfortunately nothing that simple could be done to elevate the lowered compression ratio of US-specification V8 motors. But happily, the 308GTB and GTS that soon followed found greater favour in the USA, and the GT4 was withdrawn from the US market in 1978.

Performance

The relative difficulty in sales belied the car's excellent performance and the engaging driving experience it offered. *Car* magazine, in their November 1974 road-test, praised the car's compact dimensions, which allowed their tester to 'carve through the traffic…as if you're in a 1275 Cooper' and eulogized about the V8's marvellous power delivery '…spread over an enormous rev range…the engine just gives more and more power as it revs. It is just like turning up a dial'.

Testing for *Road and Track* in the same year, ex-racing driver Paul Frère was equally complimentary about the GT4's performance, but singled out the car's ride as its most impressive driving characteristic. 'There is no low speed harshness…' he enthused, before explaining that '…at speed the road irregularities are beautifully smoothed out, damping being so good that oscillations are virtually non-existent.' Sadly, high praise could not create an upturn in demand, and the model remained a rather sluggish seller in Ferrari showrooms – with fewer units sold than its predecessor, the 246 Dino – until summer 1980, when the similarly configured Mondial 8 arrived to take its place as the practical family car in Ferrari's line-up. A few cars remained available for sale into 1981.

308GT4 models were given even-only chassis numbers, continuing the sequence begun with the Dino 206GT, and which continued even as they were built alongside the 308GTB/GTS series, those models identified according to conventional Ferrari chassis numbering arrangements in having odd-only chassis numbers.

The new V8 engine was transversely mounted in the Dino's engine bay, the cambelt end of the motor to the right side of the engine bay, and the clutch to the left. Consistent with the car's Grand Tourer aspirations, a wet sump arrangement was installed in preference to a racier dry sump configuration, though performance-oriented twin-choke Weber 40 DCNF carburettors nestled within the engine's 'V'. At first, GT4s destined for all markets would be equipped with the same twin Magneti Marelli distributors, installed at the left-side end of each camshaft cover, and driven by the two inlet valve camshafts. Second-series European cars received a single distributor driven by the forward inlet camshaft, though US and

Narrow radiator intake and exposed flanking driving lamps obvious on this first series 308GT4. Note the Dino badge between the headlamp pods.

THE 308GT4

Australian market cars continued with the original arrangement. From 1978, European cars would also feature Magnetti Marelli electronic ignition.

Initial road-test reports were critical of the car's heavy clutch action, particularly when the motor was still cold, and most road-testers found it necessary to depress the pedal fully for a consistently clean gear-change. Although further development was undertaken at the factory to improve the situation, the clutch remained hard work in heavy traffic, even on later cars.

The Dino's cooling system was of the sealed type, holding 18ltr (4gal) of coolant, with a front-mounted radiator and an expansion tank mounted at the right side of the engine bay. Twin fans drew air through the radiator from the front grille opening, while exhaust air exited through a vent on the front bonnet panel. Water pumps on early cars incorporated a rather insubstantial bearing that was prone to failure, a situation remedied by the substitution of a more substantial unit around 1979.

US and Australian market cars were hobbled by exhaust emission cleansing equipment – most significantly an air-injection system with air pumps, belt-driven from camshaft pulleys. The front bank's air pump was mounted at the cambelt end of the engine, the rear bank's at the clutch end, each providing compressed air to be injected into each cylinder head's exhaust ports via narrow diameter, tubular manifolds. The system incorporated an electromagnetic clutch to disengage the air pumps as revs rose, thereby minimizing its power-sapping action. Air-injected cars also featured pressed steel exhaust manifolds, rather than the free-breathing tubular steel items that were part of the European specification. Catalytic converters became mandatory in the US from 1978, and a fast idle system was implemented to warm them up more quickly, catalysts becoming effective only once fully warmed. On start-up a thermostatic valve increased the motor's idle speed to between 2,500 and 3,100rpm, to increase the rapidity with which the engine would warm – the unwelcome corollary being the potential for rapidly increased engine wear. Like the power-sapping air pumps, the valve was often disabled or removed entirely by US owners in the quest for improved performance and engine longevity.

ABOVE: **Beautifully understated detailing around the rear of the 308GT4. Note the discreet air intake, feeding cooling air to the car's oil radiator.**

LEFT: **308GT4 at speed.**
DANIEL HAY

Exhaust arrangements were the same on cars for all markets, with a single large transverse silencer mounted beneath the boot, culminating in two pairs of exhaust outlet pipes – dramatically slash-cut chrome affairs in all markets but the USA, where downward-facing pipes were fitted. A factory modification in mid-1975 would instruct dealers to glamorize the slow-selling Dino by installing dummy sleeves, apeing the appearance of European market cars' outlets over the drooping tailpipes.

Ferrari quoted a rather optimistic 255bhp for European specification cars, with US market cars quoted at an equally lofty 240bhp – though true figures are generally thought likely to have been around 15bhp shy of these levels. The owner's handbook quoted a 251km/h (156mph) top speed (147mph – 237km/h – for US market cars), and a 26.2sec dash across the standing kilometre (and 27sec for US market cars). While performance was certainly strong, Ferrari's figures were probably a little ambitious, the marque in this period having a tendency to bold power and performance claims.

In similar style the 308GT4 was often quoted as having a kerb weight of just 1,150kg (2,536lb) in press materials, though the car's handbook was probably a more accurate guide, stating as it did that the car weighed in at a more credible 1,365kg (3,010lb) for Europe, and a chunky 1,450kg (3,197lb) in US trim. The later US cars were not only heavy, they also suffered further constriction of their engines by catalytic converters; such cars were quoted as delivering just 205bhp, the effect being performance far short of that which had come to be expected from a Ferrari. A slightly higher first gear installed in US market cars did little to reinstate the lack of off-the-line urge.

Chassis

The chassis of the new Dino was very similar to that of the outgoing V6 car, as well as that of the Berlinetta Boxer: a tubular affair, bearing factory type reference F 106 AL 100, built atop a platform of large oval tubes, the oval profiles upright to maximize tube strength. Substantial steel box-sections served as inner sills, providing a strong perimeter for the chassis; to the front and rear, square tubes were employed to fabricate frameworks to which suspension, powerplant and bodywork would be attached. The oval tube that made the central spine for the chassis was offset slightly from the centre line – away from the driver – to allow the gearshift to be sited closer to hand, and through it ran aluminium tubes that took coolant from the engine bay to the front-mounted radiator. Chassis

Custom exhaust arrangement on this 308GT4, anti-rollbar mounted beneath.

destined for the USA would feature additional bracing around the bumper attachment points, in line with regulations governing impact resistance in that market.

Bodyshell

Glassfibre flooring, along with mouldings for the inner wheel arches and front bulkhead, were bonded to the chassis, in typical Ferrari style for the period, the V6 Dino and 400GT both sharing floor pans of similar construction. The 308GT4's steel bodywork, although designed by Bertone, would be constructed as usual by the Ferrari subsidiary Scaglietti, arriving at Ferrari's assembly plant on a wheeled trolley in readiness for mounting on the production line, where it would be protected during assembly under swathes of foam sheeting.

The steel bodyshell comprised roof panel, front pillars and front compartment slam panel; rear wing pressings, incorporating roof buttresses and rear window apertures and air intakes; rear bulkhead and deck panel with apertures for vertical rear window; and rear panel, with attachment points for rear lamps and number plate. The rear bumper was installed within this panel, a chrome-edged unit, its top edge featuring a dipped cut-out, echoing the indentation between the rear lamps into which the number plate fitted. Reversing lights were set into the ends of the rear bumper. US market cars received all-black impact bumpers with a single reversing light appended beneath it at the centre-line. Outer sill panels were of steel, rather vulnerable with relatively insubstantial corrosion proofing, painted matt-black. On some cars the matt black

■ THE 308GT4

Late model 308GT4. Note the rare steel sunroof.

finish of the sills was extended upwards to the car's belt-line, this so-called 'Boxer' paintwork usually a dealer-applied option rather than a factory scheme.

The opening front panel covered a spare wheel sat in a glassfibre well, also containing the car's toolkit. The steel-framed aluminium bonnet was hinged at its leading edge, and released by a cable pull operated from a lever mounted in the cabin, on the left side wheel-arch intrusion. US and Australian legislation meant that cars bound for those markets were supplied with a full-size tyre, not the skinny spare wheel provided for cars delivered in the European market. Doors were of steel, and featured fixed quarter windows ahead of an opening glass, both panes framed in chrome to match the rear quarter windows. Door handles were of a square design, such as was also used on several contemporary Bertone mid-engined projects of the period, including the Fiat X1/9, the Lamborghini Urraco and Lancia Stratos.

Rear opening panels were again steel-framed aluminium, though later cars usually have all-steel opening panels, the one nearer the cabin incorporating a slatted outlet vent and provided with a stay, while the lid for the boot was held open with a crude-looking sprung hinge. A sliding steel sun-roof was a rare option in European markets, though this became a standard fitment on late model US market GT4s. An emergency opening cable for each of the rear-deck covers was accessible from within the adjacent compartment.

Retractable headlamp pods reclined in apertures in the slam panel. At first a rectangular Dino badge in landscape orientation was inset between the lamps, though for later cars this was replaced by the more aspirational 'cavallino rampante' emblem as part of the car's rebranding as a Ferrari. The headlamp pods were also of steel, and held twin 5in headlamps, sealed beam units for US cars. In the event of a failure these pods could be lifted manually by turning a knob on the top of each motor, accessible beneath the front compartment lid. Below the slam panel was a wide aperture into which an elegant slim-line bumper was set, chrome-edged and with a black rubber blade featuring rectangular cut-outs into which combined indicator and sidelight lamps were installed.

On first series cars, the radiator aperture sited beneath the front bumper was a rather deep and narrow aperture filled with horizontal slats, in the familiar Ferrari so-called egg-crate style. Driving lights were installed into the valance panel to the sides of the grille, though these were fitted neither to Italian market cars nor to those bound for the USA. Series two cars received a revised full-width grille aperture, the entire opening covered with a slatted grille. Driving lamps were fitted inset within the grille behind the slats. American cars were fitted with very pronounced all-black impact bumpers, with all-amber side and indicator lamps appended to the lower edge. US bumpers were revised around 1975, and while somewhat less intrusive in design, they remained rather ugly appendages,

THE 308GT4

jarring with the otherwise svelte design. Some European market cars were fitted with all-black glassfibre bumpers, similar in style to the metal units more usually fitted.

Suspension and Steering

Double wishbone suspension has long been favoured for competition and high performance sporting cars, offering an ideal solution to the problem of keeping the wheels perpendicular to the road, and therefore providing maximum grip. Unsurprisingly, given its sweet-handling nature, the all-round double wishbone arrangement from the V6 Dino would be the reference for the larger Dino's suspension design. At the front of the car, the 308GT4 would make use of double wish-

ABOVE: **308GT4 interior. Many GT4s were delivered with seats featuring contrast-coloured cloth insert and coloured carpets.**

LEFT: **The GT4 was often ordered in colours other than the typically Ferrari Rosso Corsa: this car is presented in an attractive blue, 'Blu Scuro Dino'.**

bones with coil springs and telescopic Koni hydraulic shock absorbers, mounted at an angle between the outer end of the lower wishbones and the inboard end of the upper wishbones.

An 18mm diameter anti-rollbar was attached to the chassis, just below the line of the wheel centres, passing between upper and lower wishbones. The rear suspension was again by double wishbones, with coil springs and Koni telescopic hydraulic dampers mounted to the rear hub-carriers and extending upwards above the upper wishbones, further

exacerbating the masses perched rather too high in the rear of the car. An 11.5mm roll-bar was installed at the rear, attached low on the chassis, connecting the lower wishbones.

A rack-and-pinion steering system from Cam-Gears was fitted, again following 246GT practice; this unassisted unit offered the usual compromise in the speed of its gearing to moderate the level of driver effort to an acceptable degree. Contemporary road-test reports complained about the rather ponderous and unsporting 3.28 turns lock to lock with a wide 12m

THE 308GT4

Compact V8 comfortably contained within the 308GT4's capacious engine bay. Note the twin coils to the left side.

(39ft) turning circle, though most testers reported the system as being quite pleasant to use – *Motor Sport* magazine's October 1974 test commended feel as being '…superbly sensitive and responsive without becoming reactionary over bumps, and … light enough to make parking easy'.

First series cars reused the Cromodora light alloy wheel design conceived for the 246 Dino: a rather intricate six-hole design of 14 × 6.5J size, with a small, 'Dino'-badged, stainless-steel hubcap covering the wheel nuts. Second series cars could be ordered with the same wheels, though with exposed wheel nuts and a 'cavallino rampante' centre cap. Alternatively, the would-be owner could specify slightly wider 14 × 7J wheels of the so-called 'penta-star', these cast by Campagnolo or Speedline in aluminium alloy. Irrespective of wheel style, tyres were by Goodyear or Michelin, in 205/70/VR 14 size.

Braking System

Befitting this high performance car, the braking system was impressive for its day, offering excellent stopping ability: Ferrari claimed that the car was able to stop in an emergency in just 45m (150ft) when travelling at 100km/h (60mph), and a scant 280m (920ft) from 240km/h (150mph). The effective braking system comprised four-wheel disc brakes, the rotors ventilated front and rear. Sidestepping the danger of system failure, the braking featured dual circuits, tandem master cylinders activating one circuit for the front brakes, the other a self-contained system for the rear. A Bonaldi vacuum servo provided braking assistance, minimizing the pedal pressures required to bring the Ferrari to a rapid halt. A cable-operated handbrake was fitted, which acted directly on the rear calliper cylinders.

Fuel System

The fuel system was fed from twin flank-mounted tanks with a combined 80ltr (17.6gal) capacity, the two tanks joined by a transfer pipe running across the engine bay. Fuel was drawn by a single Corona electric fuel pump from the left-side tank, to feed the four Webers that nestled beneath a wide airbox, a large pressed unit, in a crackle black paint finish, containing a single paper element and drawing air from the right body-side air intake.

THE 308GT4

Interior Design

The Ferrari 308GT4's cabin was a most pleasant working environment, even if, in line with other low-volume cars of the time, a few design details were somewhat idiosyncratic. The driver sat in front of a dash moulding that ran the width of the car. Vinyl-covered, or optionally leather-bound, this resin moulding carried on its upper surface three ventilation outlets to convey demisting air to the windscreen. In front of the passenger there was a lockable glovebox, and ahead of the driver the moulding flared to an ovoid shape, in which three dash panels of brushed aluminium carried the instrumentation and controls. The car's fusebox was accessible from within the glovebox.

The outer of the three dash panels was angled inwards to the driver's line of sight, so that the switchgear on the left panel and the heater controls on the right panel were within easy reach of the driver's fingertips, a short reach from the steering wheel. The heater controls were attractive chromed sliders, of a design that began to appear on several Ferrari models in the latter part of the 1960s, including the 365GT two-plus-two and Daytona, though in the 308GT4, perhaps in recognition of its angular exterior design, the normally rounded plastic finger-grips were replaced with a cuboid design.

Full leather seat facings in this 308GT4. Note the choke slider to the rear of the central console beside the handbrake.

The dash panel carried comprehensive instrumentation: seven Veglia Borletti instruments were arrayed on the central dash panel, black-faced, with white script and yellow needles, and with a dimming facility via a dash-mounted knob; each bore a Dino script logo. The larger main instruments were mostly visible between the wheel spokes: a 280km/h (174mph) speedometer with odometer and trip-counter to the left, and a rev-counter redlined at 7,700rpm to the right. From 1979, the 180mph (290km/h) speedo was replaced in the US market with a revised unit that read only to 85mph (137km/h). Flanking these two were a fuel-level gauge to the left and an oil temperature gauge to the right, and between the two main instruments, arranged in an inverted triangle, were dials for oil pressure and water temperature, and a clock featuring a red second hand.

Tell-tale lights for direction indicators, lights, choke and brake system failure were integrated into the two main instrument faces, while the alternator failure lamp was a separate circular red lamp prominently overprinted with a white 'G', denoting *generatore*. Tell-tale lamps for fog lamps, hazard warning lights and ventilation fan speed were aligned beneath the appropriate function switches on the left-side dash panel, which on US market cars also contained a 'fasten seat-belt' warning lamp that operated in conjunction with a warning buzzer if the driver's belt was left unfastened.

Well stocked dashboard, conveniently angled towards the driver's line of sight at each end.

The Momo supplied and branded leather-rimmed wheel continued the aluminium theme of the dash panels, its flat three-spoke centre made from the same material. At its centre was a circular horn-push, bearing a yellow 'Dino' script badge in first series cars, replaced by the evocative 'cavallino rampante' insignia for the second series. Three column stalks were presented behind the wheel, the one to the right controlling screen washers and the two-speed plus

■ THE 308GT4

LEFT: **308GT4 with the headlamp pods raised.**

BELOW: **Marginal rear-seat accommodation very much apparent in this extensively leather-trimmed example.**

intermittent windscreen wipers, the two to the left operating lights and direction indicators. In wonderfully counter-intuitive Italian style, the single stalk controlling the headlamps raised the car's lamp pods, but the driver had to remember to push the lever *down* to bring the lamps *up*!

The central console was a low-set affair, shrouding a raised area running the length of the car's floor pan, beneath which ran the central chassis rail and coolant pipes for the front-mounted radiator. The typically Ferrari open-gated gearshift was mounted to the side of the console nearest the driver. Ahead of the gearshift was the radio slot offering an unusual vertical mounting of the chosen radio unit – never a standard fitment – and air-conditioning controls when this feature was fitted. Alongside the black plastic ball-topped gear lever were switches for electric aerial and power-operated window switches – optional on series one cars, though standardized for the second series. A wide ashtray and cigar lighter filled out the rear of the console, with a switch for rear window demisting and a slider-operated choke of the same elongated oval design used for the heater controls. At the tail end of the console was a further ashtray for rear-seat passengers.

The optional Veglia Borletti air-conditioning system was a very popular option, greatly improving the noisy and inadequate standard ventilation system; most cars were so equipped, especially in the USA, where dealers typically delivered cars that had been ordered with a comprehensively ticked options list. The freon-charged system included a compressor driven from the same end of the crankshaft as the alternator via a dedicated rubber belt, and a condenser mounted at the car's radiator and cooled by the right-hand radiator fan. Series two cars featured revised trunking arrangements so that cooled air was channelled via a pair of adjustable rectangular outlets mounted centrally below the dash moulding, instead of the earlier cars' rather unsatisfactory reuse of the three dash-top outlets. A simple, twinned, rotary knob control allowed the driver to select fan speed and moderate the intensity of cooling.

Trim and Fittings

Vinyl – often, though not exclusively, black – was very much the material of choice for the interior, covering door cards, dashboard and centre console, the headlining usually in a contrasting ribbed white vinyl. Door-release levers were borrowed from the Fiat 850. Seats were also often trimmed in vinyl with central cloth panels, sometimes in a contrasting colour and with matching cloth panels featured within the door cards. Leather trim was optionally available, sometimes for seat facings only, or in some cases swathing the entire interior, including the headlining.

The front seats were comfortable, despite the seemingly slim-line construction – an attempt to maximize rear passenger space – and while the rear seats looked inviting, nothing could reinstate the legroom compromised by the car's compact wheelbase, despite their deeply sculpted profile. All four seats were equipped with a head restraint and a seatbelt, which was relatively unusual for the period, and as a further token concession to rear passenger comfort, a lamp was fitted above the rear seats in addition to the one between the sun visors at the front.

The entire floor area, including the front wheel-arch intrusions, was carpeted, again often in a contrasting colour to the rest of the interior trim. Indeed, Ferrari's flexibility in trim selection meant that exuberant owners could go for very striking schemes, where red, tan, grey and blue carpeting contrasted with coloured vinyls; this was in addition to the more traditional black and cream selections.

Not every 308GT4 owner would see value in the necessarily compromised rear seats, and so an alternative luggage area could be installed in the rear of the cabin, its carpets protected by three aluminium rubbing rails on the floor and bulkhead, and equipped with two long leather straps to restrain luggage during spirited cornering. In practice this option was rarely selected, since all cars in any case featured a decently sized, locked luggage area accessed via a second opening panel aft of the bonnet. Useful, if prone to heat ingress as a result of the nearby engine bay and underlying exhaust silencer, the deep luggage area was carpeted with a heavy-duty hessian-

Decent-sized luggage compartment. Situated behind the engine bay and above the exhaust silencer, the contents could become very hot!

Delightful details can be found everywhere on the 308GT4.

■ THE 308GT4

ABOVE: **A brace of late GT4s at Silverstone.**

BELOW: **Compomotive alloys are popular with owners, happily also permitting them to choose from a wide range of modern performance tyres.**

style weave, and accessed by use of the opening lever fitted in the driver's side door-shut. This lever was elegantly packaged in a rectangular panel, alongside a second lever which opened the bonnet; ingeniously, both levers could be locked using the ignition key.

Generally considered a comfortable place to sit, especially when trimmed in leather and with air-conditioning installed, two aspects of the 308GT4's cabin marred its overall ambience, rather undermining Ferrari's claims that the new V8 was a viable, usable, everyday prospect. First, the pedals were rather heavily offset to the car's centreline, particularly in right-hand-drive models, making for a slightly skewed driving position. Also, cabin noise was higher than the typical GT customer might expect: in a contemporary test, *Autocar* magazine recorded a rather tiresome 81dBA at a steady 70mph (113km/h), rising to 93dBA when tested during a full-bore acceleration run in first gear.

Safety Features

Although such features had not yet become marketable, the GT4 was a reasonably safe car in which to travel. Space-frame construction made for a relatively strong passenger protection cell, and brakes that offered a good level of performance, and dual circuits, optimised opportunities to avoid an accident. Initially cars were delivered with static three-point seatbelts at the front, though these were later changed to inertia reel belts – and two-point belts were provided for rear seat passengers, though the car was built from the outset with anchor points for rear three-point seatbelts. In addition to the seatbelt warning device, US-market cars from 1976 had a pressure switch installed in the driver's seat, which disabled the fuel pump when the seat was vacated, thus cutting the engine whenever the car's controls were left unattended.

US market cars were also fitted with large and heavy, rather shelf-like bumpers, similar in shape to the elegant standard items though with a much greater protrusion, adding 19.5cm (7.7in) to the European car's overall length. US cars were also fitted with sizeable square side-marker lights chopped into the front and rear wings, though they never received the helpful driving lamps set behind the grille of cars bound elsewhere, which were wired to provide a daytime 'flash' facility. European series one cars were not fitted with any exterior mirrors at first, while the more safety-conscious US market required a rectangular metal mirror to be provided. Second series cars received a black plastic aerodynamically shaped

308GT4 (1973–80)

Layout and chassis: Two-plus-two-seat coupé with tubular steel frame and steel and steel construction body/chassis

Engine
Type:	F 106 AL mid-mounted transverse, 90-degree V8, wet-sump
Block material:	Aluminium alloy with cast-iron liners
Head material:	Aluminium alloy
Cylinders:	8 in V configuration
Cooling:	Water
Bore and stroke:	81 × 71mm
Capacity:	2926.9cc
Valves:	Actuation by twin overhead camshafts per bank, 2 valves per cylinder
Compression ratio:	8.8:1
Fuelling:	Four Weber 40 DCNF carburettors
Ignition:	Single spark plug per cylinder, two coils
Max. power (din):	255bhp at 7,700rpm
Max. torque (Nm):	283 at 5,000rpm
bhp per tonne:	187
bhp per litre:	87
Fuel capacity:	80ltr (17.6gal)

Transmission
Gearbox:	Five speed plus reverse
Clutch:	Single plate

Ratios
First:	3.418
Second:	2.353
Third:	1.693
Fourth:	1.244
Fifth:	0.952
Reverse:	3.247
Final drive:	3.71:1

Suspension and Steering
Front:	Independent, unequal length wishbones, coil springs over telescopic shock absorbers, anti-rollbar
Rear:	Independent, unequal length wishbones, coil springs over telescopic shock absorbers, anti-rollbar
Steering:	Rack and pinion
Tyres:	205/70 VR 14
Wheels:	Alloy, 14in diameter
Rim width:	6.5in
Turning circle:	12m (39ft)

Brakes
Type:	Vented disc brakes front and rear
Size:	272mm front, 277mm rear

Dimensions
Track:	Front: 1,460mm (57in)
	Rear: 1,460mm (57in)
Wheelbase:	2,550mm (100.4in)
Overall length:	4,300mm (169in)
Overall width:	1,800mm (70.8in)
Overall height:	1,180mm (46.5in)
Unladen weight:	1,365kg (3,010lb)

Performance
Top speed:	250km/h (155mph)
0–60mph (sec):	6.2 (*Car* magazine November 1974)
0–400m (sec):	14.4
Standing km (sec):	26.2

■ THE 308GT4

Vitaloni mirror to the driver side, as used on Ferrari Grand Prix cars of the day, and a passenger-side mirror could be selected from the options list. Strident twin Fiamm horns allowed the driver to make owners of lesser machinery acutely aware of the Ferrari's presence.

Scant attention was paid in this era to vehicle security, and the new Dino was no exception. Nothing more than a pair of simple keys was required to gain access to, and to start the car's engine. While the steering lock was rudimentary, the 308GT4 driver could at least partially relax in many circumstances, safe in the knowledge that their car required a certain knack to be started successfully, especially if the engine was hot. Certainly the lockable front and rear compartment levers in the door jamb were welcome protection for occupants' personal effects, operated with the door key, which also secured the glovebox; this was a different key than that for the ignition, thereby allowing secure storage of personal effects when the ignition key was handed over for valet parking. US market cars were also fitted with an easily visible plaque on the top of the steering column with the car's chassis number.

THE BERTONE RAINBOW

Bertone was clearly determined to fight to maintain credibility as an alternative design house for modern Ferraris, and set out to prove the point by building the Rainbow concept car on 308GT4 chassis number 12788, the production floor pan having been shortened by 100mm (4in) for service on this strictly two-seat car. The angular sportster made its debut at the 1976 Turin show, presented alongside Bertone's then-current production Ferrari, on the company's own show stand.

Extending themes already explored in the earlier design for Fiat's X1/9 roadster, flat planes and razor edges predominated in the Rainbow, its design eschewing completely any curves and rounded forms – even for the wheel arches. Dramatically shaped in an origami wedge, slab-sided and with a flat ramp for its nose, the angular car was the height of modernity, though it could hardly be described as beautiful. Speedline wheels in a pseudo-technical striped design completed the startling look. Those flat planes recurred even within the car, where a plank-like dash panel carried standard GT4 instrumentation and switchgear.

The Rainbow was named to emphasize perhaps the car's most interesting technical feature: a unique fold-away targa-style roof. At the press of a button, the roof's leading edge was released from the windscreen, and the intricately hinged top could be dropped down behind the seats. The driver could raise and lower the roof from his seat with a convenient handle – and as the roof folded away, it inscribed a rainbow-shaped arc.

Fully roadworthy, the Rainbow was shown by Bertone for three years, though its wilfully different lines won it few plaudits. It remained a 'one off'. On retirement it was sold to a private collector, though it was subsequently reacquired by Bertone for its museum collection.

Angular 308GT4-based concept, the Bertone Rainbow.
TINC FLAVIU

CHAPTER FOUR

THE 308GTB AND 308GTS

Mike Moore's wonderfully original glassfibre 308GTB. Note the twin radiator fans and Fiamm horns visible through the front grille.
MIKE MOORE

Beautifully pure styling of the glassfibre 308GTB.
MIKE MOORE

Is any car more readily identifiable by the majority of the public as a Ferrari than the 308GTB? With its beautifully curvaceous body and racy five-spoke wheels, low slung to emphasize its performance potential, it is a timeless design that looks fresh even as it approaches its fortieth birthday. For most people, uninformed bystander and enthusiast alike, here is the car they recall when they think of Ferrari.

The 308GTB

The 308GTB – 'B' indicating berlinetta bodywork – was the second model powered by the new 3-litre, V8 power unit, and the first non-V12 GT car built at Maranello to carry proudly the revered Ferrari emblems. Unlike its Bertone-penned stablemate, the new berlinetta would have a Pininfarina-designed body, albeit one more consistent with the aesthetic of previous Maranello models, and a body of such compact lines that this time there would be space inside for only two occupants.

In response to the perceived lack of popularity faced by Ferrari's first V8 model, it was perhaps inevitable that design duties would revert to Carrozzeria Pininfarina, whose curvaceous styling had over the previous twenty years become near synonymous with Ferrari sports cars. The scheme that Leonardo Fioravanti's team devised would amalgamate cues from Boxer and Dino, but incorporate them into a wholly original design. The finished product was strongly reminiscent of both cars, yet with its own definite personality. The Dino 308GTB – as it was often referred to in the press prior to launch – would be a compact and graceful return to the two-seat berlinetta models most sorely missed by enthusiasts since its demise in the Dino 246GT; indeed the new car would even share the V6 car's compact 2,340mm (92in) wheelbase.

■ THE 308GTB AND 308GTS

Design

The new 308 would be strongly wedge-shaped, but would shun Gandini's wilful angularity in favour of an organic whole, characterized by graceful curves: fenders arced over the wheels, meeting in an elegant dip beneath the cabin's glasshouse, and even the rear window was curved to meet the flanking buttresses in acknowledgement of Pininfarina's Dino, and in stark contrast to the Bertone car with which it would share showroom floor space. The steeply raked buttresses, between which the rear window would sit, represented one of the few areas of bodywork where straight lines ruled, a crisp, more contemporary reinterpretation of the flowing treatment Pininfarina had bestowed on its Dino predecessor. Indeed, the upright rear window and flying buttress treatment had been seen on several former Pininfarina designs that predated the Dino by more than a decade – for example, a unique 375MM produced for Roberto Rossellini and Ingrid Bergman, shown at the 1954 Paris Auto Show, featured just such a rear window treatment; this was a forward-thinking design that also featured such advanced aerodynamic details as retractable headlamps, helping to smooth its low-set nose.

Other details on the new two-seat Ferrari also referenced previous Pininfarina works: for example, the bullet-shaped air intakes extending from an aperture ahead of the rear wheel arches forward into the door were clearly cribbed from the prototype and production V6 Dino as well as the 206SP sports racer, which bore similar intakes. These distinctive intakes even adorned the sides of Pininfarina's front-engined V12-powered Ferrari 365 California Spider. Twin air radiator outlets behind the retractable headlamps were also a further reference to the V6 Dino, the functional grillework of the newer car evoking the stylized air outlets on the front lid of those cars.

A horizontal swage line, deeply inset into the panelwork and extending round the car's belt line, was also something of a Pininfarina staple, having appeared on the production Daytona, the Modulo show car and on the 400 series introduced in 1972. It would form a key element of the 308's family resemblance with its V12-powered supercar stablemate, the Berlinetta Boxer of 1971, and like the bigger mid-engined car, the innermost surface of this swage line on the 308 would be lowlighted by the application of a stripe of matt black tape. The upright Kamm-style rear panel that carried the circular rear lamps, and the number plate that nestled beneath the hint of a lipped spoiler, were also typical of Pininfarina Ferraris, a further visual link to the 246GT Dino and consistent with Pininfarina's work on earlier Maranello models: a similarly truncated tail design was first applied by the Carrozzeria to a front-engined Ferrari, the 275GTB of 1964.

While the 308GTB was clearly a relation of the 246GT Dino in its design, its more modern front aspect was first previewed, albeit in embryonic form, as early as 1968, on the Ferrari P6 concept car introduced at the Turin Auto Show that year. Its low-set front end was clearly indicative of the production cars Pininfarina would pen for Ferrari, the Berlinetta Boxer and of course the 308GTB, and its side profile was remarkably

Ferrari 365 California Spider featuring rear-wing air intake, a favoured styling cue for Pininfarina through the latter part of the 1960s and into the 1970s.
JONATHAN TREMLETT

THE 308GTB AND 308GTS

RIGHT: **An early steel car. Note the painted-on exhaust cut-out above the non-standard four-exit exhaust system.**

BELOW: **The very first right-hand-drive 308GTB; the car featured in** *Autocar*'s **road test in October 1976.**
PHOTO © FERRARIBYNEILLBRUCE.CO.UK

close to that of the 308. The rear wing-mounted air intake was even present on this prescient prototype. But not all the details on the new berlinetta referenced Pininfarina's own earlier works; for instance, the simple egg-crate style aluminium radiator grille that nestled beneath an elegantly slim-line satin black bumper was essential Ferrari, harking back to the very first of Maranello's models, those that had been bodied by Touring, and also Vignale.

By 1975 it was an open secret that Ferrari's excellent V8 engine would soon be powering a new two-seat model that would be sold alongside its relatively unloved 308GT4. Midway through the year, various magazines, including *Road and Track*, began to speculate about the new car, and some even carried images of it, either artist's impressions or grainy photographs of a prototype 308GTB, introduced in one Italian article logically – but incorrectly, as it would transpire – as the 308GT2. The photographs showed a prototype extremely close to production form, though wearing Dino-style Cromodora wheels, and with a rather different front valance treatment, lacking the full-width spoiler moulding that would feature on the production car, making for a frontal view close to that of the contemporary Berlinetta Boxer.

This prototype was extensively tested by a Ferrari team including Grand Prix driver Niki Lauda, the period reports stating that some 90,000km (56,000 miles) were covered as the car's handling, steering and brakes were tuned to ensure the controls would be usable by a wide range of drivers, including, as Lauda himself commented in one article, 'control inputs appropriate for use by a woman!'

By November 1975 the wait was over, and the car designed fully to replace the Dino 246GT was at last presented to the world at the Paris Salon. It was an instant hit, Pininfarina's gorgeous bodywork ensuring it was one of the stars of the show. To reinforce the sporty nature of the new Berlinetta, Scuderia drivers Lauda and Regazzoni appeared in launch

45

THE 308GTB AND 308GTS

imagery, including shots of the 308GTB at Fiorano, Ferrari's private racetrack, alongside the 312T Grand Prix cars. Lauda would also appear at events such as the 1976 Turin Motor Show, endorsing the car on behalf of his employers, and a 308 provided by the company permitted Ferrari to make further marketing capital from their talented driver.

Into Production

The start of 308GTB construction coincided with revisions to Ferrari's assembly lines, Ferrari perhaps anticipating that the new car might result in greater demand than their traditional factory could satisfy. The trim shop was moved into Ferrari's own factory from its prior location at Scaglietti. Acquired by Ferrari in 1971, long-term collaborator Scaglietti was now a subsidiary, thanks to the plentiful funds that arrived as part of the partnership agreement between Ferrari and the Fiat Group. Scaglietti would now focus exclusively on bodywork construction, building the new berlinetta alongside the 308GT4, and again delivering them to the Ferrari factory, painted and ready for assembly. By 1978, Ferrari had installed a state-of-the-art paint facility within its Maranello factory, and had taken over the job of finishing bodyshells in house.

Reorganizing the factory was not the only major transformation in production methodology arriving with this new model. In a surprising departure, the 308GTB's body would be constructed largely from glassfibre (or *vetroresina* as it was known at Ferrari) rather than traditional steel or exotic aluminium. Glassfibre panelwork was built round a tubular steel chassis very similar to that found in a 308GT4 Dino. Although Maranello's choice of panelwork material was unexpected, its adoption was not without logic. Certainly Scaglietti possessed extensive glassfibre experience, gained through the production of wheel wells and floor-pan mouldings used in the build of the Dino and Daytona, and more recently for 400GT and 308GT4 models. While glassfibre is perhaps frowned upon today for exclusive car construction, British rival Lotus was building an entire range from the same material, including their formidable 308GTB competitor, the mid-engined two-seat Esprit.

The simple spaceframe that underpinned every 308 and 328, altered only in detail throughout production. Note the offset central chassis tube, allowing the gear lever to be sited more conveniently nearer to the driver's hand. GAVIN MORRIS

Body panels overlaid the tubular frame, these being of a later 328, though all cars were very similar in construction.
GAVIN MORRIS

Nevertheless, while Scaglietti's work in glassfibre was of excellent quality – indeed many contemporary reviews made much of the fact that the bodywork was all but indistinguishable from steel – and brought with it the associated benefits of rust resistance and easy repair, towards the end of 1976 cars bound for the USA began to be built in more traditional pressed steel and aluminium. Models bound for the European market followed suit in mid-1977.

Press Reports

The initial glassfibre cars benefited from a further advantage over the later steel cars: that of lower kerb-weight. Unfortunately, given Ferrari's inconsistency in publishing specification figures for their cars in the period, it is difficult to state with certainty the actual weight saving this construction process bestowed. A dry-weight figure as low as 1,090kg (2,400lb) was cited in some press materials, indeed this figure could be seen in 2013 on Ferrari's own website, though the owner's handbook for the model was perhaps more realistic in presenting the car's weight in normal operation as 1,265kg (2,790lb).

But despite Ferrari's ambitious kerb-weight claim, European market cars were light and fast. While the claimed 255km/h (158mph) top speed, and the standing kilometre timing of 25.4, were perhaps somewhat optimistic, an early glassfibre car in the hands of Paul Frère, reporting for *Road and Track* magazine in March 1976, achieved some excellent numbers. The ex-racing driver executed a 0–60 dash in just 6.4sec, and reached a top speed of 248km/h (154mph).

This time the car that Frère tested was quoted as weighing 1,200kg (2,646lb), further adding to the confusion. By 1978 the handbook contained a dry-weight figure for the car – by this time constructed in steel, of course – of 1,330kg (2,930lb). Despite the confusion, whichever quoted figure is correct for the glassfibre car, there was certainly a weight saving, even if it was somewhat less significant than some specification tables promised; the true difference is likely to be something around the 65kg (143lb) spread indicated by the handbooks.

Frère's test was a most illuminating read, presenting a race driver's insight into this exciting new car's handling. 'Fast bends are really the 308GTB's element,' he expounded, 'and they can be taken in a full four-wheel drift with a feeling of utter stability.' Echoing this positive assessment, fellow racer Bob Bondurant, again in *Road and Track*, December 1976, likened driving a US Specification GTB to piloting a Ford GT40, '…so neutral you can do anything you want with it … it doesn't understeer badly or oversteer badly. It is an easy car to drive … probably the best sports car I've ever driven', concluding his judgement emphatically and personally with the statement 'I want one!' Despite being hobbled somewhat by safety and emissions rulings, US and Australian market cars were good performers, assigned performance figures by the factory of 236km/h (147mph) top speed and 26.6sec for the standing kilometre sprint.

Almost every press report for the new V8 Ferrari was, in the main, very positive. Analytical tester John Bolster was very much taken with the new two-seater when he sampled it in

Rear end of a European fibreglass 308GTB, the giveaways being the reverse lamps installed in the bumper ends, single colour indicator lenses, and no number-plate indentation in the rear panel.
MIKE MOORE

■ THE 308GTB AND 308GTS

RIGHT: **A lightly modified fibreglass 308GTB competing in the 2013 Pirelli Ferrari Classic.**

BELOW: **Early cars featured many beautiful details, including delicate Carello indicators on the front wings and door-mounted electric window switches.**

July 1976, for *Autosport* magazine, stating that 'acceleration continues surprisingly vividly past 130', though he was less keen on the hard-to-read instruments and leaky boot. Other reports, although largely complimentary, levelled further minor criticisms against the car; thus *Autocar* magazine in October 1976 was concerned with the car's directional stability, noting '…the slightest crosswind leading to a very disconcerting weaving at speeds in excess of 130mph'.

Limitations in ride also came under scrutiny, *Autocar* again commenting that 'at low speeds, on less than smooth surfaces, the 308GTB's ride is very bumpy, with potholes giving rise to much crashing and banging', though they did go on to say that 'at very high speed the ride gives great confidence with no tendency to pitch, and not a trace of float'. *Car and Driver* agreed,

an article published in their March 1977 edition bemoaning a lack of suspension travel, even going so far as to suggest they could hear a tyre touching the bodywork.

Despite such niggles, most coverage made it clear that irrespective of issue or limitation, here was a really desirable car, one that was absolutely worthy of the Ferrari badge it wore with pride. Its introduction also marked the end of Enzo Ferrari's ambition to immortalize his son in a line of cars. Nevertheless, pre-launch press speculation about the likely Dino moniker had certainly been well founded, as Ferrari's original intention was likely to have been to badge the car as a Dino – indeed a mock-up of the 308GTB had been left to languish in the factory's concept car graveyard through the 1970s, and a photograph taken of it by Hilary A. Raab Jr on a visit to the factory in 1979 clearly featured a bonnet indentation appropriate for the rectangular Dino badge, rather than the 'cavallino rampante' installed on production models.

Unlike the V6 Dinos and 308GT4, which in appearance if not intention seemed to have been offered almost apologetically under an alternative badge, the new 308 would set the template for Ferrari's future. From the 308GTB onwards, the mid-engined, V8-powered two-seater would to many become synonymous with Ferrari, supplanting Enzo's favoured front-engined GT cars as the type of car most associated with the marque. While other models were offered alongside it, it was the popularity and saleability of the 308GTB and its successors that maintained Ferrari's successful growth. And it was obvious to see why the car appealed: glamorous, purposeful, compact, aspirational, the 308GTB was a Dino for the late 1970s, and everyone's idea of a modern Ferrari. Indeed, so successful was its recipe that when the 308GTB ceased production, Ferrari's replacement was in effect an updated version of the original design, fettled mechanically, but aesthetically unaltered.

During the course of its production from 1975 to 1980, 2,897 cars were built. Unlike the 308GT4 that shared the V6 Dino's even-only chassis numbering sequence, the 308GTB – and the open GTS model described later in this chapter – would adopt the normal Ferrari odd-only chassis numbering sequence.

Engine

With expediency born out of Ferrari's low-volume approach to production, the V8 powerplant was carried forward largely unaltered from the Bertone car. The same Weber carburettors were installed, and again, high compression pistons plus a high lift camshaft could be selected from the options list. There was just one small but significant deviation from the earlier car's engine specification, and a new engine code, F106AB, was coined to indicate it: the V8 engine now featured a dry-sump lubrication system, an installation appropriate to the two-seater's more sporting character.

Such systems are favoured by racers for three reasons: first, and most importantly for the race track, a pressurized lubrication system prevents the situation in wet-sump engines where cornering forces draw oil in the sump to one side, thereby uncovering the oil pick-up pipe, and causing potentially damaging oil starvation. Second, with such a system it was possible to increase oil capacity by using a larger reservoir tank, thereby making available a greater volume of oil for engine-cooling duties. And third, dispensing with the sump presents the opportunity to mount the engine somewhat lower in the car, pushing the centre of gravity downwards and thereby improving handling.

Were these benefits realized to make sense of the investment in effort in commissioning a dry-sump arrangement at all? While the berlinetta was certainly a more overtly sporting car than the two-plus-two-seater, Ferrari would tacitly acknowledge that such a system was overkill for even this sporting road car: US market cars were fitted with a wet-sump arrangement from the start, and in time all cars, irrespective of market, would discontinue the use of this undoubtedly more expensive racing-style set-up. While it was certainly capable of sustaining oil supply on track, in spirited cornering during normal road use the worry of oil starvation was simply not an issue. Oil capacity was certainly increased. A revised sump-pan/gearbox casing, coupled with an external oil reservoir tank, tucked down in the left corner of the engine bay, hard against the bulkhead between the engine and the luggage area, made room for 11ltr (2.4gal) instead of the wet-sump V8's 9ltr (2gal).

Unfortunately, given the constraints imposed by the requirement to be able to install both dry- and wet-sump powerplants within the same engine bay, and fixed in a single location by use of the same underslung transmission as the wet-sump cars,

Engine bay of a glassfibre 308GTB. Note the oil tank for the racy dry-sump oil system.
MIKE MOORE

THE 308GTB AND 308GTS

16in alloy wheels and silver colour scheme combine with Pininfarina's timeless design, for an amazingly contemporary appearance.

Ferrari could not exploit the opportunity to lower the motor. The dry-sump system certainly added complexity to the car; while a wet-sump car managed with a single oil pump, the dry-sump-equipped V8 required no fewer than three – two scavenging oil from the bottom end of the motor and a further external pump at the belt end of the engine. An oil-cooler radiator was installed, fed air by the nearside flank aperture, while the offside one fed cool air via trunking to the quartet of Weber 40 DCNF carburettors. A crankcase emission control system deposited oil into the oil reservoir tank and vented fumes to the air intake, whereas wet-sump cars, lacking the reservoir tank, would require a small separator tank, which routed liquid oil back to the sump, and vapour into the car's air intake.

If the dry-sump installation was compromised in the 308GTB, why did Ferrari go to the trouble of devising the arrangement? The motivation for installing such a complex system was probably in pursuit of the possibility of race success; both Group 4 and the later Group B homologation papers provided for dry-sump lubrication as a result, despite the fact that Group B regulations came into effect long after production cars had reverted to a wet-sump configuration.

Dry-sump equipment aside, installation of the powerpack into the smaller car mirrored that of the 308GT4, though there were naturally some detail changes as a result of dimensional and proportional difference in bodyshells. The front-mounted radiator and twin fan arrangement was carried forward, and the catch tank was again mounted in the lower right corner of the engine bay, though the tank itself was of a different upright design. The earliest cars used a single Magneti Marelli distributor, though consistent with the 308GT4, models bound for American and Australia always had the twin distributor arrangement. Indeed the cars were considered so similar by the factory that no workshop manual would be issued, dealers having to make do with the GT4 manual when effecting repairs or maintenance on the newer car.

Exhaust System

Curiously, European cars had a rather less sporty-looking exhaust outlet arrangement: while US cars fielded a traditional exhaust system with four exhaust outlets – albeit shrouded by a large matt black covering grille – Euro cars were specified with a single tailpipe exiting beneath a lower valance that bore a single indentation to clear it. *Car* magazine's July 1976 evaluation of the model singled this out as one of the disappointments associated with the new V8 Ferrari, likening its exhaust note to the sound of a 4-cylinder Lotus – in stark contrast to comments in the same publication commending the 308GT4 for a convincing acoustic performance. An optional sports exhaust could be chosen that restored aural performance and also improved aesthetic aggression, featuring the four outlets that were by now for many synonymous with Ferrari.

The different exhaust arrangements for US- and Australia-bound cars were less to do with sound, and more to do with legislation: these GTBs wore the same kind of pressed-steel manifolds as the 308GT4, containing gas analysis probe inlets at each exhaust port, allowing service personnel to set carburettors accurately so that CO and HC levels met local legislation. Again, the fast idle device and air injection system of the two-plus-two V8 was installed. And, as with the bigger 308, US market cars featured numerous detail amendments – plaques and stickers inscribed with mandated warnings, sealed fuel-tank cap, vapour traps and valves within the fuel system – all designed to comply with varying legislation across US states.

And performance-constraining legislation would only escalate through the decade. By 1978, US cars were required to be fitted with catalytic converters, and this, combined with lower octane unleaded petrol (a narrow fuel-filler neck preventing the inadvertent use of wide bore, leaded petrol pumps), meant a further drop in power. Now only 205bhp was available, and the car was encumbered by the increasing bulk of safety and emissions equipment. US-bound GTBs weighed in at a beefy 1,433kg (3,160lb), making Ferrari's unaltered 236km/h (147mph) top speed and 27sec standing quarter claims less realistic for these later cars. In a final regulatory insult to performance aspirations for the US market cars, those equipped with catalytic converters featured a dashboard lamp marked 'slow down', warning of excessive catalyst temperatures.

Transmission

The transmission was carried forward from the GT4 largely unaltered, though a lower fifth gear was specified. Like all Ferraris of the period, clutch action was quite heavy, and required full depression to achieve consistently clean gearshifts. During Paul Frère's test for *Road and Track* in March 1976, he noted that following acceleration tests, the clutch pedal mechanism had a tendency to leave the pedal on the floor – disconcerting, and incurring the risk of over-revving the engine. It was a problem that *Autosport*'s tester, John Bolster, had previously experienced when testing a 308GT4, though when he tried the 308GTB he found no such issue.

Bodywork Dimensions

Although less impressive than Bertone's achievement of packaging four seats in such a compact car, Pininfarina could nevertheless boast that the 308GTB sat on the same wheelbase as the two-seat Dino 246GT even with the adoption of

Steel-bodied 308GTB. Note the lack of exhaust pipe cut-outs, and the migration of reversing lamps to the centres of the indicator lenses.
JO THOMAS

THE 308GTB AND 308GTS

the larger V8 power unit. Indeed the 308GTB was a most compact sportster, 70mm (2.8in) shorter than the 308GT4, 80mm (3in) narrower, and sitting a sporty 60mm (2.4in) lower: a handily diminutive performance car, its well judged dimensions making for an unintimidating and most exploitable driver's machine.

Bodywork Material

The comparatively lightweight glassfibre build of the rare early cars added further to performance capabilities (and to their desirability these days), though later steel-bodied cars were hardly portly machines, and their performance remained most acceptable, in European guise at least. Most reports suggest that 712 glassfibre cars were constructed before steel bodies became the norm through 1977, though there was a transitional period in which the factory produced cars bodied in either material. The final glassfibre car was believed to be chassis number 21289, and the first steel car 20805, these being the numbers reported by Geoff Willoughby in *Ferrari 308, 328 and Mondial*, published in 1988, though some enthusiast speculation contends that there was at least one further car built beyond this chassis number.

While the change of bodywork material made part-way through production seems dramatic, there are surprisingly few differences between steel and glassfibre cars. Self-tapping screw heads can be seen in door-shuts and at the panel edges beneath the rear compartment lid, but externally, about the only telltale feature on a glassfibre car is a small join across the top of the A pillar just beneath roof level. This line betrays the fact that glassfibre cars have steel windscreen pillars – the only steel outer panelwork on such cars – that adjoin the roof panel.

Given the lesser structural strength of glassfibre, hinge design for all opening panels differs somewhat from later steel cars. The engine cover can be detached via cable releases in hinge tubes, and door hinges are attached to lug-like brackets that are directly attached to the A-pillar chassis tubes, rather than being formed within the door-shut as on steel-bodied cars. Doors and the combined engine cover and luggage lid were made of glassfibre on resin cars, as were the lower front and rear valance panels, though the front compartment lid was of aluminium alloy. Equivalent panels on steel-bodied cars, apart from the aluminium front compartment lid, were pressed from steel, though glassfibre construction continued for front and rear valances. The rear panel did not feature the number-plate indentation that would be seen on later cars, though this indentation was present on US-delivered models.

An optional deep front valance available from around 1977 proved popular, and was also constructed of glassfibre. There are also detail differences in the framework around the cars' side glass, glassfibre cars featuring a rain gutter extending the length of the A pillar, while the equivalent on a steel car finished just a short way down the pillar.

Bodywork Features

Unlike the Dino models, which sported separate covers for engine bay and luggage boot, the 308GTB would feature a single combined engine cover and luggage lid, a large unit extending in towards the rear screen between raised buttresses, the final sections of which were incorporated into the lid itself. The cover was released using a pull lever concealed within the driver's door-shut, and once open the panel was held aloft with a rudimentary stay attached to a spring-loaded cable at its base so it could be retracted to lie flat when not in use. A secondary pull release could be used in an emergency, a loop high on the nearside of the cabin rear bulkhead provided for the purpose.

The engine was nestled between two bulkheads, one at the cabin rear, and one making the front wall of the luggage compartment at the rear. A zipped cover sealed a carpeted luggage area of 245ltr (54gal) capacity, though it did nothing to prevent heat ingress from the adjacent engine bay and exhaust silencer beneath. Cars destined for the warmer climates of the USA featured additional rows of louvres spanning the width of the engine cover aft of the twinned outlets fitted to European cars.

The wings and front panel of the car were joined as a single unit, with a front-hinged front lid inset at the centre. The lid itself was released via an under-dash lever, or by the usual pull-cable emergency release, and when lifted was propped up by an insubstantial stay, to expose a fully faired under-bonnet area. A semi-circular zipped cover offered access to the jack, toolkit and spare wheel – a skinny spare in markets where such an item was permissible.

The doors were opened from the outside via a delicate trigger-like pull handle set on the door top, located towards the rear of the window pane. The doors could be secured using the lock, low set beneath the large indentation which began the lines that would develop into the car's signature haunch-mounted air intakes. The left side intake fed air to the oil cooler, the right one provided cool air to the quartet of noisy carburettors, an installation that caused grumbles with a few

THE 308GTB AND 308GTS

RIGHT: **There were few giveaways as to the glassfibre construction of early 308GTBs; probably the most obvious was that self-tapping screws used to hold the panelwork to the spaceframe.**

BELOW LEFT: **Standard front valance, incorporating three additional cooling slots beneath the radiator air intake.**

BELOW RIGHT: **Front compartment of Mike Moore's early glassfibre 308GTB. Note the skinny spare wheel stowed beneath the neat zipped cover.**
MIKE MOORE

contemporary road-testers as intake noise dominated their experiences driving right-hand-drive cars.

Behind each rear side window was a series of satin-black finished louvres, those on the left side incorporating a hinged panel that provided access to a neatly concealed fuel filler cap.

Simple, compact satin black bumpers were installed, the one at the front carrying combined side marker lamps and indicators, and at the rear inset with rectangular reversing lamps – though US-bound cars were burdened with heavier and more prominent safety bumpers, with the reversing lamps relocated to the centre of the circular rear-indicator lamps. US market offerings could also be identified by the rectangular side marker lights set in the shapely wings. Ferrari would subsequently adopt this rear lamp design on later steel cars for all markets, thereby simplifying the rear bumpers by removing the inset reversing lamps.

THE 308GTB AND 308GTS

While simple Ferrari red paintwork was ever-present, like the 308GT4, the new berlinetta was available in a number of shades, including the usual Giallo Fly yellow hue, black, dark blue, and an attractive metallic dark red. Today rarely seen, the so-called Boxer paintwork scheme was an option, whereby the bodywork beneath the car's swage line was finished in satin black; while this device linked visually the smaller car to the Berlinetta Boxer – hence the option name – it has dated rather, and in recent years some cars finished this way have doubtless been refinished in a more contemporary paint scheme.

Perhaps it was the lack of Dino badging that precluded the re-use of the Cromodora-designed alloy wheels, but those handsome, five-spoked penta-star design alloy wheels seemed a perfect match for the simple, purposeful GTB, and would become one of Ferrari's signature motifs through the period. The wheels fitted were 14in in diameter, with a 6.5in width, though wider, 7.5in rims were a popular option, and were indeed standardized for the US market from 1978.

Suspension

The independent suspension followed the same layout as the two-plus-two-seat V8 car. Early cars suffered from a choppy ride – a characteristic noticed by many contemporary road-test reporters – borne out of the car's short wheelbase and limited wheel travel. The failing was partially mitigated by the adoption of alternative shock absorbers and coil-over springs, these items finding their way on to the earliest cars via a factory kit of parts for retrofitting – though there was no way to overcome the limited travel available within the confines of Pininfarina's low-set bodywork.

Braking System

The servo-operated braking system was also an essentially unaltered reprise of the installation found in the 308GT4, though with slightly larger diameter discs front and rear; this system effectively required a distance of 270m (885ft) to stop from 250km/h (155mph). The reservoir lid was accessed via a panel under the car's front bonnet. The handbrake was often ineffectual, the cable being unsheathed and running through a steel tube to operate on just the outer pads of the rear callipers; this system required precise adjustment to work efficiently, with further potential for problems since the cable was prone to binding within its tube.

Interior Features

While the interior of the 308GT4 was purposeful and handsome, it was rather understyled, being relatively straightforward in layout, if nicely detailed. For the berlinetta, Pininfarina conceived an elegant scheme, an interior that was practical certainly, but also with an obvious and unusual design motif to set it apart from more humdrum transport. A low-set, shelf-like dash moulding extended beneath the car's steeply

Recently refurbished rear suspension, 308.
JOHN DICKENS

308 front suspension detail.
JOHN DICKENS

THE 308GTB AND 308GTS

raked windscreen, flaring at each end to meet armrest mouldings mounted on the door-cards, to make a single arc that enveloped the car's occupants in a blended, curved effect rising up from each door and extending right across the dashboard. The familiar triplet of circular ventilation outlets were mounted to the centre of the expansive dash top, augmented by a pair of sickle-shaped vents at each end to assist in demisting duties at the screen's extremities.

In front of the driver a tall, trapezoid-shaped binnacle held the major instruments, which were installed into a brushed aluminium dashboard: speedometer on the left, rev-counter to the right, with minor instruments for fuel level, oil pressure and water temperature ranged between them. Instrument illumination dimmer and speedometer re-set knobs were mounted to the bottom of the panel, with warning lamps demarking each corner. A fifth warning light was found at the bottom centre of the panel in US market cars, reminding occupants to fasten their seatbelts.

A clock and an oil-temperature gauge were installed on a panel hung beneath the dashboard at the end closest to the driver's door, inconveniently distant from the driver's line of sight.

Steering wheel and column stalks were lifted straight from the 308GT4. On the passenger side of the dash moulding, just where a glovebox would typically be found, instead a detachable (often frustratingly self-detaching!) panel was located, which covered the fusebox. A small stowage bin was instead fitted between the seats, lidded and lockable, using the same key that secured the doors.

Switchgear and heater controls were located on the central console, while toggle switches controlling heater fan speed, wipe speed and hazard warning lamps were similar to those of the 308GT4 – though consistent with Pininfarina's curvaceous aesthetic, the finger grips for these controls were gracefully circular. Under-dash vents working in partnership with the central circular dash-top vent provided the outlets for the Veglia Borletti air-conditioning system, its rotary controls also mounted on the central console where the system was installed, alongside the cigarette lighter, behind the gear selector and ashtray, and ahead of the electric aerial switch.

The door-cards were dominated by sweeping armrest mouldings where the switches for the electric windows were

ABOVE: **Early 308GTB interior. Note the locking stowage bin between the seats.**

RIGHT: **Steel-bodied 308GTB. Note the rain gutter that stops partway down the car's A pillar.**

located, at the front of their upper surface. Beneath them were mounted the door latches, and, in typical Ferrari practice, also a removable bung to allow the windows to be raised with a small crank in the event of electric motor failure. Consistent with the two-plus-two-seat car, marker lamps were installed in the trailing edge of each door.

Seats – just two, of course, for this berlinetta – were a neat slimline design, markedly different to those of the earlier 308, eschewing the ribbed design of Bertone's car in favour of simpler decoration of just three vertical pleats adorning their faces. They could be reclined, though only as far as the bulkhead, giving the taller driver little scope for a driving position sufficiently reclined to avoid continual contact with the roof lining. Head restraints could be adjusted for height, and inertia reel belts were installed from the outset of production. An interior light was installed at the rear of the roof panel, just ahead of the rear window.

Reasonably equipped by the standards of the day, the 308GTB benefited from standard electric windows, and a Vitaloni mirror for the driver side only, though later models would feature a revised design, still in matt-black finish, though now adjustable from within the cabin. Air conditioning was optional for European cars, but standard in the USA. In an excellent example of attention to detail the wiper installation was thoughtfully refactored for right-hand-drive cars to better clear the driver's side. Similarly releases for front and rear panels switched sides to be more readily accessible to the driver.

Safety Measures

Occupant safety took another small but significant step forwards with the 308GTB design over previous Ferraris. While the chassis was certainly robust, there remained room for improvement in terms of crash protection, and so, influenced by Ralph Nader's campaigns that prompted US regulators to mandate new features to further improve occupant protection, US-market 308s were fitted with twin door beams and impact-absorbing bumpers. These regulations are the likely explanation for Ferrari curtailing the development of fully open-top versions of their cars for more than a decade, the risk of changes to regulations covering roll-over protection threatening the viability of such cars across the automotive industry through the period.

US safety and security regulations also explained some of the more nanny-like protection features 'enjoyed' by American drivers; these included seat-belt warning lamps and buzzers, and from 1979 a pressure switch within the driver seat, which would shut off the car's ignition after 30 seconds at idle if it remained unoccupied.

US- and Australia-bound cars wore a small plaque perched on the top of the steering column inscribed with the car's chassis number as a modest theft deterrent. From 1978 this sensible feature was standardized across all markets.

Immaculate glassfibre 308GTB interior.
MIKE MOORE

DESIGNER LEONARDO FIORAVANTI

While superstar designers Giuigaro and Gandini rightfully receive the credit due to them for their incredible contributions in the field of car design, Pininfarina's 1980s resident automotive artist Leonardo Fioravanti is perhaps a little less well known in comparison. Pininfarina has tended, through the years, to avoid crediting individual designers behind the firm's masterpieces, preferring credit to go to the firm itself, and by implication all of the team operating at the company at that time.

Nevertheless Fioravanti personally can be credited with nine Ferrari designs, and during his tenure at Pininfarina he oversaw development of the same number again. Initially intrigued by aerodynamics as much as by aesthetics, Fioravanti's thesis project for a degree in mechanical engineering proved sufficiently accomplished to form the basis for his employer Pininfarina's BMC 1800 concept car, presented in 1967 at Turin. His first Ferrari assignment at the Carrozzeria was to tweak the roof treatment of the mid-engined 250LM homologation special to improve its aerodynamic performance, and he was soon entrusted with an even more important project for Maranello: to transform the Dino Berlinetta Speciale concept, penned by Pininfarina designer colleague Aldo Brovarone, into a viable series-production road car.

Perhaps Fioravanti's most famous design – certainly one of his own personal favourites – was the Ferrari Daytona, beginning life as an uncommissioned project for which he drew his inspiration from the unclothed Ferrari V12 chassis he had observed in the factory. Fioravanti explained in an interview with Octane magazine of May 2008 that he had designed the big Ferrari GT in a creative flurry over a single week, bringing the rather outmoded 275GTB layout bang up to date with a sleekly modern and influential body shape. He was also responsible for penning the Berlinetta Boxer, this startling Modenese 12-cylinder supercar drawing heavily from his earlier musings on mid-engined supercars, the Ferrari-based P5 and P6 concept cars.

Fioravanti's personal favourite, the Ferrari 365GTB/4 Daytona.
JOHN DICKENS

By 1972 he was director of design at Pininfarina, and would later become managing director, though he remained personally responsible for several important design projects, including the 308GTB, the 288GTO, and the outrageous F40 supercar. Fioravanti moved into the Fiat Group in 1988 to become part of Ferrari's management team, then on to Fiat Group's Head of Centro Stile, before opting to go it alone with his own design consultancy.

He remains a huge car enthusiast, having campaigned a Lancia in classic rally racing, also becoming president of ANFIA (Italian Association of the Automobile Industry) in 2009. In an interview with *Classic & Sportscar* magazine in April 1993, he confessed to owning a small collection of Italian classics from Alfa Romeo, Lancia and, of course, a Ferrari – naturally one of his own creations – a glassfibre 308GTB, for which he clearly reserved some fondness. In the *Octane* magazine interview in May 2008, Fioravanti pronounced the 308GTB a '...simple and pure design', modestly observing that '...after the Bertone car [the Dino 308GT4], Ferrari wanted something a bit prettier, and I hope we gave them that'.

308GTB (1975–80)

Layout and chassis	Two-seat berlinetta with tubular steel frame and glassfibre construction body/chassis (later cars steel construction body)
Engine	
Type:	F 106 AB mid-mounted transverse, 90-degree V8, dry-sump (later cars wet-sump)
Block material:	Aluminium alloy with cast-iron liners
Head material:	Aluminium alloy
Cylinders:	8 in V configuration
Cooling:	Water
Bore and stroke:	81 × 71mm
Capacity:	2926.9cc
Valves:	Actuation by twin overhead camshafts per bank, 2 valves per cylinder
Compression ratio:	8.8 : 1
Fuelling:	Four Weber 40 DCNF carburettors
Ignition:	Single spark plug per cylinder, single coil
Max. power (din):	255bhp at 7,700rpm
Max. torque (Nm):	283 at 5,000rpm
bhp per tonne:	201
bhp per litre:	87
Fuel capacity:	80ltr (17.6gal)
Transmission	
Gearbox:	Five speed plus reverse
Clutch:	Single plate
Ratios	
First:	3.418
Second:	2.353
Third:	1.693
Fourth:	1.244
Fifth:	0.918
Reverse:	3.247
Final drive:	3.71:1
Suspension and Steering	
Front:	Independent, unequal-length wishbones, coil springs over telescopic shock absorbers, anti-rollbar
Rear:	Independent, unequal-length wishbones, coil springs over telescopic shock absorbers, anti-rollbar
Steering:	Rack and pinion
Tyres	205/70 VR 14
Wheels:	Alloy, 14in diameter
Rim width:	6.5in
Turning circle:	12m (39ft)
Brakes	
Type:	Vented disc brakes front and rear
Size:	274mm front, 279mm rear
Dimensions	
Track:	Front: 1,460mm (57.5in)
	Rear: 1,460mm (57.5in)
Wheelbase:	2,340mm (92in)
Overall length:	4,230mm (166.5in)
Overall width:	1,720mm (67.7in)
Overall height:	1,120mm (44in)
Unladen weight:	1,265kg (2,789lb)
Performance	
Top speed:	255km/h (158mph)
0–60 (sec):	5.8 (*Autosport* magazine July 1976)
0–400m (sec):	14.1
Standing km (sec):	25.4

The 308GTS

So positive was the 308GTB's reception, it was inevitable that Ferrari would choose to broaden the model's appeal by fielding an open-topped version alongside the popular berlinetta. Presented at the 1977 Frankfurt Salon, the 308GTS was clearly very similar to the closed version sharing most of its bodywork, and with only a few detail amendments to that car's design – aside, of course, from its convertible roof. The 'S' in the car's nomenclature denoted 'spider', though in reality the car was less than a full convertible, more similar in fact to Porsche's roof system found on their rival sports car the 911 Targa, and clearly an evolution of the scheme Pininfarina had devised for the much-missed 246GTS Dino.

Removal of the roof panel left the car open from the windscreen header rail to the roll structure joining the car's B pillars. Unlike Porsche's concertina roof panel, Ferrari opted for a solid glassfibre moulding, located at the front by two pins projecting into the header rail, and secured at the roll structure by two easily detachable swivel clamps. When removed, the roof panel stowed behind the seats in a bag provided for the purpose. The windscreen header rail was cleverly lipped to lift the flow of air passing over it, thereby minimizing buffeting within the cabin.

To further differentiate the open and closed cars, Pininfarina conceived an alternative rear-quarter window treatment, with louvred panels extending to cover the entire windows, rather

THIS PAGE:
Wet-sump engine fitted to a 308GTS.

OPPOSITE PAGE:
308GTB.
MIKE MOORE

THE 308GTB AND 308GTS

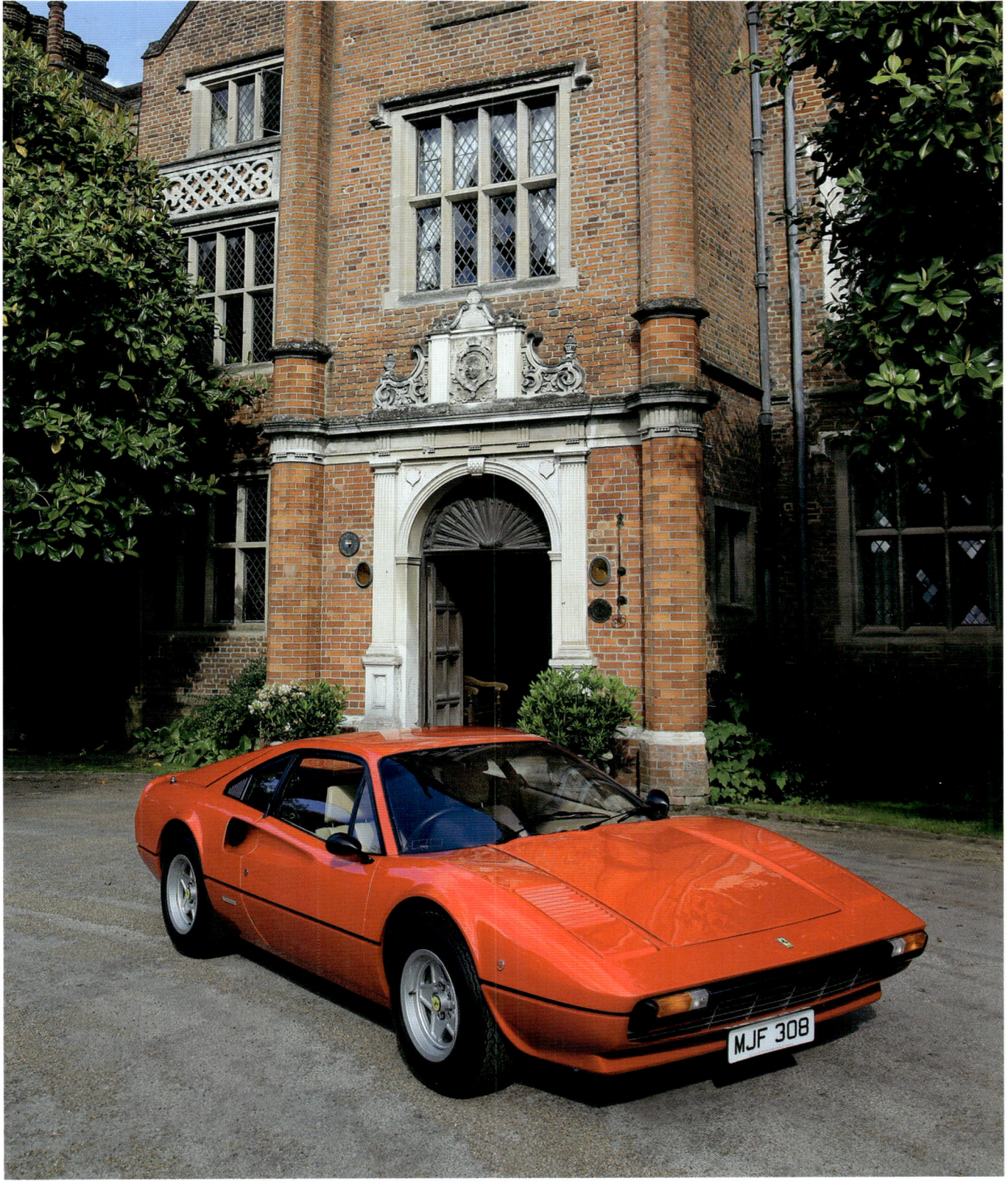

THE 308GTB AND 308GTS

US market 308GTS being enjoyed on track.
CÁSSIO MAGALHÃES DOS REIS

308GTS with non-standard F355-style wheels. Note the single exhaust outlet, standard for this model.

reminiscent of those of the 1957 250GT Tour de France coupé. The panels were hinged and lockable, facilitating access to clean the side window glasses beneath, and to reach the fuel filler on the left side.

While the roof panel, the floor mouldings, and the bumpers of the car were of glassfibre, the remainder of the 308GTS's bodywork was constructed from steel from the outset of production, though the front compartment lid was of aluminium. The GTS chassis was specially reinforced to compensate for the lack of a full roof, though strengthening incurred the cost of increased weight. Dry weight was given as 1,360kg (2,999lb), just 30kg (66lb) up on claims for the closed variant – though some experts contend that the difference was rather greater in reality – and Ferrari insisted that the 308GTS had performance parity with the 308GTB. The US specification GTS was quoted as weighing 1,463kg (3,226lb), making claims for the same 236km/h (147mph) top speed as the GTB, equally unlikely.

Mechanically there was little to tell the open car from its new sibling, though irrespective of market, every 308GTS would be built around the wet-sump motor eventually standardized for

308GTS interior. Note the gauges, situated rather out of the driver's sight-line to the lower right side of the dashboard.

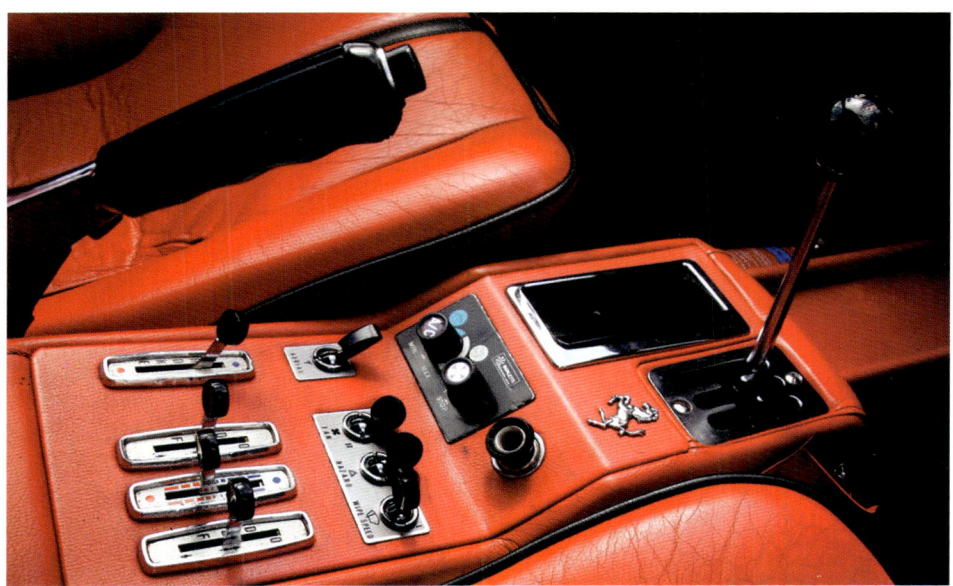

308 central console; note the Veglia Borletti air-conditioner controls next to the cigar lighter.

GTB production too. Oil capacity reverted to 9ltr (2gal), as for the 308GT4. While transmission design was the same as the other V8 cars, a different fifth-gear ratio was chosen, slightly higher at 1:0.952. This taller ratio was standardized across both open and closed US market cars from 1978 onwards, as was a lower first gear, 1:3.588 – a move doubtless intended to restore a little off-the-line sparkle from these underperforming 205bhp sportsters.

The suspension system was essentially carried over from the berlinetta, though fine-tuned for the open car, with a dif-

■ THE 308GTB AND 308GTS

ferent type of shock absorber for the front, and with amendments to the camber settings, a recommendation for lower front tyre pressures, and toe-in settings for both front and rear marginally altered. Following practice established with the 308GTB, the purposeful, deep front spoiler was optional on the open car, along with the sports exhaust system and the handsome 16in wheels, which did much to give the car a more aggressive stance. For the US and Australia, the GTS would suffer the heavier bumper assemblies and side marker lights that blighted the elegant lines of the GTB in those markets.

Inside the car, most of the changes made were due to the open car's removable roof arrangement. The interior light was re-sited to the windscreen header rail aft of the rear view mirror, and in the interests of secure stowage when the roof was down, the driver's door-card bin design was revised, a lockable flap reminiscent of that found on a satchel covering the pocket. The driver's side door pocket also contained the inspection lamp displaced from the GTB's handbrake-straddling glovebox: the latter installation was not suitable for the GTS because it would have encroached on the roof panel stowage area behind the seats.

While not a full convertible, the 308GTS was a most satisfactory open Ferrari: beautiful yet practical, relatively secure for an open car given the glassfibre roof panel, and sufficiently rigid in its bodyshell to be close in purity to the driving experience offered by the 308GTB. *Motor* magazine agreed, their August 1978 issue pitting a 308GTS against a Porsche 911 SC Targa, perhaps the benchmark for open-topped sports cars. While they still considered the German car more usable due to its faithful fuel injection and handy plus-two seating, they felt that the 308GTS stood comparison, praising in particular its good ride and commenting on its feeling of practicality and usability.

Road and Track were even more effusive in their praise, expounding in their June 1978 appraisal that: 'The Ferrari is a complete car. No aspect of its performance or its personality overpowers any other aspect…' and went on to point out the car's practicality: 'while it has a low, almost painfully pure body style, it demands no sacrifices from its driver or passenger in room or comfort.' Would-be owners must certainly have agreed with these verdicts, because shortly after production began in 1977, the factory was producing around two open cars for each berlinetta built. And when construction ceased in 1980 – at the same time as the 308GTB was discontinued – production totalled 3,219 examples, 10 per cent more than the 308GTB, despite having been in production for two years less.

308GTS (1977–80)

Layout and chassis:
Two-seat sports with removable roof panel with tubular steel frame and steel construction body/chassis

Engine
Type:	F 106 AB, mid-mounted transverse, 90-degree V8, wet-sump
Block material:	Aluminium alloy with cast-iron liners
Head material:	Aluminium alloy
Cylinders:	8 in V configuration
Cooling:	Water
Bore and stroke:	81 × 71mm
Capacity:	2926.9cc
Valves:	Actuation by twin overhead camshafts per bank, 2 valves per cylinder
Compression ratio:	8.8:1
Fuelling:	Four Weber 40 DCNF carburettors
Ignition:	Single spark plug per cylinder, single coil
Max. power (din):	255bhp at 7,700rpm
Max. torque (Nm):	283 at 5,000rpm
bhp per tonne:	188
bhp per litre:	87
Fuel capacity:	80ltr (17.6gal)

Transmission
Gearbox:	Five speed, plus reverse
Clutch:	Single plate
Ratios	
First:	3.418
Second:	2.353
Third:	1.693
Fourth:	1.244
Fifth:	0.952
Reverse:	3.247
Final drive:	3.71:1

Suspension and Steering
Front:	Independent, unequal-length wishbones, coil springs over telescopic shock absorbers, anti-rollbar
Rear:	Independent, unequal-length wishbones, coil springs over telescopic shock absorbers, anti-rollbar
Steering:	Rack and pinion
Tyres:	205/70 VR 14
Wheels:	Alloy, 14in diameter
Rim width:	6.5in
Turning circle:	12m (39ft)

Brakes
Type:	Vented disc brakes front and rear
Size:	274mm front, 279mm rear

Dimensions
Track:	Front: 1,460mm (57.5in)
	Rear: 1,460mm (57.5in)
Wheelbase:	2,340mm (92in)
Overall length:	4,230mm (166.5in)
Overall width:	1,720mm (67.7in)
Overall height:	1,120mm (44in)
Unladen weight:	1,360kg (2,999lb)

Performance
Top speed:	252km/h (157mph)
0–60 (sec):	6.6 (*Motor* magazine August 1978)
0–400m (sec):	14.1
Standing km (sec):	25.4

CHAPTER FIVE

THE FUEL-INJECTED 308

As a new decade dawned, so Ferrari would make public ambitious plans for its future, and the year 1980 would see the launch of not one, but two new important Ferrari models. A wholly new model would arrive that signalled in its name the Modena marque's intention to move away from distinct versions of each car for different markets: Ferrari's world car, the Mondial 8. Launched at the March 1980 Geneva Show, it would be the first model designed to comply with worldwide legislation, an approach gradually adopted across the range. A similar practice would be adopted for existing cars as they were refreshed and revamped, the intention being to minimize differentiation between markets, thereby simplifying the construction process. Legislative necessity emanating from the USA made such revision for the strong-selling GTB and GTS an urgent prospect, the revised models arriving on the scene late in 1980, hot on the heels of the Mondial, a car with which it would share powerplant design.

The 308GTBi and 308GTSi

Sensibly for the GTBi and GTSi, as the refreshed cars would be known, Ferrari had chosen to leave Pininfarina's masterful bodywork scheme essentially unaltered, the new car deviating in appearance from the carburetted models only in detail. Most effort had been expended in revisions to the engine, to ensure immediate compliance with emission standards coming into force in that most important of markets, the USA –

US market 308GTSi. Note the prominent bumpers mandated by Federal regulations.
JEFF GLUCKER

■ THE FUEL-INJECTED 308

PININFARINA

Ferrari 250GT SWB: to many, this was Pininfarina's finest work.
SIMON HODSON

Carrozzeria Pininfarina was founded by Battista 'Pinin' Farina in May 1930. Having learned about the business at his brother's famed Carrozzeria, Stabilimenti Farina, Pininfarina set up shop to offer bespoke bodywork for the bare chassis provided by motor manufacturers at that time. Immediately successful, handsome Pininfarina bodywork was soon adorning upmarket machines from Lancia, Hispano-Suiza, and Alfa Romeo. But Pininfarina would not constrain their efforts solely to the pursuit of excellence in conventional aesthetics: the firm was intent on influencing the future of automotive design, whether experimenting with aerodynamics through outlandish concepts such as the Lancia Aprilia Berlinetta Aerodinamica, or in the modernist reinterpretation of traditional automotive form unveiled with the pontoon-bodied 1947 Cisitalia 202 coupé – this car is now considered of such influence it has become a permanent exhibit at the Museum of Modern Art, New York.

Inevitably, a company built on expensive bespoke bodywork commissions would suffer in the period of post-war austerity, the firm's emphasis necessarily shifting to design assignments on behalf of many major manufacturers, rather than wealthy individuals. Pininfarina would create both influential concept designs such as the Lancia Florida II (a car that would have a profound impact on automotive design trends through the 1960s), and beautiful bodywork for popular series-production cars including Lancia's elegant Flaminia Coupé and Alfa Romeo's pretty and compact Giulietta Spider. Pininfarina soon extended its capabilities into vehicle construction, opening a manufacturing plant at Grugliasco in 1958, subcontracted to build lower volume cars by several major manufacturers, including the Ghia-designed Lancia Aurelia B20 Gran Turismo, and Alfa Romeo's iconic Duetto Spider. More recently, the factory has been used to produce Ford's budget roadster, the Streetka, and Alfa Romeo's spider.

Perhaps the company's most exciting and fruitful partnership was with Ferrari, and from the mid-1950s Pininfarina embarked on a series of collaborations with the marque.

though similar standards would soon also be mandated in Europe. The most efficient way of achieving the level of exhaust emission cleanliness was to ensure accuracy of fuelling, thereby avoiding a dirty – and wasteful – excess of fuel being ingested into the motor. Fuel injection would prove the answer to the problem, a solution that was by no means exclusive to Ferrari. Given its ubiquity, there would be no need for a costly, bespoke installation, as Bosch already offered a most suitable and cost-effective system, designed to be readily adaptable to pre-existing engine designs.

Bosch K-Jetronic Injection

Bosch K-Jetronic injection had already been adopted by Ferrari for their updated GT, the 400i that arrived in 1979, the large four-seater becoming the first fuel-injected road-going Ferrari. The system would subsequently become standard equipment for a Ferrari, installed from the start on the Mondial two-plus-two that replaced the 308GT4 in 1980, and fitted to the 308 range that same year. It was fitted to the Berlinetta Boxer the following year, and in 1982 found its way into the

While it was Touring and Vignale that initially won the honour of clothing the fledgling Scuderia's chassis, a commission for bodywork for the V12 212 Inter paved the way for a proliferation of projects, as Pininfarina came to achieve a near-monopoly on Ferrari design. From the late 1950s the company styled almost all road-going models: the glamorous 250GT, followed by 275- and 330-series 12-cylinder front-engined GTs and convertibles, before effortlessly moving into a sequence of mid-engined classics spanning the period from the mid-1960s through to the 1990s.

In this breathtaking burst of mid-engined creativity, Pininfarina can lay claim to the lithe Dino, the svelte Berlinetta Boxer, the 308GTB of course, along with the more practical sibling the Mondial, the mature 348 and successor F355, and the unforgettable 1980s icons – Testarossa, 288GTO and F40. After a dalliance with in-house design, Ferrari returned to Pininfarina for the 458 Italia, a more elegant mid-engined machine heralding a return to aesthetic form for Ferrari following the purposeful brutalism of its F430 predecessor.

Despite acclaim for the 458 Italia, Pininfarina's future remains uncertain. Manufacturers nowadays have the skills to design interesting cars in house, and also build economically lower volume models, reclaiming construction activities that would previously have been outsourced to Pininfarina and its competitors. An inevitable consequence has been the closure in 2008 of Pininfarina's manufacturing capability. Happily, design work continues, the management of modern Pininfarina expounding a vision for the firm that includes a return to the days of bespoke, one-off coachwork construction commissions and – we must hope – further collaboration with Maranello on beautiful new Ferrari designs, whether for one-off specials or series production models.

575GT, one of Pininfarina's more recent collaborations with Ferrari.

2-litre cars, thereby completing its standardization across the range.

K-Jetronic would bring with it the additional benefits of relative mechanical simplicity, and greatly improved starting, hot or cold, on top of those essential improvements in emissions cleanliness. Unfortunately, the pursuit of improved efficiency would require Ferrari to sacrifice a little power, and the newly injected variant of the familiar V8 was quoted as generating 215bhp, a big drop in comparison to the previously stated 255bhp figure for a European car.

While contemporary press reports expressed disappointment about the drop in horsepower, criticism was usually tempered by an acceptance that Ferrari's quoted output figures through the 1970s had almost certainly been optimistic. The general consensus was that the real-world difference between carburettor cars and injected ones was somewhat less than 40bhp, and probably rather nearer to 20–25bhp. Unfortunately, weight was up a little just as power output came down: the European market cars were now quoted by the factory as weighing 1,341kg (2,957lb) – GTBi – and 1,352kg (2,981lb)

■ THE FUEL-INJECTED 308

– GTSi – and rather portly figures of 1,505kg (3,318lb) and 1,527kg (3,367lb) were given for US cars, still laden with additional safety and emissions equipment. Interestingly, the car weights now quoted in the cars' handbooks were in respect of 'normal operation' rather than the previous 'dry weights', and it is therefore likely that in reality the true figures were not so different from those of the outgoing steel bodied, Weber-equipped cars.

ABOVE: **308GTSi; this example wears the buttress-mounted spoiler from a later model.**

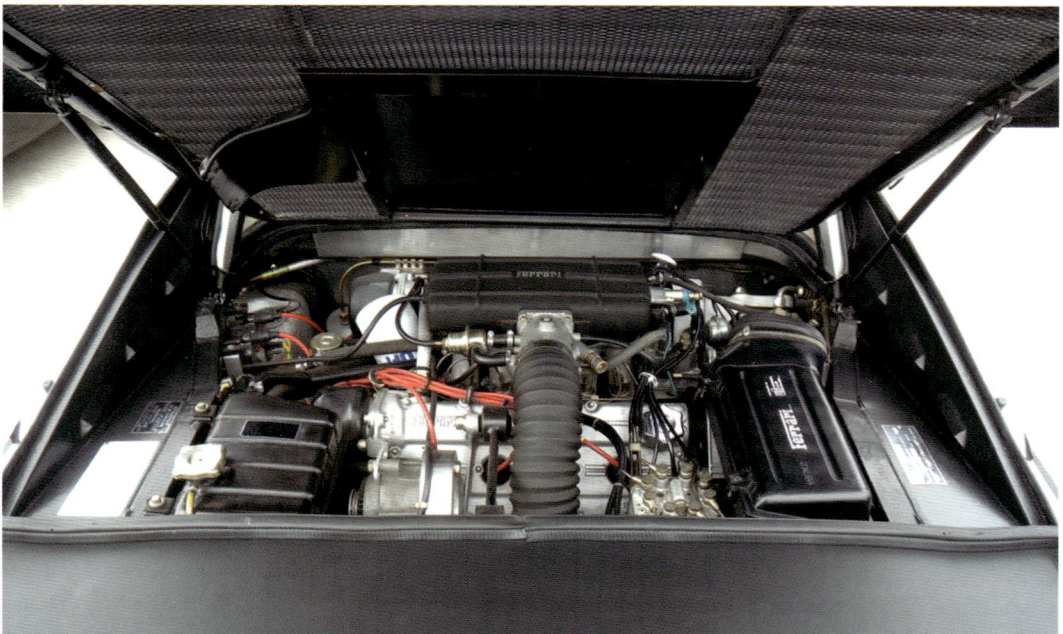

LEFT: **308GTSi engine bay. Note the gas struts conveniently holding the engine cover aloft.**
CARBON MCCOY

THE FUEL-INJECTED 308

Naturally performance suffered; European cars – both the GTBi and GTSi – were now capable of achieving the standing kilometre in 27sec and a top speed of 240km/h (149mph), while US market cars were attributed the same standing kilometre time, though the claimed maximum speed was slightly inferior, if a still respectable 236kmh (147mph). While European magazines bemoaned the downturn in 308 performance, American publications, such as *Road and Track* testing an injected car in October 1980, had fewer complaints, due in part to the relatively poor performance of preceding US-bound Maranello models, and tempered no doubt by the endemic lethargy of most Clean Air Act compliant vehicles on sale at the time. Nevertheless, concern about the relative lack of speed meant that the GTBi and GTSi would remain in production for barely eighteen months, from late 1980 through to 1982, during which time 494 berlinettas and 1,749 open cars were produced.

Detail Revisions

A series of detail revisions were made to the familiar V8 for the injected cars. The dry-sump 308s were a thing of the past, and in addition to the new Bosch K-Jetronic fuel-injection system that made sense of the car's new nomenclature, the 308GTBi and GTSi were notable also for the introduction of the Marelli MED 803A Digiplex electronic ignition system. Although advanced in comparison to previous Ferrari installations, this system was relatively rudimentary, incorporating a coil, distributor and ignition module to serve each bank of cylinders, and featuring eight timing curves within its stored memory. Even so, contemporary reports boasted of a 15 per cent improvement in highway economy. A diagnostic port to review engine health was accessible at the left of the engine bay, adjacent to the intake plenum.

In opening the engine cover, the most obvious difference was the modest sized, cast aluminium, alloy plenum chamber, decorated simply with an understated Ferrari script, which replaced the wide, flat air-filter box of carburetted cars. A large plastic air-filter housing sat in the lower right corner of the engine bay, displacing the cooling system expansion bottle to the lower left side, just where a dry-sump car's oil reservoir would previously have been. The Bosch mixture control unit, attached to the injectors by eight spindly pipes, was prominent at the rear of the engine bay, adjacent to the air-filter box, while the system's warm-up valve nestled in the V of the engine at the cambelt end.

The injected cars' transmission had been subject to the same detail evolution as the motor: it was much the same as

Slightly revised interior for the injected cars; note the earlier style of console mounting for supplementary gauges.
JEFF GLUCKER

■ THE FUEL-INJECTED 308

THE 308 SPIDERS

For the most devoted sun-worshipping car enthusiast, the removable roof panel of the GTS provided insufficient exposure to the elements. These enthusiasts, eager for a full Ferrari spider experience, turned to firms operating in an exclusive cottage industry that could offer a suite of modifications to 308 bodywork, effectively refactoring a GTS to become a fully convertible car.

As Ferrari was introducing the injected 308 range, Ekkehard Zimmermann, a former Ford Motor Company designer, was founding a company to construct special sports-car bodywork for Kremer-Porsche. The logo of dP Design, as it would be known – a distinctive, stylized lowercase 'd' and uppercase 'P' logo – soon began to feature on the tail panel of another conversion: a full 308 Spider, the model dubbed GTRi by its creators. Like other 308 Spider conversions, the rear buttresses were completely removed for a fully flat rear deck, the louvred engine cooling vents more exposed and therefore more visible, abutted by a rather awkward-looking tonneau cover that hid the stowed fabric roof. The fabric roof when erected was rather makeshift in appearance, truncated and rather ungainly – though owners presumably considered this unimportant, since most cars of this type were bought to be driven with the roof lowered.

Similar conversions were offered by various companies, including the German dealership Auto Becker, which supplied several full spiders, and Gunther Artz, a specialist in unusual vehicle conversions such as shooting brake Porsches and Porsche-powered Volkswagens. The Artz conversion was professionally detailed, though the example that famously appeared in the 1988 coffee-table book Dream Cars was finished in a very 1980s all-white paint scheme, the colour coding extending even to wheels and bumpers. Clearly spiders were in demand in Germany: Lorenz and Rankl, based in Wolfratshausen, offered a spider conversion service, the cost to convert a GTS in 1985 being 35,000 Deutsche marks, then equivalent to a substantial £9,000. One 208GT4

Handsome one-off spider, converted from a 308GTS.

308 Spider spotted at Silverstone, 1992.
LUCY FOSKETT

Spider was constructed – reputedly by Bertone, at the factory's request – cleverly replacing the air vents from the removed C pillar with similar shaped intakes let into the rear wings immediately ahead of the rear wheel arches.

The idea of a 308 Spider continues to hold a fascination even today. Though certainly not a project for the novice DIYer, more than one intrepid owner has embarked on a spider project of their own; for example, UK enthusiast, Andy Garrett, removed the buttresses of his GTS, and devised an elegantly sculpted rear-deck treatment incorporating a small rollbar at the driver's side to create a Ferrari spider that is very attractive and truly unique.

that fitted to earlier V8 cars, though with such detail revisions as a new gearbox-specific oil pump mounted on the rear cover, operated by the output shaft, and minor tweaks in the interests of reducing noise and improving synchromesh reliability. The final drive was changed from the carburettor cars' 3.71:1 to 4.06:1 in European markets, while US versions retained the old cars' final drive, but instead were fitted with lower first and fifth gears: 3.588 verses 3.419, and 0.952 verses 0.919. The clutch mechanism also received some fettling: a refactored clutch-pedal return spring brought pedal effort down to 17kg (37lb), thereby easing significantly the driver's work rate from the tiresome 27kg (60lb) effort of early 308s.

Benefits of Fuel Injection

Seen as a great innovation by the uninitiated as it began to feature on many road cars through the late 1970s and early 1980s, fuel injection was by no means a new concept. Gasmotorenfabik Deutz was manufacturing plunger pumps for injecting fuel as far back as 1898, though carburettor technology advanced sufficiently quickly thereafter to dominate fuelling systems through the earliest days of motor manufacture. Bosch began experimenting with fuel injection in 1912, though it would be 1937 before an aircraft equipped with Bosch fuel injection took to the air. The benefits for aviation associated with carburettor icing were largely meaningless from the perspective of potential automotive use, but performance potential was another matter, and Bosch injection was specified for the potent road-going Mercedes 300SL of 1954, while luxury sporting car rival Maserati added a Lucas-produced system for their elegant 3500GTi of 1961. Lucas fuel injection also featured on Triumph sports cars from the late 1960s.

But it would be Bosch systems that came to dominate the industry, as the original Jetronic system of 1967 evolved into the air-flow-controlled L-Jetronic and then K-Jetronic systems widely adopted by many manufacturers. In K-Jetronic system documentation, Bosch explained the virtues inherent in their own – or indeed any – efficient fuel-injection systems as those of 'economy of operation, high output power, and – last but not least – improvements to the quality of the exhaust gases emitted by the vehicle'. Earlier systems had been used by race teams in the pursuit of higher performance, and mechanical injection systems based on the now famed Kugelfischer high pressure pump found their way into race and fast road vehicles from Porsche and Ferrari, among others. But as efficiency and emissions cleanliness became more pressing con-

Matt black dash panel for the GTB/Si.
JEFF GLUCKER

cerns, particularly for manufacturers wishing to offer cars in the USA, so fuel injection became an important means of achieving the necessary efficiency to remain compliant with prevailing legislation.

Bosch K-Jetronic injection, despite the electronic promise of its name, was actually a mechanically and hydraulically controlled system. Relatively straightforward, but efficient and accurate, the system greatly enhanced the driveability of the 308GTBi, making the car much easier to start, banishing the hit-and-miss nature of the carburetted cars' hot-starting performance, and improving fuel economy and exhaust gas cleanliness. An electric fuel pump delivered petrol to the fuel distributor via a fuel accumulator and a filter. The fuel distributor allocated the fuel to the injectors for each individual cylinder, each in effect a simple check valve that continuously provided fuel to each valve once a pre-determined pressure was reached. While the intake valve was closed, the fuel was in effect stored until it reopened. The amount of air drawn in by the engine was controlled by a throttle valve, measured by an air-flow sensor which determined the appropriate amount of fuel to be provided by the fuel distributor.

The system enriched the mixture in certain circumstances: warm-up, idle and full load, and an accumulator was installed to maintain fuel pressure for a while after the motor was switched off, to make the car easier to restart while hot. Consistent with US market carburetted 308s built from 1978 onwards, the unpopular fast-idle arrangement was also installed, similarly

THE FUEL-INJECTED 308

PININFARINA MILLECHIODI

In 1977 Pininfarina presented an experimental 308GTB at several shows, concocted from a largely standard steel 308GTB (serial number 23611), though adorned with several aerodynamic amendments: wheel-arch blisters, tail spoiler, and a large front air-dam featuring large square driving lamps inset into the grille. Amendments to the car had been made and presented in an aluminium finish, the panels riveted to the standard bodywork, making sense of the prototype's nickname 'Millechiodi' or 'thousand rivets'. The car also featured a rear spoiler mounted directly behind the cabin across the tops of the buttresses.

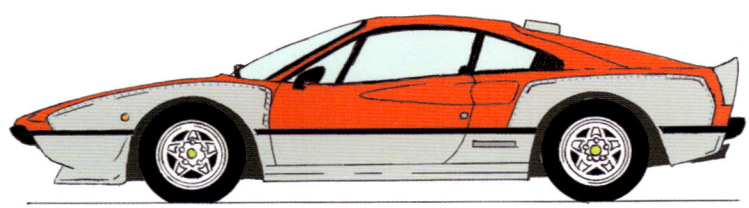

Pininfarina Millechiodi.

The interior was lightly though attractively modified from the standard car, with red-striped bucket seats and bright red carpets, and an instrument panel containing instruments from the Berlinetta Boxer in a dash design similar to that car. Fully wind-tunnel tested, this prototype was as advanced as it was prescient, featuring as it did all the necessary aerodynamic amendments to transform the shape of the 308GTB to that of the 288GTO, though the roof spoiler would be seen on a production Ferrari very much sooner, a similar item available for the 308 from 1982. Perhaps more importantly in terms of 308 evolution, the Millechiodi wore TRX road wheels of the style to become standard during the short production run of the fuel-injected 308s, as well as the Mondial 8.

Incredibly this unique car languished for a time in Ferrari's factory scrapyard, famously photographed by Hilary A. Raab Jr on a visit to the factory in 1979 before the incredible treasure trove of forlorn exotica was cleared for factory extensions. It is believed that the car was subsequently rescued, being spotted at Ferrari events during the 1980s, and a video can even be found online of the Millechiodi in action, apparently fitted with 16in wheels rather than the TRX rims it wore originally.

increasing the risk of premature bore wear on these cars' engines. US-bound cars were also fitted with catalytic converters, two warning lights on the dashboard denoting catalyst overheating.

Outward Appearance

Apart from revised tail badging, car spotters could identify a fuel-injected 308 from earlier models by looking at the front wing-mounted radiator outlet grilles, which now wore a satin black finish. Four exhaust tail-pipes were now standardized across all markets, and the rear valance of European cars now featured twin exhaust-pipe cut-outs, rather than the single indentation or entirely horizontal lower panels of the carburetted cars. Combined rear indicator and reversing lamps were also standardized across all markets.

Emphasizing the marketing link between Ferrari and Michelin, Grand Prix tyre supplier to the Scuderia, TRX metric wheels soon became standard equipment across the range. While the new metric wheels cast by Speedline in the famous five-pointed star design remained visually similar to the older wheels, they featured a wider rim width of 165mm and a larger inset, bringing the spokes near level with the face of the rim. Michelin 220/55 VR390 TRX tyres, one of the few choices available in this unusual metric size, would be the default option.

THE FUEL-INJECTED 308

RIGHT: **Impact bumpers and catalyst warning light, details mandated by ever-tighter US safety and emissions legislation.** JEFF GLUCKER

BELOW: **TRX Metric road wheels.** JOHN DICKENS

But although they gave a consistent level of grip, and were claimed to improve stability, they also proved expensive come replacement time. Imperial measurement wheels could still be had from the options list: Michelin XWX tyres on 14in wheels, or the popular 16in wheels, which allowed fitment of well regarded, low profile Pirelli P7 tyres. The rather chunky-looking wider and higher profile TRX tyres necessitated some revision to spring rates, and apparently also required a small modification to the inner wheel arches to accommodate full lock.

Though many contemporary road tests of the injected cars commented favourably on the improved handling bestowed by the metric wheels, *Road and Track*, testing a 308GTSi in March 1981, were surprised to discover that the wider tyres appeared actually to have reduced the car's lateral grip. A figure of 0.810g was recorded on the skidpan, down in comparison to an earlier test of a 308GTS shod with Michelin XWX tyres, which achieved a lateral grip of 0.852g. *Road and Track* were not impressed, noting that '…what had formerly been a neutral-handling automobile now tended towards oversteer'. Ferrari cited the car's improved all-weather (wet and dry) performance, presumably accepting a reduction in overall grip as a fair exchange for better behaviour in certain low-grip situations.

■ THE FUEL-INJECTED 308

LEFT: **Second console design found in this GTBi.**
MANGOPULP2008@FLICKR

BELOW: **Always attracting attention: the 308GTSi.**
LUTZ LEMKE

Interior

Inside the injected cars, a few small but worthwhile alterations had been made. The clock and oil-temperature gauges were moved from the hard-to-read panel on the lower part of the dash moulding, and now sat side by side in an upswept moulding at the front of the central console, immediately ahead of the gearshift gate. Strangely some early US-market cars had a slightly different configuration at the console front end, the dials vertically stacked with a small oddments stowage bin added to the very front of the central console. Rather 'tacked on' in appearance, this arrangement soon gave way to a neater-looking, curved console design.

Aft of the gearlever, at the spot where a carburetted car's console was adorned with a handsome Ferrari 'cavallino rampante' chromed emblem, a pair of window switches were now located instead, having migrated from their previous position on the door-card tops. Ahead of the driver, the dashboard panel was now finished in matt black, and the steering wheel spokes, now a slotted design rather than solid, were also finished in satin black paint.

Interior trim had advanced a little in terms of quality: Connolly leather facings for the seats were now decorated with a more intricate, geometric pleat motif, and the door cards had been amended, carpet now covering the lower portions including the door bins. The 308GTSi did away with the fussy, satchel-like door pocket of its predecessor, secure stowage now offered in a covered pocket attached to the driver's seat back. Even the rear compartment lid was more user-friendly, lifted easily by a pair of gas struts, rather than the amateurish prop stick of the carburettor-equipped 308s.

A rather gawky-looking, square, black plastic door mirror design was specified for the European market, electrically adjustable from within the cockpit, the control neatly if not very ergonomically sited beneath the armrest moulding on the driver's door-card, though some cars were delivered with the earlier bullet-shaped mirror design. The US-market GTBi was delivered at first with the simple cabin lamp carried forward from where it would be in the carburetted equivalent, whereas European GTBis received a more luxurious-looking roof console extending forwards from just ahead of the rear screen, carrying the cabin lamp plus a swivelling map-reading light; this installation arrived in the US for 1981. US-market 308s were fitted with a comical 85mph (137km/h) US speedometer, though the peril this legislative idiocy was designed to ward off must have disappeared the following year, and they were quietly discontinued.

308GTBI/308GTSI (1980–82)

Layout and chassis: Two-seat berlinetta or sports with removable roof with tubular steel frame and steel construction body/chassis

Engine
- Type: F 106 BB mid-mounted transverse, 90-degree V8, wet-sump
- Block material: Aluminium alloy with cast-iron liners
- Head material: Aluminium alloy
- Cylinders: 8 in V configuration
- Cooling: Water
- Bore and stroke: 81 × 71mm
- Capacity: 2926.9cc
- Valves: Actuation by twin overhead camshafts per bank, 2 valves per cylinder
- Compression ratio: 8.8:1
- Fuelling: Bosch K Jetronic fuel injection
- Ignition: Marelli MED 803A Digiplex electronic ignition system
- Max. power (din): 214bhp at 6,600rpm
- Max. torque (Nm): 243 at 4,600rpm
- bhp per tonne: 160 (GTSi 158)
- bhp per litre: 73
- Fuel capacity: 74ltr (16gal)

Transmission
- Gearbox: Five speed plus reverse
- Clutch: Single plate

Ratios
- First: 3.419
- Second: 2.353
- Third: 1.693
- Fourth: 1.244
- Fifth: 0.919
- Reverse: 3.248
- Final drive: 4.06:1

Suspension and Steering
- Front: Independent, unequal-length wishbones, coil springs over telescopic shock absorbers, anti-rollbar
- Rear: Independent, unequal-length wishbones, coil springs over telescopic shock absorbers, anti-rollbar
- Steering: Rack and pinion
- Tyres: 240/55 VR 390
- Wheels: Alloy, 390mm diameter
- Rim width: 165mm
- Turning circle: 12m (39ft)

Brakes
- Type: Vented disc brakes front and rear
- Size: 274mm front, 279 mm rear

Dimensions
- Track: Front: 1,460mm (57.5in); Rear: 1,460mm (57.5in)
- Wheelbase: 2,340mm (92in)
- Overall length: 4,230mm (166.5in)
- Overall width: 1,720mm (67.7in)
- Overall height: 1,120mm (44in)
- Unladen weight: 1,341kg (2,957lb); GTSi 1,352kg (2,981lb)

Performance
- Top speed: 240km/h (149mph)
- 0–60 (sec): 6.7 (Car magazine, June 1981)
- 0–400m (sec): 14.9
- Standing km (sec): 27.1

MONDIAL 8, THE EVERYDAY FERRARI

First presented at the 1980 Geneva Salon, the Mondial 8 four-seater adopted one of Ferrari's historic model names – that of a 4-cylinder sports car, the Mondial 500. That car had been named in honour of Ascari's second Grand Prix world championship, but for the new Mondial the number of cylinders would be appended to the moniker rather than the cubic capacity of a single cylinder, as had been the Ferrari numbering convention in the 1950s.

It was Ferrari's second attempt at building a mid-engined sports car that could seat four, and this one would be less compromised in its passenger accommodation than its predecessor. Pininfarina requested, and received, approval to extend the wheelbase by a full 100mm (4in) over the 308GT4's 2,550mm (100in), allowing sufficient room at last for rear-seat passengers to travel in relative comfort. Indeed the Mondial was a bigger car all round than the car it succeeded: its track was wider front and rear, the roofline was 70mm (2.8in) taller, and the car a full 280mm (11in) longer. But additional scale inevitably brought additional weight, and the substantially built and comprehensively galvanized Mondial was well over 10 per cent heavier than the 308GT4.

Performance was not impressive, and weight was not the only reason. The Mondial 8 was the first Ferrari fitted with fuel injection as standard from the outset, and used the same constricted motor as its siblings, the 308GTBi and 308GTSi. Ferrari claimed a 230km/h (143mph) top speed, and around 8sec to achieve 60mph, aided in large part by a long second gear extending to 108km/h (67mph). Its relatively 'unFerrari' turn of speed attracted negative criticism in contemporary press reports – for example, American magazine *Car and Driver* grumbled that the Mondial's '… extra mass burdens it down to the point of being dog meat for the turbocharged Porsche 924 and Datsun 280-ZX. A Ferrari that is slow is certainly an enigma and maybe even a contradiction in terms'.

But those who decried its lack of pace were, at least in part, missing the point. Ferrari felt sure that there were potential buyers who wanted more than raw speed: some required a car durable enough to withstand everyday usage, and demanded a more refined, ergonomic car offering civilized, docile road manners. Viewed in those terms, the Mondial 8 really delivered: the car was relatively

Not everyone's idea of a Ferrari, the Mondial really came into its own aesthetically in later cabriolet guise.
JASON VANDERHILL

undemanding to drive, and there was plenty of room for four occupants, cosseted in armchair-like leather seats, enjoying the benefits of a comprehensively equipped luxury interior. Standard air conditioning featured, and an electronic systems monitor was fitted to the centre console, which looked more Mercedes than Maranello.

Pininfarina's body styling was equally controversial. Elegant from certain angles, but rather elongated next to the compact 308GT4 – oddly both cars were featured at the Turin Motor Show in 1980 – and decidedly less glamorous than its 308 stablemates, the Mondial was not everyone's idea of what a Ferrari should look like. Its decidedly cab-forward stance led to a very forward-placed driving seat – the driver looking very short-legged through the side window – and chunky impact bumpers and matt black details were too heavy handed to be harmonious. Particularly controversial were the haunch-mounted air intakes protected by rather prominent trapezoidal latticed covers, somewhat 'art deco' in style. Fioravanti blamed German safety regulations for their presence, and they would always look uncomfortably aftermarket, even after they were colour-keyed to the bodywork instead of the satin black of the earliest examples.

While reviews were mixed for its styling, *Car* magazine loved the civilized new Ferrari, dubbing it 'Mondial la magnifica' and lauding its 'Porsche-like build quality'. But even such glowing endorsements, not to mention patronage by celebrities including French footballing superstar Michel Platini, could broaden its appeal, and the Mondial 8 sold only 703 units worldwide in its three years of production.

CHAPTER SIX

THE 2-LITRE AND TURBOCHARGED RELATIVES

The 1970s and 1980s were tough times for performance-car enthusiasts based in Italy. A swingeing 'IVA' tax, representing 38 per cent of the car's purchase price, was imposed on citizens who had the temerity to buy a car with an engine capacity beyond 2 litres; this was more than double the 18 per cent levied on smaller-engined machines. Unfortunately this legislation rather made a mockery of the illustrious output of many of Italy's revered car makers. Acting with patriotism, Alfa Romeo Maserati, Lamborghini and, of course, Ferrari began to offer tax-efficient alternatives to their brawnier export models. Italian market cars often featured engine bays under-filled with smaller motors, latterly turbocharged to mitigate the performance deficit of smaller capacities and fewer cylinders.

Ferrari's first efforts at a tax-break special were based around a smaller capacity version of the same engine that powered the export models, initially avoiding the turbocharging technology that was still in its infancy in terms of road-car usage. The first such car arrived in 1975, when the 308GT4 was joined by a 2-litre variant in Maranello's line-up. The 208GT4, as it was known, made its debut at that year's Geneva Motor Show, becoming the first 2-litre V8-powered production car in Ferrari's history. And it would not be the last, because the offer of a 2-litre equivalent for the home market would be a practice that persisted until the advent of the 348; by this time the tax legislation that had imposed the capacity compromise had been revised.

A battered 208GT4, still appealing despite its battle-scarred bumper and aftermarket wheels.
STEFAN SOBOT

■ THE 2-LITRE AND TURBOCHARGED RELATIVES

The 208GT4

The new 208GT4 was fitted with a smaller V8 motor, though externally it was the same as the 3-litre version. Given a type designation F 106 C 000 by the factory, it shared the bigger motor's 71mm stroke, but new shrunk-in cylinder liners constricted bore size to 66.8mm, making for a tax-friendly cylinder capacity of 1991cc. The compression ratio remained consistent with the larger engine's figure of 9:1. Four twin-choke Weber carburettors – smaller 34DCNF versions – topped the motor, and a single Marelli distributor was installed rather than the twin distributor arrangement of earlier 308GT4 cars. The motor produced 170bhp, though some sources, such as the owner's manual, mentioned a power output figure of 180bhp.

To make best possible use of the available motive power, the 2-litre car received alterations to the gearing. A lower

208GT4. Note the lack of driving lamps, and the radiator exhaust air outlet in aluminium silver finish. MAURIZIO BOI

208GT4 interior. Note the matt black finish for the dash panel.
DANIEL HAY

208GT4 featured a different exhaust treatment than that of the larger-engined variant.
STEFAN KOSCHMINDER

fifth-gear ratio and a new 4.6:1 final drive ratio replaced the 3-litre cars' components – some mitigation for the unavoidable loss of power and torque resulting from the capacity reduction. Kerb weight was barely changed from that of the larger car at a quoted 1,305kg (2,878lb), and inevitably performance suffered somewhat, some enthusiasts naturally arguing that the smaller car's abilities were unworthy of a machine from Maranello. Nevertheless, the car was quite sprightly, with top speed claimed to be more than 220km/h (137mph), and a standing kilometre sprint executed in 29.5sec, which was impressive for a 2-litre car of the day. And its engine note was no less strident, perhaps rather softer sounding, but with a similar vocal charm as the larger-engined car, making every drive a real event.

With a bodyshell identical to that of its 3-litre equivalent, aside from the Dino 208GT4 script badge fitted on the bootlid, there was little to tell the cars apart. A single exhaust outlet was the obvious external giveaway at the car's rear, and at the front a bare aluminium finish for the radiator exhaust grille similarly betrayed the car as a smaller-capacity home-market Ferrari. The radiator air intake beneath the front bumper and air outlet in the engine cover were also of a bare aluminium finish, and there were no driving lamps at the front of the 208. Smaller 195/70/14 Michelin XDX tyres were fitted.

Despite its diminutive engine capacity, the 208GT4 was marketed as a premium car. Ferrari publicity emphasized the luxury nature of the smaller car, brochure photography

208GT4 (1975–80)

Layout and chassis	Two-plus-two seat coupé with tubular steel frame, and steel and steel construction body/chassis
Engine	
Type:	F 106 C mid-mounted transverse, 90-degree V8, wet-sump
Block material:	Aluminium alloy with cast-iron liners
Head material:	Aluminium alloy
Cylinders:	8 in V configuration
Cooling:	Water
Bore and stroke:	66.8 × 71mm
Capacity:	1990.64cc
Valves:	Actuation by twin overhead camshafts per bank, 2 valves per cylinder
Compression ratio:	9:1
Fuelling:	Four Weber 34 DCNF carburettors
Ignition:	Single spark plug per cylinder, two coils
Max. power (din):	170bhp at 7,700rpm
Max. torque (Nm):	186 at 4,900rpm
bhp per tonne:	130
bhp per litre:	85
Fuel capacity:	80ltr (17.6gal)
Transmission	
Gearbox:	Five speed plus reverse
Clutch:	Single plate
Ratios	
First:	3.418
Second:	2.353
Third:	1.693
Fourth:	1.244
Fifth:	0.881
Reverse:	3.248
Final drive:	4.6:1
Suspension and Steering	
Front:	Independent, unequal-length wishbones, coil springs over telescopic shock absorbers, anti-rollbar
Rear:	Independent, unequal-length wishbones, coil springs over telescopic shock absorbers, anti-rollbar
Steering:	Rack and pinion
Tyres:	195/70 VR 14
Wheels:	Alloy, 14in diameter
Rim width:	6.5in
Turning circle:	12m (39ft)
Brakes	
Type:	Vented disc brakes front and rear
Size:	272mm front, 277mm rear
Dimensions	
Track:	Front: 1,460mm (57.5in)
	Rear: 1,460mm (57.5in)
Wheelbase:	2,550mm (100in)
Overall length:	4,300mm (169in)
Overall width:	1,800mm (70.9in)
Overall height:	1,180mm (46.5in)
Unladen weight:	1,305kg (2,878lb)
Performance	
Top speed:	215km/h (134mph)
0–400m (sec):	16
Standing km (sec):	29.5

■ THE 2-LITRE AND TURBOCHARGED RELATIVES

208GTS, very crisp in white paint finish. Aside from the badging, there is very little to tell this model apart from the larger-engined version. JONATHAN TREMLETT

presenting the 208GT4 beside an aircraft hangar in which a private plane was stowed, thereby linking the tax-break Ferrari with aspirational aircraft ownership. And it needed to be seen as a fully fledged luxury, because the 208GT4 faced stiff competition in the home market from arch rivals Lamborghini and Maserati. Both marques offered 2-litre versions of their conceptually similar two-plus-two-seat mid-engined sports cars in the Urraco P200 and the Merak 2000. Available in left-hand-drive format only – as appropriate for Italian roads – and with its relative paucity of performance, the 208GT4 was destined from the outset to be something of a rarity: despite its five-year production run, at the cessation of production in 1980 just 840 examples had left the factory.

The 208GTB

When sales of the 308GT4 model proved disappointing, the introduction of an additional two-seat model to sit alongside it in showrooms was a most sensible response. Given the tiny volumes in which the 208 variant would sell in its home market, a similar option to offer small capacity versions of both cars was simply not viable. And so the 208GT4 would fill the role of smaller capacity Ferrari until it was discontinued in 1980, superseded by two new cars based closely on Pininfarina's 308

open and closed variants, named 208GTB and 208GTS. The new two-seaters were powered by an updated – if not uprated – version of the 2-litre V8 motor from their predecessor.

Visually all but identical to their 3-litre equivalents, to some these 2-litre cars were once again rather lacking sufficient brawn to match their aesthetic appeal, and again there were criticisms that these Ferraris were short of the performance that buyers had come to expect. With the same bore and stroke of 66.8 × 71mm, and the same 9:1 compression ratio as the 208GT4, the F 106 CB 000 engine made do without the Bosch fuel injection installed the same year on the 3-litre equivalents, the 208s continuing with an array of four twin-choke Weber 34 DCNF carburettors. Nevertheless, just like the 3-litre cars, the 2-litre motor for 1980 was down on power in comparison to preceding models, power output claims from Ferrari now quoted at a modest and realistic output of 155bhp at 6,800rpm. Maximum torque was a little down on the 208GT4's output of 137.4lb/ft at 4,900rpm, the newer 2-litre said to offer 129lb/ft, albeit at a slightly more usable 4,200rpm. Gear ratios were the same as those installed into the 208GT4's gearbox, though the final drive ratio reverted to the 3.71:1 of the 3-litre cars.

The berlinetta tipped the scales at 1,305kg (2,878lb), the open car naturally a little weightier at a claimed 1,365kg (3,010lb); these not insubstantial weights conspired with the

208GTB/208GTS (1980–82)

Layout and chassis	Two-seat berlinetta or sports with removable roof with tubular steel frame and steel construction body/chassis
Engine	
Type:	F 106 CB, mid-mounted transverse, 90-degree V8, wet-sump
Block material:	Aluminium alloy with cast-iron liners
Head material:	Aluminium alloy
Cylinders:	8 in V configuration
Cooling:	Water
Bore and stroke:	66.8 × 71mm
Capacity:	1990.64cc
Valves:	Actuation by twin overhead camshafts per bank, 2 valves per cylinder
Compression ratio:	9:1
Fuelling:	Four Weber 34 DCNF carburettors
Ignition:	Single spark plug per cylinder, single coil
Max. power (din):	155bhp at 6,800rpm
Max. torque (Nm):	170 at 4,200rpm
bhp per tonne:	119 (GTS 114)
bhp per litre:	78
Fuel capacity:	74ltr (16.3gal)
Transmission	
Gearbox:	Five speed plus reverse
Clutch:	Single plate
Ratios	
First:	3.418
Second:	2.353
Third:	1.693
Fourth:	1.244
Fifth:	0.881
Reverse:	3.248
Final drive:	3.71:1
Suspension and Steering	
Front:	Independent, unequal-length wishbones, coil springs over telescopic shock absorbers, anti-rollbar
Rear:	Independent, unequal-length wishbones, coil springs over telescopic shock absorbers, anti-rollbar
Steering:	Rack and pinion
Tyres:	205/70 VR 14
Wheels:	Alloy, 14in diameter
Rim width:	6.5in
Turning circle:	12m (39ft)
Brakes	
Type:	Vented disc brakes front and rear
Size:	274mm front, 279mm rear
Dimensions	
Track:	Front: 1,460mm (57.5in)
	Rear: 1,460mm (57.5in)
Wheelbase:	2,340mm (92in)
Overall length:	4,230mm (166.5in)
Overall width:	1,720mm (67.7in)
Overall height:	1,120mm (44in)
Unladen weight:	1,305kg (2878lb); GTS 1365kg (3,010lb)
Performance	
Top speed:	215km/h (134mph)
0–400m (sec):	17.1
Standing km (sec):	31.3

reduced power output to make for decidedly un-Ferrari-like performance statistics, the standing quarter despatched in an unexceptional 17.1sec, and the standing kilometre taking an unhurried 31.3sec. Top speed was quoted at 215km/h (134mph).

A mere 300 of the pretty but rather under-achieving two-seaters left the factory, 160 examples of the berlinetta and just 140 open cars, before this understandably rare model was superseded by a harder-hitting home-market 208.

The 208GTB Turbo

Scuderia Ferrari's rabidly enthusiastic fans, the Tifosi, had high hopes for Grand Prix glory in 1982. The team was in a strong position at the season's start, fielding a talented driver pairing in Gilles Villeneuve and Didier Pironi, and retaining a rising star on the technical front in the person of Harvey Postlethwaite, the British designer at last providing a modern aluminium honeycomb monocoque chassis for the powerful V6 of Formula 1 design legend Mauro Forghieri. But tragedy robbed both drivers of their respective opportunities to achieve the world championship that year: Villeneuve perished in an appalling accident, his judgement clouded by bitterness following perceived dishonour from a teammate who ignored pit signals to rob him of a certain win, while Pironi's Formula 1 career came to an immediate end when his legs were damaged in a serious qualifying accident. But the inherent speed of Ferrari's turbocharged challenger was undeniable, a fact that would be underlined emphatically as Maranello secured the constructor's championship despite the tumult of the team's horrifically disrupted season.

Ferrari had truly mastered the art of turbocharging, the 126C2 of 1982 generating from its diminutive 1500cc V6 more than 650bhp in qualifying trim, boosted by twin KKK turbochargers. Inevitably the experience gained on track would transfer to the road, and so it was that in that same year – 1982 – forced induction made its debut on a Ferrari road car. Turbocharging technology was the perfect answer to the criticisms levelled at Maranello's previous 2-litre offerings for the home market. Here was a technology that could redress the imbalance in performance, and at last a 208 owner could experience levels of performance previously available only to drivers of the 3-litre cars. Presented at the 1982 Turin Motor Show, the 208GTB Turbo represented a very credible, exciting new two-seater for the home market, one with all the go to match the show! The launch brochure even featured a picture

THE 2-LITRE AND TURBOCHARGED RELATIVES

of Didier Pironi with the new car as Maranello sought to reinforce the exchange from the race team of turbocharging technology that could endow the small motor with powerful punch.

Essentially the same V8 motor from the previous 208GTB and GTS models was the starting point for the turbocharged power unit, though there was a significant reduction in its compression ratio because of a revision to piston design: down to just 7:1, to compensate for the pressurizing effect of the exhaust-driven KKK turbocharger unit; this unit nestled aft of the rear cylinder bank, above the transmission and differential. The K26 turbocharger unit was an obvious choice, being supplied by the Grand Prix team's then collaborator in forced induction, KKK, thus reinforcing the link with the Formula 1 cars. It was a particularly neat installation, the compressor feeding charged intake air upwards to a smart cast plenum chamber – naturally emblazoned with a 'turbo' script – which sat in the V of the cylinder heads, motivating exhaust gases fed to the compressor by convoluted manifolding, which led down to a broad transverse silencer. Spring-loaded expansion joints prevented the huge heat of the turbocharged installation from cracking the pipework.

The tail-pipes were distinctively different to those fitted to the naturally aspirated V8 cars, the paired outlets at each end of the silencer shrouded in an ovoid chrome-effect outer sleeve. A waste gate was installed just ahead of the left side of the exhaust silencer, its function to regulate the exhaust gas passed into the turbocharger. In situations where engine speed exceeded 3,500rpm, boost was pegged at around 0.6bar. Bosch K-Jetronic fuel injection and Marelli MED 804A electronic ignition completed the new motor installation, giving a peppy powerpack, capable of generating a worthwhile 220bhp at 7,000rpm. The rev limiter was set a little higher for the 2-litre car, at a frenetic 7,800rpm.

Typically, the transmission received only minor amendments to gearing, a slightly higher first gear being installed in place of the cog fitted to naturally aspirated 208 cars, the remaining ratios unaltered, though a higher final drive ratio was fitted to better exploit the turbocharged engine's much improved power output. Performance was dramatically improved over preceding models: the 242km/h (150mph) top speed was most respectable for a 2-litre car, and the standing quarter and standing kilometre times of 15.2sec and 27.5sec respectively were very close to those quoted for the outgoing GTBi and GTSi models, despite giving away a whole litre of cylinder capacity.

Outward Appearance

Initially intended only to be offered in berlinetta form, Maranello bowed to customer clamour and added a GTS variant to the range in 1983. While bodywork fitted to the 208GTB and 208GTS models was faithful to that of the larger-engined cars, there were subtle features that enabled the cognoscenti to identify Ferrari's first ever turbocharged road car. The standard roof spoiler and deeper front spoiler were by no means specific to this model, but the row of five additional cooling slots that punctuated the lower portion of the front spoiler moulding beneath the car's radiator grill were certainly unique.

An additional radiator exhaust grille was installed on the car's front lid to allow the greater volume of incoming air to exit once it had passed through the radiator. This was the same as the grill subsequently fitted to the Quattrovalvole 308s, though here it was finished in satin black paint to match the similarly painted front wing vents. Engine-lid louvres were also extended backwards and across the lid in a U-shaped arrangement that would later feature on the 328 series.

208GTB Turbo.
CÁSSIO MAGALHÃES DOS REIS

THE 2-LITRE AND TURBOCHARGED RELATIVES

The most obvious alteration was the incorporation of additional NACA-style ducts on the lower body sides, just ahead of the rear wheel arches; these drew much needed cool air into the busy engine bay. The Pininfarina badging was displaced to a spot just aft of the rear wheel arches.

At the car's rear, a split rear bumper was fitted with a cooling grille bridging the gap, and a new tail badge pronouncing 'Turbo' was attached – a rather over-designed affair, the 'b' uncomfortably similar to a 'd', a potentially embarrassing misread for the automotive illiterate! At launch, metric Michelin TRX tyres were standard equipment – though as always, there was a 16in alternative available in the popular Pirelli P7.

The car's interior was barely different from that of the larger engine equivalent, just a 'turbo' badge installed on the fuse-

RIGHT: **208GTB Turbo**; note the unusual sleeved exhaust outlet treatment. CÁSSIO MAGALHÃES DOS REIS

BELOW: **208GTS Turbo**; note the location of the **Pininfarina** badging, displaced to the back of the rear wing by the **NACA** cooling duct. MAURIZIO BOI

81

THE 2-LITRE AND TURBOCHARGED RELATIVES

box cover ahead of the passenger, and a boost gauge giving the game away; this dial replaced the 3-litre car's clock at the front of the central console beside the oil temperature gauge. Seats were part trimmed in attractive light brown 'Zelna' cloth, though full leather trim was always optional on the 2-litre cars.

Into Production

Production of the first iteration of 208GTB and 208GTS Turbo models ran from 1982 (the berlinetta) and 1983 (the open-topped car) until 1985, when a significant upgrade would refactor the model visually to bring it in line with the incoming 328 range, in a model which further improved on the capabilities of this already strongly performing smaller-engined Ferrari. During this period, 437 examples of the 208GTB Turbo, and 250 208GTS Turbos were constructed.

The GTB and GTS Turbo

Although turbocharging is something of a quick win to increase engine-power output, the gains that are made are necessarily compromised by a drawback that is inherent in the physics of compressing air. Compression allows a greater volume to be crammed into each cylinder, thereby providing more fuel for power-rich combustion, but it also inevitably increases the temperature of that incoming air, reducing the efficiency of its burn. The ingestion of hotter air also increases the likelihood of potentially damaging pre-detonation, or 'knock' as it is often informally known. Early turbocharger installations minimized the impact of this increase in temperature by limiting the level of compression – or 'boost' as it is more commonly referred to – so that the heating effect was confined to manageable levels.

But higher boost means greater power, and so inevitably engineers conceived methods for increasing intake air compression – Formula 1 race teams were at the forefront of such initiatives. But what was suited to the track – heat-tolerant specialist fuels, and water injection to cool charged intake air – would not be the answer for road cars, though German tuning firm Koenig did experiment with water-injection systems for their specialist road cars. Instead the solution that was settled on industry wide was the introduction of an intercooler, an example of this device specified by Ferrari for the latest, most powerful incarnation of its 208 Turbo model.

Once the new 328 range was launched, generating a buzz in the press and showrooms, in 1986 Ferrari's attention turned to the introduction of a new home-market equivalent.

ABOVE: **208 Turbo badging.**
DAVID RIPAMONTI

RIGHT: **208GTB Turbo.**
CÁSSIO MAGALHÃES DOS REIS

208GTB/208GTS TURBO (1982–85)

Layout and chassis	Two-seat berlinetta or sports with removable roof, with tubular steel frame and steel construction body/chassis
Engine	
Type:	F 106 D, mid-mounted transverse, 90-degree V8, wet-sump
Block material:	Aluminium alloy with cast-iron liners
Head material:	Aluminium alloy
Cylinders:	8 in V configuration
Cooling:	Water
Bore and stroke:	66.8 × 71mm
Capacity:	1990.64cc
Valves:	Actuation by twin overhead camshafts per bank, 2 valves per cylinder
Compression ratio:	7:1
Fuelling:	KKK turbocharger unit with waste gate, Bosch K Jetronic fuel injection
Ignition:	Marelli MED 804A electronic ignition
Max. power (din):	220bhp at 7,000rpm
Max. torque (Nm):	240 at 4,800rpm
bhp per tonne:	171
bhp per litre:	111
Fuel capacity:	74ltr (16.3gal)
Transmission	
Gearbox:	Five speed plus reverse
Clutch:	Single plate
Ratios	
First:	3.59
Second:	2.353
Third:	1.693
Fourth:	1.244
Fifth:	0.881
Reverse:	3.248
Final drive:	4.31:1
Suspension and Steering	
Front:	Independent, unequal-length wishbones, coil springs over telescopic shock absorbers, anti-rollbar
Rear:	Independent, unequal-length wishbones, coil springs over telescopic shock absorbers, anti-rollbar
Steering:	Rack and pinion
Tyres:	205/55 VR 16 front tyres, 225/50 VR 16 rear
Wheels:	Alloy, 16in diameter
Rim width:	7in front, 8in rear
Turning circle:	12m (39ft)
Brakes	
Type:	Vented disc brakes front and rear
Size:	274mm front, 279mm rear
Dimensions	
Track:	Front: 1,460mm (57.5in)
	Rear: 1,460mm (57.5in)
Wheelbase:	2,340mm (92in)
Overall length:	4,230mm (166.5in)
Overall width:	1,720mm (67.7in)
Overall height:	1,120mm (44in)
Unladen weight:	1,283kg (2,829lb)
Performance	
Top speed:	242km/h (150mph)
0–62mph (sec):	6.6
0–400m (sec):	15.2
Standing km (sec):	27.5

THE 2-LITRE AND TURBOCHARGED RELATIVES

Performance

The GTB and GTS Turbo models would therefore bring the 2-litre range into line with the exterior and interior updates premiered on the 328 range. With the increase to 3.2 litres cylinder capacity, the performance capability of the new V8-powered two-seat Ferrari took a determined step forwards to outpace the stiffening challenge from Porsche's 911 Carrera of similar capacity. Constrained by tax regulation, capacity increases were out of bounds for the home market, so to enable the 2-litre variant to maintain near parity of performance with its larger-engine sibling, Ferrari revisited the turbocharger installation conceived for the first 208 Turbos. A Japanese-sourced water-cooled IHI turbo replaced the previous unit, while a Behr Intercooler sat atop the engine between the V of the cylinder heads, allowing the safe increase of maximum boost by more than one third again over previous cars, to a heady 1.05 bar. Indeed the charge cooling action was so effective the engine compression ratio could also be increased to 7.5:1, to improve off-boost efficiency. Engine power was a generous 254bhp at 6,500rpm, and output per litre a heady 128bhp per litre.

Performance increased dramatically. While top speed at 253km/h (157mph) was some 10km/h (6mph) less than the 3.2-litre car, acceleration and standing quarter and kilometre sprint timings were about equal with the 328, an amazing performance from the small V8. Driveability was improved over the sometimes rather peaky 208 Turbo models, courtesy of a huge increase in torque, the new turbo bettering the outgoing

208GTB Turbo. Note the turbo boost gauge just visible behind the gearlever.
CÁSSIO MAGALHÃES DOS REIS

■ THE 2-LITRE AND TURBOCHARGED RELATIVES

THE 288GTO

Surely the most famous 308-derived turbocharged Ferrari must be the incredible GTO, unveiled to a rapturous reception at the Geneva Motor Show in 1984. It was bravery indeed to resurrect the GTO nomenclature, the 250GTO having achieved unsurpassable, iconic status with many Ferrari cognoscenti who considered it to be the finest Ferrari ever built. But the new supercar certainly had the credentials to live up to its illustrious ancestor.

Ferrari's new GTO was indeed conceived as a homologation special, hence its designation 'Gran Turismo Omologato', a dramatic reimagining of the original 308 design with the potential to become a Group B racer. Its breathtakingly beautiful bodywork was subtly altered almost everywhere from its 308 ancestor, Fioravanti working magic to adapt the original lines to the longer 2,450mm (96.5in) wheelbase necessitated by installation of a longitudinally mounted V8 motor, with a similarly oriented new transmission. More aggressively styled wings offered space for larger tyres, and the rear wings were perforated by three slash-like vents, recalling those seen behind the front wheels of the original 250GTO. A substantial front spoiler underlined a front grille arrangement reminiscent of Pininfarina's Millechiodi concept, this time housing four large, squared driving lamps rather than the concept's pair.

At the rear, a pronounced lip spoiler again recalled that seen first on the concept car, though it was now smoothly integrated, rather than a tacked-on appendage. So tall was the spoiler that new, flag-like door mirrors with elongated mounting stalks were necessary to allow the driver to see over it. Much of the new car's bodywork would be constructed from exotic Formula One-derived composite materials: kevlar, aluminium honeycomb, nomex and glassfibre, all featuring on tub and panels overlying a traditional Ferrari tubular chassis.

Ferrari 288GTO.

model's 240Nm at 4,800rpm with a muscular 328Nm at a very usable 4,100rpm. Indeed it was the engine's relative flexibility in comparison to earlier turbo-charged efforts that was perhaps the car's standout achievement, with boost available from as low as 3,000rpm, making this a much more tractable and user-friendly car. Indeed, such was the turbo motor's tractability that Ferrari was at last able to reuse the same gearbox and final drive ratios as those for the 328.

Bodywork and Interior Design

As with previous models, the smaller car would inherit the bodywork and interior design of its larger stablemate, though as before, it was possible for the dedicated car spotter to determine that this was a turbocharged Ferrari and not a regular 328, particularly by the NACA ducts inset into the rear wings ahead of the wheel arches. These had grown in size,

Intensive louvring of the engine cover hinted at the potency of the car's new powerpack. Clearly a derivation of earlier V8 designs, the type F 114 B engine was a 90-degree V8 unit with bore and stroke of 80mm and 71mm for a cylinder capacity of 2855cc, this figure giving rise to the model designation 288: 2.8 litres and 8 cylinders. Predating the Mondial T and 348, this was the first V8 Ferrari to have its motor installed longitudinally, mated to a new transmission unit that would later find use in the even more outlandish F40. Twin camshafts, 4 valves per cylinder, and the Weber-Marelli IAW combined ignition/fuel injection system were specified. The motor was topped by a pair of IHI turbochargers and Behr intercoolers, and with a compression ratio of 7.6:1, generated 400bhp at 7,000rpm.

All 288GTOs were finished in red paintwork, complemented by either all-black leather interior trim, or a black leather and orange cloth combination, the orange a match for the markings on the 328-style instruments. The cabin was very much an amalgamation of 308 and 328 cues and components. As befitted a driver's car of the highest order, the dashboard moulding was at last trimmed in alcantara – and at last the V8 Ferrari owner could enjoy a forward view without the distraction of dash-top reflections in their windscreen!

With a power output of 140bhp per litre, in a remarkably lightweight package – the GTO weighed just 1,160kg (2,558lb)

Taking performance to the next level, the 288GTO's successor, the incredible Ferrari F40.

(dry) – its performance was exceptional: acceleration from 0 to 62mph was achieved in a scant 4.9sec, and the standing kilometre despatched in 21.8sec, and the car did not run out of steam until it reached an indicated speed of 304km/h (189mph).

Given the rise of four-wheel drive in rallying, the 288GTO is unlikely ever to have achieved success in competition, though by the time examples began to roll off the production line, motivation to acquire Ferrari's wonder car was driven by investment potential rather than track capability, as the 1980s supercar investment boom inflated the values of exotic cars to unprecedented levels. Always intended to be highly exclusive but with the added benefit of appreciation, the initial run of 200 sold out so quickly that even Ferrari legend Niki Lauda missed out, though he did get one of the further seventy-two examples that Ferrari produced to meet demand.

thereby allowing a greater volume of cooling air to circulate around the hardworking powerplant.

At the rear, five horizontal slots in the valancing expelled the heated air, and the engine cover lid featured a prominent and heavily louvred hump allowing clearance for the intercooler. The roof-mounted spoiler remained a standard fitment for this model, though the shrouded exhaust tips were discontinued in favour of a tail-pipe style indistinguishable from the 3-litre car. Happily, the tail badging denoting the car's model designation was revised, with 'GTB Turbo' or 'GTS Turbo' now presented in a simpler, unambiguous lower-case script, and the 208 designation no longer featuring in the cars' naming.

The turbo-boost gauge was relocated, sensibly now joining the oil-pressure and water-temperature gauges on the dash panel, forming an inverted triangle of instruments between speedometer and rev-counter in the refreshed 2-litre cars.

■ THE 2-LITRE AND TURBOCHARGED RELATIVES

The GTS Turbo. Note the increase in size of the rear-wing NACA ducts for this model.
TIZIANO CASARETO

GTB TURBO/GTS TURBO (1986–89)

Layout and chassis Two-seat berlinetta or sports with removable roof with tubular steel frame and steel construction body/chassis

Engine
Type: F 106 N, mid-mounted transverse, 90-degree V8, wet-sump
Block material: Aluminium alloy with cast-iron liners
Head material: Aluminium alloy
Cylinders: 8 in V-configuration
Cooling: Water
Bore and stroke: 66.8 × 71mm
Capacity: 1990.64cc
Valves: Actuation by twin overhead camshafts per bank, 2 valves per cylinder
Compression ratio: 7.5:1
Fuelling: IHI turbocharger unit with Behr intercooler, Bosch K Jetronic fuel injection
Ignition: Marelli MED 807A electronic ignition
Max. power (din): 254bhp at 6,500rpm
Max. torque (Nm): 328 at 4,100rpm
bhp per tonne: 201 (GTS 199)
bhp per litre: 128
Fuel capacity: 74ltr (16gal)

Transmission
Gearbox: Five speed plus reverse
Clutch: Single plate
Ratios
First: 3.419
Second: 2.353
Third: 1.693
Fourth: 1.244
Fifth: 0.919
Reverse: 3.248
Final drive: 3.7:1

Suspension and Steering
Front: Independent, unequal-length wishbones, coil springs over telescopic shock absorbers, anti-rollbar
Rear: Independent, unequal-length wishbones, coil springs over telescopic shock absorbers, anti-rollbar
Steering: Rack and pinion
Tyres: 205/55 VR 16 front tyres 225/50 VR 16 rear
Wheels: Alloy, 16in diameter
Rim width: 7in front, 8in rear
Turning circle: 12m (39ft)

Brakes
Type: Vented disc brakes front and rear
Size: 282mm front, 280mm rear

Dimensions
Track: Front: 1,485mm (58.5in)
Rear: 1,465mm (57.8in)
Wheelbase: 2,350mm (92.5in)
Overall length: 4,255mm (167.5in)
Overall width: 1,730mm (68in)
Overall height: 1,128mm (44.4in)
Unladen weight: 1,265kg (2,789lb); GTS 1,275kg (2,811lb)

Performance
Top speed: 253km/h (157mph)
0–62mph (sec): 6.3
0–400 m (sec): 14.3
Standing km (sec): 25.7

THE 2-LITRE AND TURBOCHARGED RELATIVES

GTS Turbo engine lid raised. Note the extensive cooling louvres surrounding the raised portion, making room for the intercooler beneath. TIZIANO CASARETO

Sales Figures

Remaining in production for three years, the GTB and GTS Turbo followed the usual sales trend whereby the open variant significantly outsold the berlinetta: when the model was discontinued in 1989, 308 GTB Turbos had been constructed in comparison to no fewer than 828 examples of the GTS Turbo.

TOP: **GTS Turbo engine bay.** TIZIANO CASARETO

ABOVE: **Cabin design: essentially the same as the 328 series.** TIZIANO CASARETO

LEFT: **GTS Turbo.** Note the additional cooling vents incorporated into the rear bumper. TIZIANO CASARETO

CHAPTER SEVEN

THE 4-VALVES

Seven years into a production run, the two-seat Ferrari V8s were starting to show their age, and while time had been kind to them in terms of appearance, the performance credentials of the 308GTB and GTS had certainly not stood up nearly so well. The imposition of regulations requiring a clean-up of exhaust emissions, particularly in the US, had led to a gradual emasculation of the cars to the point that they were becoming unacceptably slow in comparison to more modern competition.

It was essential, therefore, that Ferrari restored the performance necessary to justify their reputation – after all, owners required a turn of speed in line with the promise of their car's aggressive design, not to mention its substantial price. At the time of launch, the list price for a Ferrari 308 Quattrovalvole made it 10 per cent more costly than a Porsche 911SC, and nearly 40 per cent more expensive than a Lotus Esprit Turbo, though discounts could be negotiated with a friendly dealer. Typically, a GTB bought new in 1984 could be had for around £23,000 in the UK, provided they had bargained a substantial discount of perhaps 15 to 20 per cent with the dealer.

The 308GTBi and 308GTSi Quattrovalvole

To stay abreast of the competition, Ferrari went to the challenge of improving performance, evaluating several possible solutions along the way. Surprisingly, the technical solution they settled on as the optimal one for all their V8 cars – the Mondial included – was to redesign the cylinder heads so they could

308GTB Quattrovalvole.
JOHN DICKENS

308GTB Quattrovalvole. Note the new side-marker lamps and mirrors.
JOHN DICKENS

accommodate 4 valves per cylinder. What might be seen as an unexpected choice of performance-boosting technology, especially given the Scuderia's expertise in turbocharging both for the road and on track, was in fact a sensible choice. 4-valve technology was an eminently practical, tried and tested, soundly engineered solution to the GTBi's relative lack of power. Just as turbocharging had become fashionable technology in the late 1970s, so multi-valve technology was growing in popularity in the industry through the early part of the 1980s.

Multi-Valve Engine Technology

Maserati showcased a clever 3-valve head to help the breathing of the small capacity, turbocharged V6 in their otherwise surprisingly conventional Biturbo saloon of 1982, while Mercedes and Ford had both turned to Cosworth, transferring their 4-valve Formula 1 and 2 experiences to 16-valve head designs for exciting performance versions of their dowdy 190 saloon and Sierra hatchback respectively. They were by no means the only adopters. Here was a race technology destined for the mainstream: in the hot hatchback power struggle of the decade, Volkswagen discounted the more obvious forced induction deployed by Ford in their hatchback RS Turbo Escort, or the more ingenious twin-spark arrangement Alfa Romeo installed into their 75 and 155 saloons, favouring a 16-valve head to uprate their iconic Golf GTi in 1986.

Quite significant rework would be necessary at the top of the engine, but the rest of the car was remarkably faithful to earlier versions, Ferrari as always evolving their design with just a few comparatively minor tweaks that they hoped would stand the 308 in good stead until replacement. Both models

■ THE 4-VALVES

were presented simultaneously at the 1982 Paris Salon. Launch materials from Maranello revealed the reasoning behind the selection of 4-valve technology, insisting this was a 'more valid technical result, increasing power and torque while ensuring the highest standards of reliability'. Enzo Ferrari reminded motoring journalists in his 1983 annual press conference that 4-valve head design was nothing new, somewhat misleadingly implying that the 4-valve heads fitted to the Ferrari-powered, rally-dominating Lancia Stratos had been inspired by Ferrari's 12-cylinder Boxer Grand Prix motor design – though such technology had been available even before World War I!

Increasing the number of valves allows for a more efficient flow of the fuel-air mixture into the combustion chamber, and similarly speeds the exit of exhaust gases, improving the

US-market cars continued with the satin black finish to radiator exhaust grilles. Note the so-called **Boxer** paintwork, where the lower sections of the car were also finished in satin black.
CHAD HORWEDEL

So-called **Green Giant** milling machines arrived at the Ferrari factory in 1983, working twenty-four hours a day to finish engine and gearbox castings.
© FERRARIBYNEILLBRUCE.CO.UK

motor's volumetric efficiency. Smaller valves can be used while still delivering a net increase in gas flow efficiency, the reduction in scale and weight of valve gear making the engine more resilient in high rpm situations, reducing the likelihood of valve bounce. Drawbacks are few, and limited largely to the additional complexity and therefore cost of building and maintaining such valve gear, though oil consumption often increases due to the doubling of valve-stem seals.

Peugeot and Bugatti had introduced multi-valve engine technology to their racing cars as far back as 1912 in the quest for Grand Prix success, and the same technological solution would eventually find its way on to the road. Triumph, aiming to keep abreast of rival BMW's 2002Ti and turbo models, forged ahead with a clever 16-valve configuration for their familiar 1850cc Dolomite motor, creatively and expediently designing a cylinder head on which all valves were operated by a single camshaft. The result, the Dolomite Sprint of 1973, would be the first mass-produced road car to deploy 4-valve technology, the understated saloon's power output benefiting to the tune of up to 135bhp – a highly creditable figure for a sub-2-litre car of its day.

The Quattrovalvole Unit

Ferrari was already intimately acquainted with the multi-valve engine technology. Their experience of multi-valve breathing stretched back to certain of the Alfa Romeos campaigned by the Scuderia, and the concept was by now an essential element of their own Grand Prix and sports racer engine designs. Denoting the significance of the V8 redesign, a new engine code of F105A was given to the Quattrovalvole unit, a delightfully idiosyncratic numbering increment given that all preceding Ferrari V8 units has been given identifiers commencing with F106! The revised design also allowed space for an additional litre of oil, making for a capacity of 10ltr (2gal). Cast from hardened and tempered silicium, aluminium alloy, the new 4-valve heads featured valve seats in cast iron, and valve guides of tellurium copper-bronze. Exhaust valves were of nimonic type.

Naturally, there was an overall increase in valve area, and with it, breathing efficiency. Ferrari claimed gas flow increase was 37 per cent up on the inlet side and 41 per cent on the exhaust side, even though the individual valves themselves were significantly smaller. Intake valves were now 29mm in diameter, those fitted to a 2-valve head being 42mm, while exhaust valves were of 26mm diameter, compared to the outgoing single 36.8mm valve design. Valve angle was decreased in comparison to the 2-valve head design, now being 33 degrees rather than 46. Valve clearances still required manual adjustment via the addition and removal of hardened shims, and despite the theoretical increase in resilience in higher RPM situations, the rev-limiter was set at 7,700rpm, as before.

The new combustion chamber configuration necessitated new pistons, carefully matched to rods that were numbered to indicate which cylinder they were to be fitted into, and marked with a letter that indicated their weight. Pistons were installed into Nikasil liners, and compression ratio went up from 8.8:1 to 9.2:1, though US cars continued with a lower 8.6:1 ratio. Bosch K-Jetronic fuel injection and Marelli MED 803A

Quattrovalvole engine bay.

Substantial exhaust shrouding blighted the rear aspect of US-market cars.

■ THE 4-VALVES

Digiplex electronic ignition systems were carried forward to the new model from the preceding 2-valve cars, each bank of cylinders being fed sparks from its own coil, distributor and ignition module, as before. A new intake plenum chamber sat on the revised motor, raised ribbing contrasting beautifully with its red paint finish, and proudly displaying a 'Ferrari' script cast at the top left and 'quattrovalvole' emblazoned across the bottom.

Performance

Claimed power output for European cars was now a realistic 240bhp at 7,000rpm, or 230bhp, then 235bhp at 6,800rpm for 1983 and 1984 US market cars respectively. Maximum torque was now 260Nm at 5,000rpm, or 255Nm at a slightly higher 5,500rpm for US-bound vehicles. The slight upturn in output for the 1984 model year was the result of a new, single three-way catalytic converter that replaced earlier cars' twin catalyst arrangement, the updated system incorporating an exhaust-gas oxygen sensor to feed data to the ECU.

A revised gearbox oil-pump arrangement was installed, now mounted on the gearbox front cover, though as before it was motivated by the output shaft. The gearbox contained the same ratios as had been installed in the European GTBi/GTSi, though now partnered with a slightly lower 3.82 final drive, albeit still higher than that of the original carburetted cars. Gearing was close to ideal; the Quattrovalvole could pull all the way to the redline in fifth gear, making for a frenetic and noisy top speed of 255kmh (158mph)! Quattrovalvole drivers enjoyed a lighter clutch action than before, and while in the real world the gearing was beautifully judged, the new ratios required a change up to third at 93km/h (58mph), masking the true performance of the car to those who judged automotive capability solely on the hackneyed, yet often repeated, 0–60mph yardstick.

The Quattrovalvole's abilities shone through: despite the need for two gearchanges, *Motor* magazine still managed in October 1983 to record a highly impressive 0–60mph sprint time of just 5.7sec. US market cars would share the same gear ratios as their European counterparts, though they would retain the outgoing model's slightly higher 4.06 final drive ratio. The Swiss market version had a lower 3.588 first gear and higher fifth speed ratio of 0.952, teamed with a 3.71 final drive.

Outward Appearance

All but the most ardent car spotter would struggle to spot the external differences incoming with the new model. Apart from the 'quattrovalvole' script attached to the car's tail panel, the most obvious revision was an additional radiator exhaust

308GTB Quattrovalvole, this car with the deep front spoiler fitted, as would become standard for berlinettas during the Quattrovalvole's production run.
JOHN DICKENS

THE 4-VALVES

outlet, fitted on the front compartment lid and running parallel to the leading edges of the wing-mounted outlets. For Europe, all three outlet grilles would be finished to match the adjacent bodywork, while grilles fitted to US-bound cars wore the same satin black finish seen on the earlier injected cars. The radiator grille was revised, with rectangular driving lamps that could be flashed during the daytime now fitted at each end, beneath a slightly amended bumper design. Side repeater lamps were now rectangular for all markets, though as before, European market cars were spared the rear-wing mounted side markers and heavier impact-absorbing bumpers that were demanded elsewhere.

Quattrovalvole cars are often identified by the rear aerofoil that spans the rear buttresses just aft of the cockpit, an attractive appendage clearly derived from the Pininfarina Millechiodi design concept. However, this popular spoiler was actually optional in all markets other than Japan, installed on the car in its original black plastic finish, though often painted as a factory option or by the dealer to match the car's bodywork.

Ferrari continued their quest to improve construction quality, and around 1983, the factory began to coat bodywork prior to painting with a treatment known as Zincrox – as the name implies, a zinc-based coating designed to improve resistance to corrosion. Beside such technological advances, charmingly old-world hand-finishing techniques persisted on the production line: bodywork was carefully finished by craftsmen skilled in traditional techniques such as lead-loading, a process that was used to smooth bodywork joins and pressings, particularly important around the intricately sculpted, rear wing-mounted air intakes.

By now, the 308 weighed 1,330kg (2,933lb) in GTB form and 1,341kg (2,957lb) for the GTS, and a rather podgy 1,492kg (3,290lb) (GTB) and 1,515kg (3,341lb) (GTS) in US trim, though these quoted figures fell to 1,447kg/1,465kg (3,191lb/3,230lb) for the 1984 model year, in part due to simplification in exhaust arrangements courtesy of the more compact three-way catalytic converter design. Despite its inevitable middle-age weight gain, the 308 was as fast as ever it had been, Euro specification cars managing the standing 400m drag in just 14.4sec, and the standing kilometre in a creditable 26.2sec. The US car offered

ABOVE: **308GTB Quattrovalvole.**
JOHN DICKENS

RIGHT: **Classic interior colour scheme in this 308GTB Quattrovalvole.**
JOHN DICKENS

■ THE 4-VALVES

near parity in the same tests at 14.5sec and 26.4sec respectively. Despite the increase in weight and performance over its predecessor, factory claims for braking performance were not revised for the new model, and the same sub-250m (820ft) braking distance from 235kmh (146mph) was quoted – even for the heaviest US-market cars.

At launch, the standard-fit wheels were the same TRX items installed on the 2-valve cars, though this would soon change. At the November 1983 annual Ferrari press conference, eighty-six-year-old Enzo Ferrari himself gave the rationale for abandoning Michelin TRX tyres for his production, explaining: '…40 per cent of Ferrari's own production ends up in America – we hope to do even better – and how can Ferrari send cars with the TRX Michelin, which requires a metric wheel, to America when it is equally feasible to fit the cars with imperial measurement wheels and tyres….'

This was rational, certainly, but perhaps also at least partly motivated by a loss of faith in Michelin, reportedly unwilling at the time to strike a three-year deal with the Scuderia for Formula 1 tyres. A lengthy and stable partnership would help negotiate with success the transition in Formula 1 rules from normal aspiration to turbocharged racers, and a move to Goodyear tyres on track no doubt eased the return of previously optional imperial measurement road wheels, and the demise of the unloved TRX items. Ferrari fitted Pirelli or Goodyear tyres, the 16in-size wheels becoming standard equipment, with sizes 205/55/VR16 at the front, and 225/50VR16 for the rear wheels.

If the return to genuine levels of Ferrari performance did not drive home the message, the profusion of badging certainly would! The modesty of the Dino era was long behind the V8 models, and on the Quattrovalvole, Ferrari's emblems proliferated, with a 'cavallino' badge installed on the ashtray lid, and tiny rectangular badges carried on the newly designed, remote-controlled rear-view mirrors.

Interior

Several thoughtful touches made the car more user-friendly than before. The mirror adjustment controls were much more readily accessible by expedient of actually being visible to the driver, installed on the side of the driver's door armrest rather than hidden beneath it, and central locking made a welcome appearance on the options list.

Further interior amendments were minor in nature, detail improvements rather than dramatic changes. A revised three-spoke steering-wheel design arrived from Momo, still matt

The roof spoiler was a popular Quattrovalvole option, often finished in the body colour for a more harmonious appearance.
JOHN DICKENS

THE 4-VALVES

RIGHT: **308GTS Quattrovalvole**, Silverstone 2013.

BELOW: **308GTB Quattrovalvole. Note the optional 16in wheels on this example.** JOHN DICKENS

308GTBI/308GTSI QUATTROVALVOLE (1982–85)

Layout and chassis	Two-seat berlinetta or sports with removable roof with tubular steel frame and steel construction body/chassis
Engine	
Type:	F 105 AB, mid-mounted transverse, 90-degree V8, wet-sump
Block material:	Aluminium alloy with Nikasil liners
Head material:	Aluminium alloy
Cylinders:	8 in V configuration
Cooling:	Water
Bore and stroke:	81 × 71mm
Capacity:	2926.9cc
Valves:	Actuation by twin overhead camshafts per bank, 4 valves per cylinder
Compression ratio:	9.2:1
Fuelling:	Bosch K Jetronic fuel injection
Ignition:	Marelli MED 803A Digiplex electronic ignition
Max. power (din):	240bhp at 7,000rpm
Max. torque (Nm):	260 at 5,000rpm
bhp per tonne:	180 (GTSi 179)
bhp per litre:	82
Fuel capacity:	74ltr
Transmission	
Gearbox:	Five speed plus reverse
Clutch:	Single plate
Ratios	
First:	3.417
Second:	2.352
Third:	1.692
Fourth:	1.244
Fifth:	0.918
Reverse:	3.247
Final drive:	3.82
Suspension and Steering	
Front:	Independent, unequal-length wishbones, coil springs over telescopic shock absorbers, anti-rollbar
Rear:	Independent, unequal-length wishbones, coil springs over telescopic shock absorbers, anti-rollbar
Steering:	Rack and pinion
Tyres:	225/55 VR 390
Wheels:	Alloy 390mm diameter
Rim width:	165mm
Turning circle:	12m (39ft)
Brakes	
Type:	Vented disc brakes front and rear
Size:	274mm front, 279mm rear
Dimensions	
Track:	Front: 1,460mm (57.5in)
	Rear: 1,460mm (57.5in)
Wheelbase:	2,340mm (92in)
Overall length:	4,230mm (166.5in)
Overall width:	1,720mm (67.7in)
Overall height:	1,120mm (44in)
Unladen weight:	1,330kg (2,933lb), GTSi 1,341kg (2,957lb)
Performance	
Top speed:	255km/h (158mph)
0–60 (sec):	5.7 (*Motor* magazine October 1983)
0–400m (sec):	14.5
Standing km (sec):	26.2

black finished, though now with a triangular centre section, and cloth seat centres were optionally available for those who preferred this to the standard and comprehensive leather trimming. A woollen headlining lifted the cabin ambience, and a very 1980s anti-glare tinting strip could be specified at the top of the windscreen, though this encroached on the line of sight for taller drivers. A handy fold-down coat hook was conveniently provided to the rear of the seats, and a new fog-lamp toggle switch appeared at the tail end of the console for markets in which these lamps were fitted.

Into Production

The Quattrovalvole package of upgrades was clearly enough to keep the market engaged with Ferrari's most popular two-seater: between the late 1982 launch and the cessation of production in 1985, a very respectable 3,970 units were produced. The open car continued to gain in popularity relative to the berlinetta, Ferrari producing cars at a ratio of four GTS for each GTB constructed (3,042 to 748). Furthermore, despite its age, Hollywood certainly agreed that the 308 still had star quality, film makers casting the Quattrovalvole in several feature films including teen comedy *One Crazy Summer* – at one point the car's Quattrovalvole motor finds its way into a yacht, converting it into a powerboat with a 308-style tail panel complete with round rear lamps and 'cavallino rampante' badging! The model also appeared in *To Live and Die in LA*, and perhaps most memorably, a black 308GTSi Quattrovalvole starred in the 1984 film *Against All Odds* in its most memorable sequence, where James Woods wins a breathtaking Los Angeles road race against Jeff Bridges in a Porsche 911 Cabriolet.

The 328GTB and 328GTS

No matter how beautifully designed, it is unlikely that any sports car – perhaps Morgan roadster aside – can continue in production perpetually without requiring refreshment. So, some ten years after it was first presented to the world, Pininfarina's remarkably relevant 308 body shape received a modernizing facelift. The outcome would be presented at the 1985 Auto Show of Frankfurt, remarkably faithful to the original 308 scheme, albeit with a more homogenized, smoothed-over appearance, lending the new 328 range a refined, if rather less edgy and dynamic aesthetic.

4-VALVE MONDIALS

Rather unfairly maligned as being underpowered and unlovely, Ferrari nevertheless persevered with the Mondial format, the four-seater car enhanced in parallel with its sportier two-seat siblings. First addressed was the lack of pace; some early 1980s motoring magazines had tested the Mondial and found it incapable of exceeding 225km/h (140mph), so the family supercar was in urgent need of a boost to reinstate the model to Ferrari's customary position at the top of the sports-car performance league. To make this happen, Ferrari installed 4 valve heads at the top of their familiar 3-litre V8. The 32 valve heads attached to the 1982 Mondial Quattrovalvole's V8 motor lifted power to 240bhp (230bhp in US-market specification), and its top speed figure rose to a more satisfactory 240km/h (149mph). Like all Mondial models, the motor was mounted into a sub-frame, along with the gearbox and rear suspension assemblies, facilitating rapid removal for maintenance.

The mechanical fettling was underplayed, in that little aside from tail-panel badging and some amended cockpit detailing betrayed this as a more potent Mondial. A fresh and glamorous new look did, however, reach the four-seat range in 1983, as Ferrari launched its first full cabriolet since the 365GTS/4 Daytona was discontinued nine years earlier. A slight constriction of rear-seat accommodation made room for a very elegant soft roof, profiled to emulate the metal roof and buttresses it supplanted. Roof up, and especially roof down, the Mondial Quattrovalvole Cabriolet was a very attractive car, and it would improve still further with more cosmetic work in 1985.

While the Mondial 3.2 by no means received a comprehensive reskinning, new bumpers effected a remarkable transformation, harmonizing its appearance with the newly upgraded two-seat 328 range. A neat, full-width radiator grille opening held revised lamp clusters, and the rear of the car looked considerably sleeker, exhaust outlets neatly framed by openings in the rear bumper and valance assembly, and there were again some tweaks to the interior. The modest capacity increase substantially boosted performance, the bigger V8's 270bhp able to propel the 1,410kg (3,109lb) car to 250km/h (155mph). New, convex-dished five-spoke wheels were fitted to all 3.2s, allowing space for the negative offset suspension geometry imposed by the optional ABS braking system, where it was fitted.

While the coupé was perhaps a little staid in design terms – for a Ferrari, at least – Hollywood was really won over by the glamorous style of the Mondial Cabriolet. A red 3-litre car featured in the teen film *Weird Science*, and a white cabriolet appeared in the Michael Caine/Steve Martin film *Dirty Rotten Scoundrels*, in both cases acting as visual shorthand to indicate the luxurious and privileged lifestyle with which this glamorous model was associated.

Mondial 3.2.
JOHN DICKENS

■ THE 4-VALVES

LEFT: **328GTS**.
PAWEŁ SKRZYPCZYŃSKI

BELOW: **US-specification 328GTB. Note the side-marker lamps and more protruberant rear bumper.**
CHAD HORWEDEL

Outward Appearance

The makeover was functional as well as visual, and aerodynamics were improved both in terms of overall cD value, and importantly in the reduction of lift at speed. In tune with the more aerodynamic-aware age, the crisp, shark-like front-wing profile of the 308 models gave way to a softer, more rounded motif, bringing the car in line with both the Testarossa supercar and the Mondial 3.2 with which it was introduced at the 1985 Frankfurt Salon. Those curvaceous front wing lines met a fully integrated, wraparound bumper that incorporated a pair of neatly clustered driving lamps and indicators set at either side of a simple rectangular front grille, underscored by a low-set front spoiler. The rear aspect was also neatened, with a similarly integrated bumper and lower valance assembly, Pininfarina having succeeded in simplifying their original design for a more mature appearance.

At the rear of the car the lower portion of the bumper and valance moulding carried a full-width slatted grille through which the exhaust outlets protruded, and into which the rear fog lamps were mounted, outboard of the exhaust pipes. Bumpers fitted to US-market cars were of a more prominent, impact-absorbing design, the rear unit lacking the integrated fog lamps that were installed for European cars.

In addition to the softened front wings and integrated bumpers, there were other detail changes: the louvres installed behind the retractable headlight pods of the 308 series were gone, radiator cooling air now exiting through a single, large louvred panel inset into the front lid. Also the dainty trigger-style door handles of earlier cars were replaced by lozenge-shaped pull-release handles, initially set flush in the upper surface of the door, but later superseded by a style that incorporated a mounting for the handle itself.

Pininfarina's 328 was a more substantial-looking car, the body appearing deeper and bulkier because of those integrated

THE 4-VALVES

Modern detailing for the 328 series.
PAWEŁ SKRZYPCZYŃSKI

328 Cabriolet; this car is the factory prototype.
EMILIO PALTRINIERI

bumpers, despite the visual slimming trick of painting their lower portions black to match the sill panels. Praise for the revised design was fulsome: Michael Scarlett, reporting for *Autocar* in December 1985, appraised the refreshed appearance as a '... gracefully purposeful machine, one of the loveliest shapes in my opinion ever to spring from Pininfarina's drawing boards', and considered it a match for such classic Maranello machinery as the Dino and California spider.

Available from the outset in both GTB berlinetta and removable roof GTS body styles, it is rumoured that Ferrari toyed

THE 4-VALVES

328GTS; this example was first delivered and registered in the Isle of Man to Ferrari Grand Prix driver Nigel Mansell, three months after winning for the Scuderia at Rio, 1989.
STEVE BAMBER

with the idea of releasing a full spider variant. Dirk-Michael Conradt asserted in his 1990 book *Ferrari 308/328 GTB/GTS – Autos die Geschichte Machten* that a prototype was built in 1984, based on a 308 chassis. Some reports go so far as to specify a chassis number of 49543 for this car, consistent with the reported build year, though the prototype spider wore 328-style bodywork. With a fully flat rear deck and a cloth roof incorporating the flying buttresses that had been removed from the car's metalwork, the car was apparently tested at Fiorano and even on the road – spy-shots of the car, albeit heavily camouflaged, were printed in magazines in the summer of 1985.

Nothing came of the experiment, however, many speculating that Ferrari was concerned that such a model would rob the Mondial cabriolet of sales, a theory with some merit, given that the 348 Spider would arrive as the Mondial T was being withdrawn from sale in 1993.

Into Production

Build quality was better again, Ferrari now having the confidence to introduce a twenty-four-month warranty. A better build, coupled with the car's intrinsic desirability despite the age of its initial design, meant that the 328 would prove every bit as popular as its predecessor. In its short four-year production lifespan, more than 7,000 examples left the factory: 1,344 berlinettas and 6,068 open cars. The earlier part of the series was numbered in the Ferrari odd-number road-car chassis sequence, with later examples (post chassis number 75000) adopting a continuous number sequence. The car's desirability was assisted by efforts to peg pricing so it would be comparable to key rivals; in mid-1986 the GTB model was listed for sale in the UK at £34,750, undercutting Lamborghini's exotic Jalpa 350 at £36,577, and arch-rival Porsche's 911 Carrera Sport at £36,676, though Lotus's Turbo Esprit boasting near parity in performance was a relative bargain at £23,440.

The factory gave the revised berlinetta's dry weight as 1,263kg (2,785lb) for European markets, and 1,273kg (2,807lb) in US trim. Workshop manuals suggested more realistic 1,375kg (3,032lb) and 1,422kg (3,136lb) kerb weights for the cars, and 1,380kg (3,043lb) or 1,435kg (3,164lb) respectively for the GTS variant in European or US trim. With this minimal increase in weight over the outgoing cars, and extra motive power, performance took a determined stride forwards, the berlinetta now offering a 262km/h (163mph) top speed and standing kilometre of 25.7sec, with 251km/h (156mph) and 26.4 sec for US-market cars.

The figures showed the car was fast, certainly, but more impressive was the flexibility of its power delivery. *Motor* magazine, testing the car in June 1986, noticed that it could despatch each 32km/h (20mph) increment between 32 and 177km/h (110mph) in around 4.5sec, using just fourth gear. It was therefore some half a second quicker in each increment than its already rapid predecessor.

Now refreshed with smart new clothes and with accessible additional power, the capable and beautiful 328 would prove a seductive package. Indeed, *Motor*'s road tester was comprehensively won over, describing the 328GTB as a '…rare and beautiful work of art…that is also faster than ever and easier to live with…a car you ache to own'.

While much press coverage was complementary, the age of the car's basic design was beginning to show in places. The GTS in particular began to receive criticism regarding its relative lack of structural rigidity, especially evident on rough road surfaces, as the open car's enemy, so-called 'scuttle shake', became apparent. Betraying the 328's 1970s roots was its increasingly outdated construction. There were just a few minor revisions to the 308's tubular chassis, including some strengthening of rear suspension attachments, which resulted in a new factory type reference: F 106 MB 100 for the berlinetta, and F 106

THE 4-VALVES

328GTB at speed, very much at home on the race track.
SIMON WATLING

MS 100 for the spider. But it would take a whole new body design, and a whole new method of construction, before Ferrari addressed these criticisms – and plans were in place to do just that.

In a way, the 328 was no more than a stop-gap model for Ferrari, albeit a very popular one – it continued in production until the autumn of 1989, when Ferrari unveiled a radical (for the marque) new design: the 348tb. Until then the 308 sufficed, refreshed in modernized 328 guise, successfully upholding the firm's honour until the new car came on stream.

The 3.2-litre Engine

A model number change signified the 328's biggest engineering amendment. The engine, while largely the same design as that fitted to the preceding 308 Quattrovalvole models, had been slightly reworked to release more power. The new F 105 motor still used a block made of aluminium alloy, though it now featured a revised bore and stroke of 83 × 73mm – the stroke marginally longer in proportion to bore than before – for a new capacity of 3185cc. The block now incorporated shrunken-in

Smart new intake plenum design for the 328 series.

■ THE 4-VALVES

328GTS.

PAWEŁ SKRZYPCZYŃSKI

liners made of aluminium, replacing the steel items of earlier cars.

Compact 12mm-diameter sparking plugs were installed, in a revised combustion chamber configured to maximize squish effect in conjunction with an increased compression ratio of 9.8:1. Valve-gear configuration was carried forward unchanged from the Quattrovalvole motor, although the intake and exhaust valves received chrome-plated stems during 1988.

Bosch's dependable K-Jetronic system was a constant, though it was now partnered with an updated Marelli MED 806A electronic ignition system, again featuring twin coils. Power output was up to 270bhp, though US- and Swiss-market cars with a rather lower compression ratio of 9.2:1 made do with 260bhp and 255bhp respectively. Perhaps even more important in terms of driveability, the larger capacity power-plant offered a very worthwhile torque boost for greater flexibility across the rev-range, a maximum of 304Nm delivered at 5,500rpm (289Nm at 5,500rpm for US cars), a significant increase on the preceding car's already strong values.

Yet another intake plenum chamber design arrived with the capacity increase, similar to the previous design, though largely unpainted. Its intricately cast upper surface was finished in red paint, contrasting beautifully with the bare aluminium raised ribbing and model designation, to which '3200' was now appended. The same configuration of three-way catalytic converters was carried forwards from the later quattrovalvole

THE 4-VALVES

RIGHT: **Convex wheels arrived towards the end of the 328 series production run.**

BELOW: **Handbrake lever repositioned on the driver's side sill.**

cars, incorporating oxygen sensor feedback to the engine management system, and as before the air-injection system remained a standard fitment for the US. From mid-1988 all catalyst-equipped cars also featured a CO/HC sensor probe in the catalyst, a fitment necessary to facilitate compliance with incoming emissions regulations.

Engine cooling improvements extended to more effective oil radiators, though system capacity remained the same as that of the later 3-litre cars, at 10ltr (2.2gal). Further cooling system fettling was apparent in the revised arrangement for the nose-mounted water radiator: this was now offset to the right side of the car, leaving a portion at the left side of the grille to supply cool air to the cockpit ventilation fans, both now installed at the left side of the car's nose instead of flanking the water radiator, as in 308 models.

Transmission

There was some minor tweaking of transmission, too – while European cars retained the same gearing as that installed on the Quattrovalvole, the final drive now reverted to the 3.7:1 ratio of the earliest 308s. Further refinement of the cable-clutch mechanism once more slightly reduced pedal effort to 15.9kg (35lb). US cars carried a higher final drive at 4.06, partnered with a slightly lower ratio for each of the five forward gears, and while Swiss market cars were fitted with the same lower final drive as those for Europe, all five forward gears were of a slightly lower ratio. The Swiss car could achieve a top speed of 255km/h (158mph), the same as had been quoted by the factory for European market Quattrovalvole models.

Wheels and Steering

The 16in wheels fitted to the 328 were again of the familiar penta-star pattern, though like those fitted to the 412GT and Mondial four-seaters, the classic design had been modernized with a rather more angular, stylized moulding of the spoke indentations, and a simplified pentagonal central section carrying 'cavallino' badging, through which the wheel-fixing bolts attached. Tyre sizes were resolutely imperial in measurement: 205/55 on 7in rims at the front, and 225/50 on 8in rims at the rear. The unloved Michelin TRX tyres were a thing of the past, though in about 1988 Michelin MXW tyres in imperial sizes began to be offered alongside the now standardized Goodyear rubber for certain markets, with Pirelli alternatives also available on the options list. The skinny spare wheel was standardized across all markets.

Steering was still unassisted, the steering rack receiving the slightest of modification, with a barely higher ratio of 3.25 turns lock to lock for the same 12m (39ft) turning circle.

Safety Equipment: ABS

The last major upgrade to the 328 came shortly before the model's demise, in late 1988. By now, industry emphasis was transferring somewhat from the performance-at-all-costs engineering of homologation racers and rally cars for the road, towards more rounded, user-friendly models that augmented performance with safety-enhancing equipment such as four-wheel-drive and anti-lock braking (ABS). To maintain credibility with safety-aware buyers, ABS would need to become an element of the Ferrari driving experience, at least on an optional basis. So while such relatively mainstream cars as Ford's Granada would make their debut with ABS as standard equipment on all models in the range, Ferrari began to offer ABS as an option for would-be Mondial 3.2 and 328 owners who considered such features sufficiently important to pay a bit more for them. By necessity, new suspension geometry arrived at the same time, the revised configuration installed irrespective of whether ABS was present.

The new set-up included amendment to track, caster and camber, though toe-in remained the same as before. A small tweak to rear tyre pressures (up .1 bar) and the 328 suspension geometry now provided the negative offset that was more appropriate for use in conjunction with ABS-equipped brakes. Road wheel design was revised simultaneously, the wheel spokes and centres bulging subtly to offer additional space behind for the ECU-controlled Teves Mk2 system. Solenoid-operated valves provided the ABS brake-force modulation. These wheels were installed on all subsequent 328s, as well as 3.2 Mondials, whether or not ABS was installed.

A new handbrake lever, sill-mounted rather than sited on top of the central console, signalled a much needed improvement in parking brake performance, the new lever now acting on small brake shoes mounted within the centre of the rear brake discs. Long overdue, this system finally offered the driver the possibility of incline parking without the necessity of leaving the car in gear, though the owner's handbook sensibly continued to recommend this practice for maximum safety.

Interior

Inside the car, Pininfarina had cleverly updated many key interior details, bringing a modern style to the rather dated 308 cabin design. The dash moulding was in essence unaltered, the only real differences being the addition of a small speaker, inset into each end of the upper surface adjacent to the area in which the door-card moulding was adjoined, and some reprofiling of the instrument binnacle. The full-length armrest design was gone, and rather than continuing the sweep of the dash moulding through the entire door-card, a truncated moulding was substituted, offering a curious grab-handle, behind which the door switches were rather unergonomically hidden. At the driver's side, the controls for the remote door mirrors were mounted in front of this grab-handle.

The door-cards were more luxurious in appearance, containing pull-out door pockets, part of an arrangement that incorporated a small armrest to the upper surface. Loudspeakers were mounted at the lower front of each door-card, as before.

The dashboard panel was simplified, now carrying just two minor instruments (unlike contemporary 2-litre GTB/GTS Turbo equivalents) showing oil pressure and water temperature, stacked vertically between the speedometer and rev-counter. The car's white-needled instruments were still sourced from Veglia, and had a new modernist, orange-coloured typeface. Although certainly more contemporary in feel, these instruments were rather annoyingly harder to read than those installed in the outgoing model. The displaced

THE 4-VALVES

RIGHT: **328GTS. Note the extensive use of leather coverings in the business-like interior.** STEVE BAMBER

BELOW: **328GTS.** STEVE BAMBER

■ THE 4-VALVES

LEFT: **328GTB** prepared for track use in the Pirelli Ferrari Formula Classic series, 2013.

BELOW: **328GTS.**
PAWEŁ SKRZYPCZYŃSKI

dashboard instrument joined the other auxiliary gauges in a row sited at the centre of the dashboard moulding, directly above the radio mounting aperture: clock to the left, oil temperature at the centre, and fuel level to the right, each conveniently angled slightly towards the driver's line of sight.

The central console beneath them was comprehensively revised and modernized, slightly bland plastic switchgear supplanting the charismatic chromed sliders of the 328's 3-litre ancestors. Rotary and switch controls for the ventilation system sat ahead of a stylized line of large rectangular rocker-switches, each with a bar-graph comprising six small lights to indicate the level of operation. Behind these, simple rectangular push switches controlled the front and rear fog lamps, the electric aerial and parking lights. Naturally, the traditional Ferrari open gate gearshift remained a constant at the front of the console, with the ashtray alongside as usual.

To the rear of the console there was a lockable storage, the design differing in detail according to whether it was for the GTB or the GTS: for the berlinetta the storage was larger, extending upwards between the seats to adjoin the bulkhead, whereas that installed in the GTS was smaller and lower, and sited further forward in the console moulding to allow storage of the roof panel behind the seats. A plaque on the underside of the storage area lid recorded tyre pressure information.

The steering-wheel design was carried forwards from the Quattrovalvole, though the column stalks were revised, receiving chunkier grips. Functionality was the same as before, though the stalk to the right, controlling windscreen wipe functions, now incorporated a knob at the end to vary wipe speed. The seat-trims wore a straightforward, stitched repeating rectangle pattern, more cossetting than before due to additional luxurious padding. The quality interior feel could be enhanced further by specifying an optional leather makeover for the entire cabin, including the headlining. Other options available for the 328 included metallic paint, central locking, passenger side mirror, and the popular rear aerofoil, a standard fit for Japanese market cars. Air-conditioning, now with a compressor sourced from Sankyo, was standardized for US-bound cars, but remained on the European options list.

Other small but worthwhile improvements included the fitting of a 3ltr (0.6gal) windscreen washer bottle, one third bigger than that of the outgoing 308. European cars received standard rear foglamps integrated within the lower portion of the valance. Cars headed for the US received a third brake light within the rear window opening; and as always they carried the 'check engine' and 'fasten seatbelt' warning lamps.

328GTB / 328GTS (1985–89)

Layout and chassis	Two-seat berlinetta or sports with removable roof with tubular steel frame and steel construction body/chassis
Engine	
Type:	F 105 CB, mid-mounted transverse, 90-degree V8, wet-sump
Block material:	Aluminium alloy with Nikasil liners
Head material:	Aluminium alloy
Cylinders:	8 in V configuration
Cooling:	Water
Bore and stroke:	83 × 73.6mm
Capacity:	3185.76 cc
Valves:	Actuation by twin overhead camshafts per bank, 4 valves per cylinder
Compression ratio:	9.8:1
Fuelling:	Bosch K Jetronic fuel injection
Ignition:	Marelli MED 806 A electronic ignition
Max. power (din):	270bhp at 7,000rpm
Max. torque (Nm):	304 at 5,500rpm
bhp per tonne:	196 (GTS 190)
bhp per litre:	85
Fuel capacity:	74ltr (16.3gal)
Transmission	
Gearbox:	Five speed plus reverse
Clutch:	Single plate
Ratios	
First:	3.419
Second:	2.353
Third:	1.693
Fourth:	1.244
Fifth:	0.919
Reverse:	3.248
Final drive:	3.7:1
Suspension and Steering	
Front:	Independent, unequal-length wishbones, coil springs over telescopic shock absorbers, anti-rollbar
Rear:	Independent, unequal-length wishbones, coil springs over telescopic shock absorbers, anti-rollbar
Steering:	Rack and pinion
Tyres:	205/55 VR 16 front tyres, 225/50 VR 16 rear
Wheels:	Alloy, 16in diameter
Rim width:	7in front, 8in rear
Turning circle:	12m (39ft)
Brake	
Type:	Vented disc brakes front and rear
Size:	282mm front, 280mm rear
Dimensions	
Track:	Front: 1,485mm (58.5in)/1,473mm (58in) ABS Rear: 1,465mm (57.7in)/1,468mm (57.8in) ABS
Wheelbase:	2,350mm (92.5in)
Overall length:	4,255mm (167.5in)
Overall width:	1,730mm (68in)
Overall height:	1,128mm (44.4in)
Unladen weight:	1,375kg (3,032lb); 1,422kg (3,135.5lb)
Performance	
Top speed:	263kmh (163mph)
0–60 (sec):	5.5 (*Motor* magazine June 1986)
0–62mph (sec):	6.4 (factory figure)
0–400m (sec):	14.3
Standing km (sec):	25.7

■ THE 4-VALVES

A FOUR-DOOR FERRARI

Announced at the Turin Motor Show in 1986, the Lancia Thema 8.32 was a more conservative reprise of a theme Pininfarina had explored previously with the 1980 Pinin concept car. Here was a car that could legitimately qualify for the title of 'four-door Ferrari', even if it lacked the prestigious 'prancing horse' emblem. Less ambitious in concept than the expansive 12-cylinder Pinin, the Lancia Thema 8.32 was a pragmatic reinvention of that car's scheme, a luxury saloon propelled by Maranello muscle.

Lancia's Thema of 1984 was the output of a platform-sharing arrangement between the Fiat Group and Saab, sharing development and component production costs across their collective output, thereby rendering each individual manufacturer's previously uneconomic luxury car project viable. While the Thema was a competent car, a more exclusive, Ferrari-powered version of the Thema soon became a favoured project of Vittorio Ghidella, then Fiat Group boss, who would receive one of the first batch of production cars himself.

The exciting Thema 8.32 was assembled in the same dedicated area within Lancia's San Paulo plant in Turin, where staid Thema limousines were completed. Luxuriously trimmed with Poltrona Frau leather covering most surfaces, including the entire dashboard moulding, the 8.32 was as handsomely finished as it was comprehensively equipped. Thoughtful touches included stereo headphones for rear-seat passengers, and a car telephone fitted inside the central armrest. Hand-applied pinstriping and a column-stalk controlled retractable spoiler installed in the bootlid completed the car's elevated specification.

Power was provided by a V8 motor made at Maranello, though some later motors were assembled by Ducati. Based heavily on the engine that powered the contemporary 308 and Mondial Quattrovalvole models, the 32-valve V8 shared its block design, though in the pursuit of smoothness a new crank design giving 90-degree throws replaced Ferrari's 180-degree flat-plane item.

Lancia Thema 832.
MARCUS ROBINSON

The compression ratio was 10.5:1. Bosch KE3 Jetronic fuel injection and Marelli Microplex ignition were used, though there were changes to the firing order, to improve tractability and refinement. Lancia's plans for a four-wheel-drive variant came to nothing, and all 8.32 Themas would deploy their power via front wheels only; indeed, at launch the 8.32 was the most powerful front-wheel-drive car available on the European market. The saloon boasted 215bhp at 6,750rpm, 25bhp down on the 308 Quattrovalvole, though there was more torque, the refactored Ferrari motor generating 284Nm at 4,500rpm.

The engine was designated F 105 L, in line with Ferrari's usual engine-type numbering system. Its inlet plenum was proudly adorned with a script stating 'Lancia, by Ferrari', the sole reference to Ferrari anywhere on the saloon, though five-spoke wheels and yellow 8.32 badging hinted at the collaboration. Nevertheless, in-period publicity materials emphasized the Lancia-Ferrari link, referencing past collaborations including the D50 Grand Prix car, and Enzo Ferrari himself cannot have been wholly disapproving of the saloon, as it is reported he was often chauffeured in one. But perhaps the 8.32 suffered from its lack of direct Ferrari badging, because the big saloon did not sell well and fewer than 5,000 units were delivered in a production run spanning seven years.

CHAPTER EIGHT

THE 348

The continued popularity of the 328 could not disguise the fact that as a car born in the 1970s, Ferrari's two-seat V8 was now well behind the times. Despite the 1980s makeover, the car's interior was rather old-fashioned, and its construction method was unquestionably outdated. Building a car based on a space-frame chassis was a somewhat manual process and therefore rather expensive and imprecise, and the outcome, while undeniably beautiful, exhibited something of a lack of structural rigidity, particularly in GTS form. Calling upon the expertise of parent company Fiat in the creation of its successor, the new Ferrari for the new decade, the first all-new Ferrari to be launched after the death of Enzo Ferrari would be a much more modern construction.

The 348tb and 348ts

Presented at the 1989 Frankfurt Salon, the latest in a line of V8 Ferraris differed in several significant respects from its antecedents. Its crisp new body style was certainly a new take from Pininfarina on the compact Ferrari theme, cues from 1980s icon the V12 Testarossa providing visual interest for an otherwise rather formal, understated and conservative mid-engined sports-car design.

But if the car's design was understated, the manner of its construction was nothing short of revolutionary in comparison with previous Ferrari practices. The 348 was the very first series-production Ferrari to be built with monocoque

Ferrari 348tb.
JONATHAN TREMLETT

THE 348

A more modern Ferrari for the 1990s.
EDUARDO CARO CABRERO

RIGHT: **Ferrari 348ts at Brooklands Motor Museum.**

BELOW: **Ferrari 348tb engine bay.**
MICHAEL DÖRING

bodywork, abandoning the full-length spaceframe of its predecessors, and instead was built around a robotically welded and pressed-steel structural bodyshell. Strictly speaking, the car was a semi-monocoque in that construction of the monocoque extended from the front of the car to the rear bulkhead between cabin and engine bay, with a substantial tubular sub-frame bolted behind carrying body panels, suspension and drivetrain components. Identified by new chassis type designation F 119 A, Ferrari had taken the opportunity inherent in a wholly new design to tweak key dimensions, adding 100mm (4in) to the new car's wheelbase over the 328 model it succeeded, for a 2,450mm (96.5in) gap between wheel centres.

Drivetrain installation was similarly reconsidered, the enlarged V8 motor now installed longitudinally within the engine bay, with the gearbox in line aft of the engine – though rather than reusing the lengthy transmission devised for 288GTO and F40's longitudinally mounted motors, a space-efficient, highly innovative and incredibly compact new transverse gearbox was devised for the new model. Even its naming broke with recent convention: 348 did indeed denote its cylinder capacity and count, but the GT moniker was gone, replaced with a 't' to spotlight the new gearbox, of which the factory was justifiably very proud, followed by either 'b' for berlinetta or 's' for spider, depending on the body style chosen. Both bodywork configurations were readied simultaneously, and buyers could order either variant right from the car's introduction.

Discreet air intake shadowing the rear side glass.
EDUARDO CARO CABRERO

Outward Appearance

The 348 would be the final Ferrari project during Leonardo Fioravanti's tenure as head of Centro Studie Richerche at Pininfarina. Perhaps not as effortlessly beautiful as its predecessors, it was nevertheless a superbly executed design, perfectly in tune with the late 1980s, harmonious, simple and functional in appearance; its only frivolity consisted of dramatic side radiator cooling air-intake strakes that referenced its V12 stablemate, spanning the lower section of each door and extending down into the sill area. Matching grillework extended across the rear lamp clusters.

The 348 was a more substantial, almost chunky design in comparison to the delicate 308, a swage line at bumper top height encircling the bodywork, delimiting the upper surface of the broad panels that clad the lower sides of the cars; the lower extremities of bumpers and side panels were finished in satin black. Surprisingly, the impression of a much larger car was not borne out in dimensions, the 348 some 25mm (1in) shorter than the 328, and a scant 42mm (1.7in) taller. It was significantly wider, however, side-mounted radiators and fatter rubber making the 348 a massive 164mm (6.5in) broader than its antecedent. But despite the new car's additional girth, Pininfarina's careful aerodynamic detailing – near flush side glasses and a largely flat underbody – had given the car a surprisingly efficient shape, the wider car registering a cD factor of 0.32, a worthwhile improvement on the 328GTB's 0.36.

While the new design was crisply modern, two details in particular were curiously reminiscent of Maranello's past. The function of the 308's sculptural rear-wing air intakes – drawing intake air on one side and cooling an oil radiator at the other – would be executed differently for the 348. While the oil cooling air would now be provided by one of the substantial slatted air intakes on the lower body sides, two discreet intakes shadowing the trailing edge of the rear side glasses ducted intake air to the motor. These intakes were of a style rather reminiscent of those Bertone had conceived for the 308GT4. The de-rigeur egg crate-style front grille – a feature of so many historic Ferrari designs – was once again in evidence, though closer inspection would reveal it to be a sham. Rather undermining the efficient function-to-the-fore design ethic, the grille was a dummy moulding; water radiators were now fitted to the sides of the car, so only a small intake to one side of the lower portion of the bumper was truly functional, passing air to the cabin air-conditioner.

Flanking this grille were handsome new lamp clusters comprising direction indicators, fog lamps and daytime flasher units. In an interesting exercise in design exchange, the 348, so clearly influenced at its sides and rear by the appearance of the Testarossa, would in turn provide the inspiration when the Testarossa received a facelift in 1992. The front aspect of the resulting 512TR, previously rather similar to the 328 and Mondial 3.2 models, became closer in style to the 348, adopting lower lamp clusters, and bumper and grille treatment very close to those of the smaller Ferrari. European market cars had tiny circular repeater lamps on the front wings, above the swage line that bisected the car's side and at the top level of the bumper, just aft of the wheel arches. US-market cars dispensed with these lamps in favour of larger rectangular side-marker

■ THE 348

lamps inset into the sides of the front bumper, with similar lamps also fitted to the sides of the rear bumper.

Anticipating the New Ferrari V8

The world eagerly anticipated the new Ferrari V8. Through the late 1980s a classic car boom gathered momentum as many speculators entered this rising market, eagerly snapping up cars that had previously been the preserve of the automotive enthusiast, confident in ever growing returns on desirable metal. Models from Maranello were in particular demand. But if the investors were keen, so were the enthusiasts, and the imminent arrival of a new Ferrari triggered the usual journalistic speculation. In June 1988 *Autocar* ran a short piece entitled 'Enzo's new hit', in which certain details of the forthcoming 328 replacement were previewed. In the article, the 3.4-litre V8 motor was confirmed, though there was no mention of its longitudinal positioning. The Testarossa-style side strakes were correctly assumed to be confirmed for production, and there was speculation about a weight reduction over the outgoing car, though extensive use of exotic materials had already been ruled out by factory sources. There was even a picture of a prototype 348 on test, angular cladding partially disguising the rear bodywork, and misleadingly fitted with split-rim alloy wheels.

Exterior Design

When it arrived on the market it was clear that, unlike the 308, both berlinetta and spider had been created simultaneously as part of an overall design scheme; the Pininfarina-designed body was essentially the same on both cars save for that removable roof panel, which could be stowed as usual behind the seat-backs when not fitted. Elegant and well proportioned, it

ABOVE: **348tb tackling the challenging Shelsey Walsh hillclimb.**
SIMON HODSON

RIGHT: **Intricately louvred surfacing of the 348 series, reminiscent of the iconic 1980s Ferrari Testarossa supercar.**

LEFT: **US-market 348ts finished in unusual white paintwork.**
DANIEL F. HUGHES

BELOW: **Orange dial markings introduced with the 328 continued with the 348 series. Note the 300km/h speedometer.**
EDUARDO CARO CABRERO

was a design sufficiently timeless and resilient to serve for a decade, evolving with a series of subtle tweaks to become the breathtaking F355. Like the 328 that it succeeded, the bodywork configuration was straightforward. the large bumpers at each end carrying integrated valancing, grilles and spoilers to enclose the extremities of the car from the beltline downwards; this line was set rather higher than on previous models. The smoothed nose once again featured pop-up headlamps – with the usual facility for emergency manual operation – though the lamps themselves were now the same rectangular homofocal units installed in the recently introduced Mondial T.

Extending forwards between the headlamps, and hinged at its leading edge, the front bonnet exposed a deep if relatively narrow luggage well, reclaiming the space between the front wheel wells freed up by the removal of the nose-mounted radiator. The area was smartly trimmed and contained the usual toolkit, now packed into a nicely finished leather case, though in the interest of maximizing luggage space, there would be no spare wheel at all in this model. A tyre-sealing spray bottle was provided, allowing the driver to re-inflate a damaged tyre and complete their journey, albeit at speeds not exceeding 150km/h (90mph).

Like the engine cover, the front bonnet was made from aluminium. This would be the only stowage space available, since the longer wheelbase of this short car pushed the rear wheels closer to the rear extremities, leaving no spare room behind the engine. The battery was located initially within the engine

compartment, though it was re-sited during the course of 1992 –93 to a bay ahead of the left front wheel arch; battery access therefore now required removal of the wheel and gravel-guard within.

The extensively louvred engine cover extended from the wraparound rear windscreen, between the car's flying buttresses, to culminate in a lip that met the grillework across the rear lamp clusters; this carried the car's model designation on an embossed badge. The rear grille masked a pair of rather

THE 348

bland lamp assemblies. Paired gas struts conveniently held the engine lid and luggage cover open.

The detailing on the steel doors was subdued – apart from the busily striated radiator air intakes – with a discreet, lozenge-shaped combined door-lock and opening pushbutton, the pull-handle a recess within the underside of the first of the door intake strakes. In the pursuit of cost-efficient parts commonality, both closed berlinetta and open ts doors carried frameless single-pane side windows, and both cars also featured the same rear quarter and rear window glasses. Mirrors were rather long-necked affairs, and like the door-lock assemblies, were painted to match the car's body colour.

Into Production

The announcement of the new 348 models generated the usual press frenzy, with most reports full of praise for the appearance and capabilities of the new cars. But adulation was by no means unanimous: *Fast Lane* magazine queried the credibility of the new car, running a preview article entitled 'More attractive than it looks', though respected writer Peter Dron did go on to express his view that the new 348 was '… from a dynamic point of view…a serious and important step forward from the 328'. It wasn't just the aesthetics that were subjected to scrutiny: *Car* magazine of October 1989 hinted at the discovery of some rather unforgiving handling traits, noting that hard acceleration on exiting corners could invoke '… terrific tail slides, but if you try too hard the tail will never return, unless you pull a full 360'. This criticism was, however, tempered by the note that such behaviour would be unrealistic in normal road use.

Such criticisms were by no means the biggest risk to the incoming model's future success. Arriving in 1989, just as superheated demand for sports cars was at an all-time high, the 348's production run faced the misfortune of coinciding with the comprehensive collapse of the investment car market. Speculators learned the hard lesson that classic cars as investment vehicles were often costly to maintain, and were deeply susceptible to fluctuating demand. As they offloaded these unwanted commodities, investors quickly flooded the market with barely used cars for which there had previously been massive factory waiting lists. Porsche suddenly had to contend with huge over-capacity, as would-be 911 buyers disappeared in droves.

The 348 was similarly affected: the market was suddenly awash with immediately available cars, just at the same time as certain commentators became more open in their view that

348ts.

the model just might be less than perfect as a driving experience. It was enough to cause many to waver, and the 348 waiting lists all but disappeared as investors abandoned their reserved build slots and few new enthusiasts were motivated to join the queue. It became easy to procure a new 348, and second-hand values crumbled as a result.

The Ferrari Challenge Series

Attempting to address dwindling demand, Ferrari sanctioned a race series to reignite interest in their range, reinforcing the closeness of connection between the Ferrari built for the road and the one seen out on track. The Ferrari Challenge series for 348 cars, either tb or ts models, began in 1993. Amateur 'gentlemen' drivers were offered a kit of safety and performance equipment for their cars, and the factory provided assistance and support throughout the season for this crowd-pleasing and closely contested race series.

It was the start of a most popular series for contemporary two-seat V8 Ferraris, and one that continues to this day, though the 348 has, of course, long since been superseded, each new V8 model introduction triggering a change in cars eligible for the series. Despite the falling market into which they were born, production volumes for the 348tb/ts series were by no means disastrous: 2,894 berlinettas and 4,228 ts models left the factory between 1989 and 1993, as they gave way to updated versions, evocatively rebranded the GTB and GTS.

THE 348

ABOVE: **348 badged in celebration of the Challenge race series, conceived to stimulate demand in the depressed sports-car market.** PAWEŁ SKRZYPCZYŃSKI

RIGHT: **Robotized construction of the 348 series' semi-monocoque chassis.**
PHOTO © FERRARIBYNEILLBRUCE.CO.UK

A Revolutionary Build Process

Although the 348 would be built on the same lines as were employed for the 328, its pressed-steel build would by necessity alter the factory's approach to its construction. Even though time and money had been invested in investigating the possibility of aluminium construction through the 1980s with a series of mysterious prototypes, this Ferrari would still be made from steel. But a new methodology for construction would arrive with the new model, Ferrari proudly unveiling its new flexible manufacturing system, drawing advanced techniques from specialists such as Comau for bodyshell welding, and Mandelli for mechanical assembly. The 348 production line would at last give Ferrari's facilities the appearance of a high-tech automotive factory.

The Scaglietti facility would be dramatically refreshed to undertake this revolutionary build process. Huge orange jigs were employed to ensure that assembly of the body substructure was millimetre perfect, a pair of robots positioned each side of the body-in-build, following a computer programme to land every spot-weld precisely. The resulting bodyshell in berlinetta form was an impressive 59 per cent more resistant to torsional loadings than its predecessor, though the 348ts could improve on the 328GTS shell's stiffness by only 5 per cent.

Despite the advances in precision welding, body building was by no means an entirely automated affair: panelwork was still

115

■ THE 348

Despite the arrival of monocoque methodology in Ferrari bodyshell construction, extensive structural tubing remained a significant part of the formula. Note the palletized rear sub-frame assemblies in the front of the jig used in their construction.
PHOTO © FERRARIBYNEILLBRUCE.CO.UK

largely hand assembled, with significant craftsman effort being expended in spot-welding, deburring and sanding to ensure accurate panel fit. Paintwork would be applied by hand within the Ferrari factory itself, the bodies arriving by truck from Scaglietti following immersion in a cataphoretic primer dip-tank and the application of primer by machine.

The 3.4-litre Engine

The heart of the car – the engine – would, as always, be built in house. So-called Green Giant milling machines, originally introduced into the factory in 1983, finished the rough castings produced by the factory's own foundry, the machine automatically switching bits as it progressed from one pre-programmed task to the next. To keep pace with construction, Ferrari's flexible machining system operated twenty-four hours a day, completing one engine block per hour of operation. Crankshafts and camshafts were also finished on site, though these components were now cast by suppliers outside the factory.

Engine Assembly

Engine assembly was in a separate wing of the factory rather than alongside the line, as had been the case before. As build progressed, motors were moved around on wheeled trolleys, and once completed, each was spun over by an electric motor prior to being run for four hours on one of five dynamometers to ensure its readiness for installation. It was by no means just the motor that was an in-house effort: approximately 70 per cent of the components comprising the new V8 Ferrari would be made in the factory, its foundry, or in its own trim shop.

Engine and bodywork would be united on the production line, where automated lifts along the line adjusted the work height to facilitate the installation of groups of components under and around the car. For a short period both 328s and 348s progressed down the lines together as the still popular older car's production run came to a reluctant conclusion. By 1990 there were four assembly lines in the factory, the V8 cars being built on the two central lines, flanked by Testarossa and F40 assembly.

Eight 348s came off the line each day in 1990, along with three Mondials, two Testarossas, and an F40. While there was still an unusually high degree of manual intervention, Ferrari's production line was by now all but unrecognizable from early efforts. In formative years, mere handfuls of cars were hand-built by craftsmen in a seemingly ad hoc process. Indeed, when a true assembly line was finally commissioned at Maranello in 1958, productivity went through the roof (relatively speaking),

LEFT: **348s passing down the variable-height production line. Note the largely flat underside and the pressed-steel lower wishbones at the front of the car under construction.**
PHOTO © FERRARIBYNEILLBRUCE.CO.UK

BELOW: **Inviting and enduringly popular: red, cream and black interior colour scheme.**

as annual production doubled to a heady 183 cars! One of Ferrari's old traditions, the road test, survived the onslaught of efficiency in construction process, and each 348 – wearing those evocative 'prova' plates – would be assessed by a test driver before delivery, though the previous 200km (124 miles) trial was shortened to around 100 to 150km (60 to 90 miles).

Engine Design

Designed from the outset to run on unleaded fuel, a new factory type reference of 119 was assigned to the 348's new motor design. Once again, a 90-degree configuration V8 with 4 valves per cylinder, and as before, block and head were cast in aluminium-silicon alloy featuring Nikasil-coated steel cylinder liners. Compression ratio was set at 10.4:1, and a bore of 85mm and stroke of 75mm gave a total cylinder capacity of 3405cc. The heads featured cast-iron valve seats and bronze guides, the valves themselves set at the same rather narrow 33-degree angle as their quattrovalvole ancestors.

Reverting to original 308 practice, all 348s would feature dry-sump lubrication, with two gear-driven oil pumps, and a substantial oil reservoir located towards the right-side rear of the engine compartment, the same side of the car as the large oil radiator with thermostatic fan, fed cooling air from bodyside air intakes. The oil filter was sited conveniently at the rear of the engine, mounted on the upper surface between

the V. A closed-loop crankcase emission system vented oil vapour from the heads back into the oil reservoir; the system capacity was 11ltr (2.4gal), and synthetic Agip 10W40 was recommended by the factory.

Rather than the one-belt-per-bank design of preceding Ferrari V8s, a single rubber toothed belt drove all four camshafts and also the water pump at the centre of the motor, a pair of idlers flanking the drive gear fulfilling tensioning duties. Ferrari advised a check of belt condition at each scheduled service –

every 10,000km (6,200 miles) or annually, whichever arrived sooner – and replacement at between 35,000 and 45,000km (22,000 and 28,000-mile) intervals; this was no small undertaking given the lack of clearance between motor and bulkhead, and incredibly, this routine maintenance activity would necessitate full motor removal! The alternator and air-conditioning compressor were each powered by a dedicated rubber belt.

Marelli ignition was discontinued in favour of an integrated Bosch Motronic M2.5 system that combined fuel injection and ignition. It was later upgraded to Bosch's incoming M2.7 system incorporating a self-diagnosis capability, part way through production; this arrived with the 1990 model year US cars, and a year later in Europe. Controlled by a pair of sophisticated ECUs – one for each bank – which measured throttle position, engine temperature and engine revolutions per minute, the system featured a hot-wire air-flow sensor to report the volume of air ingested by the engine, thus ensuring accuracy of fuel introduced into the intake. Where catalysts were fitted, an oxygen sensor was installed into the inlet of each catalyst body, the ECUs thus able to analyse exhaust gases and adjust the mixture as necessary for optimum emissions cleanliness.

Two heavily ribbed, cast-aluminium plenum chambers sat within the motor's V, each drawing air via a butterfly valve from a shared, square air-filter housing to the rear of the engine bay, emblazoned with the Ferrari script.

The Motronic system was a distributorless arrangement, operating two coils per bank, both installed into a single 'pack'. Each coil fired two sparking plugs simultaneously in a so-called 'lost spark' system, one firing at the end of the compression stroke for combustion, with its paired plug firing at the end of the exhaust stroke. The 'lost spark' arrangement offers the benefit of cleaner emissions by combusting any mixture remaining unburned prior to exit via the exhaust valve. Sparking plugs were again of 12mm diameter.

The expansive width of this new V8 Ferrari – not to mention its curious dummy front grille – is explained by the location of its water radiators. Paired water radiators were installed in the rear wings, the radiator installed in the right side of the car being smaller than the one in the left side, thus allowing room beneath it for the oil radiator. Both radiators were fitted with electric cooling fans to the rear. An expansion tank was located towards the front of the engine bay on the right side, and the voluminous cooling system held 20ltr (4.4gal) of fluid.

The first European 348s did not receive catalytic convertors, though cars for all markets would incorporate an air-injection system that introduced secondary air into the exhaust manifolds to activate post-combustion; as a secondary benefit it also sped up warming, and therefore efficiency of catalysts where these were installed. Catalytic converters were mandatory from the outset in certain markets, including the US, though during the course of the 348's final years of production their installation would be standardized everywhere. The exhaust manifolds directed spent gases rearwards – via the twin catalysts where these were fitted – and through to a large transverse exhaust box perched on top of the gearbox; this in turn fed a second transverse box behind the engine/transmission

The substantial thickness of the doors necessary to accommodate the radiator intakes is very much apparent in this view.
MICHAEL DÖRING

assembly, each end of the silencer culminating in typically Ferrari twinned tailpipes.

Despite its longitudinal positioning, the new powerpack was nearly 10cm (4in) shorter than that of the 328, and also set very much lower within the chassis. Contemporary press reports asserted that the new powerpack benefited from a centre of gravity some 13cm (5in) lower than that of the outgoing transverse installation, the centre of gravity for the car as a whole now some 5cm (2in) lower overall as a result. This was partially attributable to the dry-sump arrangement – though the key factor in such elegantly compact powerplant packaging was a brand new gearbox design.

Gearbox

Accepting drive from a longitudinally mounted motor, the new so-called trasversale five-speed gearbox turned the engine's power through 90 degrees before feeding into gearshafts lying transversally across the gearbox, which passed drive on to a limited slip differential sited above the gears. This beautifully executed casting carried the gearbox and differential, and a gearbox oil pump, and offered a 4ltr (0.9gal) oil capacity within its decidedly diminutive form. Lobro driveshafts took power to the wheels.

The clutch – usually twin plate, though sometimes a single plate variation – was located to the rear of the gearbox, and featured hydraulic actuation. Housed in a domed casting, with the Ferrari script cast at the lower edge of the backplate, the outboard clutch assembly was easily accessible for maintenance, and equally easy to spot by any enthusiast sufficiently knowledgeable and motivated to crouch low for a peek at this clever transmission arrangement. Curiously, the quirky and complex Valeo automatic clutch system that was offered on the Mondial T never found its way on to the options list for the 348: this arrangement for shifting gears manually but without the need for a clutch pedal was presumably considered inconsistent with the more clearly sporting intent of the two-seat car.

Performance

Every gear in the new gearbox was of a lower ratio, and the final drive ratio of 3.44:1 was lower than any previous V8 two-seat Ferrari. Catalyst-equipped cars for any market were fitted with a slightly different final drive ratio of 3.56:1. The longitudinally mounted engine produced 300bhp (221kW), and installed in Ferrari's relatively lightweight semi-monocoque bodywork – 1,393kg (3,072lb) for the tb and 1,398kg (3,083lb) in ts format – provided sufficient power for another performance increment over the outgoing 328. Slashing 0.8sec from the 0–62mph dash, the 348 could reach the benchmark speed in a punchy 5.6sec. The standing kilometre time was cut by a

348ts.

Ferrari's innovative and compact trasversale gearbox.

■ THE 348

FERRARI'S TRASVERSALE GEARBOX

When Ferrari finally accepted the unquestionable mass-distribution benefits of mid-mounting engines in their racing cars, like other manufacturers, their first solution situated the gearbox aft of the differential, therefore extending far behind the rear wheel centres. While this was certainly an improvement in terms of weight distribution in comparison to a front-mounted motor, it did make for a rather long and tail-heavy powerpack, particularly when this layout incorporated Ferrari's large Formula 1 12-cylinder engine. Thus for the 1975 season, legendary race-car designer Mauro Forghieri conceived a gearbox containing gearshafts that ran parallel to the car's driveshafts – a short and wide gearbox that would allow a more compact mid-engined installation than before, and a shorter, more agile racer: the Ferrari 312T.

Adopting the same layout for the road-going Mondial T some fourteen years later, a short trasversale gearbox allowed the motor to be mounted longitudinally within the same wheelbase that the car had featured when powered by a transverse engine. Furthermore, as the motor would no longer sit above the gearbox, it could be installed a significant 13cm (5in) nearer the road. Unlike the Formula 1 gearbox from which it drew inspiration, the road car's differential was mounted close to the engine, with the clutch positioned to the rear of the powerpack. Engine power was transmitted right through the gearbox casing via a shaft running beneath the differential, to an outboard clutch unit.

Ferrari 312T Grand Prix car, its trasversale gearbox responsible for the short wheelbase despite this car's lengthy 12-cylinder boxer engine.
ANTHONY FOSH

Here was yet another mechanical feature inspired by competition, Vittorio Jano having fitted similar clutch units to Ferrari's Grand Prix cars in 1960. An enclosed twin-disc clutch fed power back into the gearbox via a short hollow shaft mounted concentric to the first shaft, which carried at its end a gear that turned the drive through 90 degrees to power the gearbox mainshaft. Despite the advanced design, the gearchange mechanism remained quite stiff in use and very traditionally Ferrari in feel.

Very compact by virtue of clever packaging, strong and user-friendly – synchro was fitted to all gears including reverse – the five-speed trasversale gearbox was a great success; it was installed in both Mondial T and 348, and subsequently formed the basis for a six-speed gearbox for the F355 range.

full second over the 328, and top speed rose to more than 275km/h (171mph) – which is not surprising, given the aerodynamically optimized bodywork of the new car. Interestingly, the performance figures quoted for the US-market cars were just the same as those for Europe; the US-market cars shared the European variants' power output but were somewhat heavier, the tb quoted in Ferrari literature as weighing 1,460kg (3219lb) – later 1,478kg (3,259lb) – dry, and the ts just 5kg (11lb) more.

Suspension and Steering

While similar in overall configuration, the 348 suspension design did diverge somewhat from historic Ferrari V8 construction practice in that the top and bottom wishbones, both front and rear, were now fabricated from welded high-tensile steel sheet pressings. Designed to incorporate very low kingpin offset, Ferrari promised that the system would offer greater braking stability and minimal steering kickback. There was an

THE 348

Blade-like spokes were a modern reinterpretation of the classic Ferrari penta-star wheel design.

Braking System

A servo-assisted, hydraulic dual-circuit braking system was installed, supplemented by Teves MkII ECU-controlled anti-lock braking – this important safety feature now standardized at last. This sophisticated system featured separate brake pumps for front and rear axles, and the ability to modulate braking pressure up to fifteen times per second, once the onset of wheel locking was detected by the sensors mounted to the king-pins at the front, and the hub carriers at the rear of the car. An ABS failure warning lamp was installed within the array to the right of the instrument panel, supplementing the brake failure warning lamp at the bottom of the dash. The ABS warning lamp also conveyed any failure codes detected by the Teves system's self-diagnostic capabilities via a sequence of flashes.

Confidence in braking was further inspired in non-emergency situations because each of the aluminium brake callipers contained four cylinders, and offered excellent braking performance – the car was capable of stopping from 96km/h (60mph) in just 42.36m (138.98ft). A cable-operated handbrake activated small brake shoes in the centres of the rear brake discs.

anti-rollbar both front and rear, the one to the front mounted quite high and almost level with the wheel centres, with the steering rack directly above it.

Steering was once again by unassisted rack and pinion, hampered by the same rather restricted turning circle as previous V8 Ferraris. In their handbooks for 1989 the factory quoted a turning circle of 11.85m (38.88ft), though some sources attribute a rather larger 12.05m (39.54ft) to the model; whatever the case, the steering wheel now required a slightly improved three turns to go from lock to lock, a quarter of a turn less than the outgoing car.

The suspension received some updating during the course of the car's production run, as more compact so-called third-generation wheel bearings were introduced. According to Ferrari publications these lightweight units were specifically designed for performance vehicles.

Aluminium alloy wheels (17in) were fitted throughout the production run (aside from special edition models), of a modernized Ferrari penta-star design: this was a rather stylized dynamic reinterpretation, the spokes thrusting forwards and with a recessed trailing edge, making for a blade-like appearance. The wheels were cast in mirror image from side to side of the car, so the 'bladed' edge always trailed the direction of rotation. Bridgestone tyres, in sizes 215/50 at the front and 255/45 at the rear, were standard wear, though Pirelli P Zeros in the same sizes were offered as an alternative.

Fuel System

Fuel was no longer retained in paired haunch-mounted tanks: instead the new car carried a single broad and deep tank directly behind the cabin, offering a substantially increased capacity of 95ltr (20.9gal). The fuel system was sealed by a lockable fuel-filler cap located on the upper surface of the left-side rear wing, and an evaporative control system with active carbon filter prevented the escape of polluting fuel vapours. Despite the adoption of a single fuel tank, the fuel system nevertheless featured twin fuel pumps, each supplying a single bank of cylinders.

Interior

The new V8 car's interior was a radical reimagining of the cockpit design first seen on the 308GTB: a modern aesthetic, if rather generic in some of its detailing, but still incorporating a hearty acknowledgement in its details of past Ferrari cabin designs. Ergonomically improved over the outgoing cars in almost all respects, the cabin was modernized and improved in both layout and function; there was more room in the footwell, and the steering wheel was more closely aligned with the

THE 348

LEFT: **The dashboard design was criticized in some contemporary reports for lacking Ferrari character, and being rather too similar to designs found in the cabins of lesser Fiat Group marques.**

BELOW: **Despite the mechanization in the factory, interior trimming remained very much a hands-on affair.**
PHOTO © FERRARIBYNEILLBRUCE.CO.UK

centreline of the comfortable, if still less than fully supportive driver's seat.

Like the 308GTB, the dashboard moulding featured an upper surface inclined away from the occupants, rather low set, and sweeping curvaceously into matching mouldings at the top of each door. The entire dash was padded, and swathed in leather-look vinyl. At the front, close to the windscreen, nestled four slot-like demister vents, and on the inclined surface four grid-like fresh-air ventilation outlets were inset at a rather reclined angle, an identical pair at the centre, and smaller units at each end of the dash, sharing a moulding with a small loudspeaker. In front of the passenger seat a glovebox was accessible via a cover that followed the contour of the dash moulding; facing the driver was a trapezoid-shaped instrument binnacle, very familiar in proportion and prominence to any 308 or 328 owner.

The dashboard panel now carried four instruments: to the left a 200mph or 300km/h speedometer, depending on market, and a rev-counter to the right, redlined at 7,500rpm. The speedometer incorporated a trip counter, the re-set button extending from the lower portion of the instrument glass, while the rev-counter featured a similar button that controlled a rheostat altering the intensity of instrument illumination. Between these dials were two smaller gauges arranged vertically, for oil pressure and water temperature readings. All instruments – supplied as usual by Veglia – were black-faced with orange markings, drawn in a curiously squared off and italicized font. Black plastic strips following the bottom edge of the binnacle and extending up each side concealed the various warning and tell-tale lamps required by increasingly sophisticated engine and braking management systems.

The steering wheel was of a similar style to that fitted to the 328 range, though the centre was now trimmed and padded rather than with a painted metal finish. The 'cavallino rampante' badge at the wheel's centre once again doubled as the horn button. Three column stalks flanked the wheel in a column

THE 348

RIGHT: **Functional pushbutton heater controls.**
MICHAEL DÖRING

BELOW: **Modified 348ts. Note the 360-style wheels, painted lower bodywork and lift-out roof panel.**

123

■ THE 348

that was height-adjustable via a lever at its underside. A lever for opening the luggage area was installed in the driver's side-kick panel, next to a useful clutch foot-rest, and there was a similar lever to open the engine cover next to the sill-mounted handbrake lever.

The central console moulding extended at an angle from the lower dashboard moulding, in the berlinetta passing between the seats to meet the bulkhead, in the open car stopping short as usual to leave room for roof panel stowage. Matching the lower dashboard moulding, the console was trimmed in leather in the same colour as the seats. At the top of the console was a lidded radio installation compartment, with a row of five square pushbuttons beneath, their tell-tale lamps in a single strip above them indicating operating parking lights, fog lamps front and rear, hazard warning lamps, and the rear window heater (it also controlled heating elements installed in the rear-view mirrors). Directly beneath these buttons was a further pair of Veglia dials indicating engine oil temperature and fuel level.

Sandwiched between these dials and a small oddments storage area situated directly in front of the traditional exposed gearchange gate was a cluster of pushbuttons: these managed the car's sophisticated, digitally controlled ventilation and standard air-conditioning system with climate control, and a digital clock. Beside the gearlever a series of square pushbuttons controlled the standard central locking and electrically operated fuel-filler flap. Between the seats the console moulding carried a wide ashtray with a cigar lighter; behind this was a panel of coin slots, typical for the period, and finally a lockable stowage box.

The door-cards were heavily sculpted, featuring a tick-shaped strip that adjoined the dashboard at the door's leading edge. On each door a combined door-pull and opening handle was fitted towards the front of this strip, which was heavily sculpted, with a deep indentation extending down from the handle to the occupants' elbow, before rising upwards to the door's trailing edge. At the front this strip carried electric window switches, and on the driver's side, a remote control switch for mirror adjustment. The V-shaped panel above it was vinyl wrapped to match the upper surface of the dashboard moulding, the panel beneath partially leather covered in a repeat of the tick motif featured in the panel above, and carpeted at its lowest extremities. A loudspeaker was installed to the lower front of the door-card.

The seats were substantially constructed and deeply bolstered, and were manually adjustable. They were trimmed in leather that matched the leather covering the lower dashboard panel and lower door-card portions, in an attractive pleated design. Each seat carried a small guide for the inertia-reel seat-belt to ensure accurate location of the belt at the occupant's shoulders.

348tb parked next to its predecessor at Brooklands Motor Museum.

The roof panel for the ts was a rigid panel, attached to the car's rear roll-over structure at the back by a pair of locating pins, and to the header rail by a pair of levers. Supports behind the seats allowed this panel to be stored against the rear bulkhead within the cabin, in a soft cover provided for the purpose. A small overhead panel adjacent to the rear window in both open and closed variants carried the illumination panel containing the interior lamp and a map-reading spot lamp.

Safety Features

Ferrari took the opportunity presented by the creation of this brand new model to improve and standardize safety features, standard fitment of ABS being the most significant. Unlike previous V8 Ferrari models, the bumper design complied with the regulations that prevailed in all markets, and with the exception of discreet side-marker lights and a slimline third brake light in the trailing edge of the engine-cover lid, it was difficult to tell for which market a given car was destined.

Cars for all markets were fitted at first with three-point inertia-reel seatbelts, though US-bound cars from the 1990 model year onwards received a more sophisticated arrangement. The so-called 'passive type safety systems' consisted of a retracting lap-belt, and a further belt anchored at the top of the cabin's rear bulkhead between the seats, the other end of the belt attached to a track following the door aperture. The guide at this end of the belt was motor-driven along the track as the door opened, drawing the belt forward and away to facilitate entry, then draw the belt to the correct location automatically as the door was closed. Two hooks were fitted between the sun-visors to allow the occupant to stow the belt away so that it was easier to get in and out of the cabin.

Security features were much more seriously considered for this modern Ferrari. Vehicle theft had reached epidemic proportions through the 1980s, and rising insurance premiums had made vehicle immobilizers all but essential in most markets. Similarly vulnerable – and usually expensive – audio equipment put vehicles at risk of a break-in, but this issue was effectively dealt with by Ferrari interior designers, who had devised a trimmed lid that covered any hi-fi equipment when the car was left unattended.

The vehicle chassis number was stamped into the spring-top mounting plate in the engine bay, and like the 308 and 328 that preceded it, this number was restated on a plaque on top of the steering column shroud behind the steering wheel.

348tb/348ts (1989–93)

Layout and chassis Two-seat berlinetta or sports with removable roof with steel monocoque body/chassis with tubular steel rear sub-frame

Engine
Type:	F 119 D mid-mounted longitudinal, 90-degree V8, dry-sump
Block material:	Aluminium alloy with steel liners
Head material:	Aluminium alloy
Cylinders:	8 in V-configuration
Cooling:	Water
Bore and stroke:	85 × 75mm
Capacity:	3404.70cc
Valves:	Actuation by twin overhead camshafts per bank, 4 valves per cylinder
Compression ratio:	10.4:1
Fuelling and Ignition:	Bosch Motronic M2.5 combined fuel injection and ignition
Max. power (din):	300bhp at 7,200rpm
Max. torque (Nm):	323 at 4,200rpm
bhp per tonne:	215/214
bhp per litre:	88
Fuel capacity:	95ltr (20.9gal)

Transmission
Gearbox:	Transverse five speed, plus reverse
Clutch:	Twin plate
Ratios	
First:	3.214
Second:	2.105
Third:	1.458
Fourth:	1.093
Fifth:	0.861
Reverse:	2.785
Final drive:	3.44:1 (3.56:1 for cars equipped with catalysts)

Suspension and Steering
Front:	Independent, unequal-length wishbones, coil springs over gas-filled telescopic shock absorbers, anti-rollbar
Rear:	Independent, unequal-length wishbones, coil springs over gas-filled telescopic shock absorbers, anti-rollbar
Steering:	Rack and pinion
Tyres:	215/50 ZR 17 front, 255/50 ZR 17 rear
Wheels:	Alloy, 17in diameter
Rim width:	7.5in front, 9in rear
Turning circle:	11.85m (38.88ft)

Brakes
Type:	Vented discs with ATE anti-skid
Size:	300mm front, 305mm rear

Dimensions
Track:	Front: 1,502mm (59in)
	Rear: 1,578mm (62in)
Wheelbase:	2,450mm (96.5in)
Overall length:	4,230mm (166.5in)
Overall width:	1,894mm (74.6in)
Overall height:	1,170mm (46in)
Unladen weight:	1,393kg (3,072lb)/1,398kg (3,082lb)

Performance
Top speed:	Over 275km/h (170mph)
0–60 (sec):	5.5 (*Fast Lane* magazine Jan 1990)
0–62mph (sec):	5.6
0–400m (sec):	14.3 (*Road and Track* magazine January 1990)
Standing km (sec):	24.7

■ THE 348

The 348GTB and 348GTS

Quite why Ferrari reverted to the former model designations of GTB and GTS for the 1993 update of the 348 is not clear, as the revisions introduced in this model were by no means significant. Indeed, by 1993, the tb and ts were leaving the factory with Motronic 2.7 fitted and the battery repositioned to the front of the car (some enthusiasts considered that this alteration gave a marginal improvement in handling as a result of improved weight distribution).

While American customers were still offered the tb and ts models, the European buyer interested in a late model 348 would benefit from three notable mechanical alterations that were all new in the GTB and GTS: the engine's compression ratio was raised to 10.8:1, a larger air-intake plenum design was fitted, and a free-flowing exhaust system was introduced, all of which contributed to a worthwhile increase in power output, this value rising by 20bhp over the earlier cars. Three-way catalytic converters were standardized for all markets, while behind the catalysts a single silencer box replaced the earlier 348's twinned transverse units, though the detailed design of this varied according to the market in which the car was sold.

The only visual amendment of any note was that the matt black paintwork for the lower extremities was discontinued in favour of continuous body colour. The car did look rather deeper-sided as a result, though the scheme was more contemporary and made the car appear less fussy in side profile. A 'cavallino rampante' emblem was installed on the centre of that controversial dummy front grille, a match for one installed between the rear lamps since the start of 348 production.

Kerb-weight figures were quoted in the owners' handbooks as 1,500kg (3,308lb) for the berlinetta, and 1,510kg (3,330lb) for the open car. The standing kilometre time had slowed by around one second on the ts models, though as with all Ferrari performance and weight figures, there is some ambiguity as a result of contradictory figures being presented elsewhere.

Despite the increase in weight, the additional engine power made the GTB and GTS models even more rapid sports cars, with a top speed approaching 280km/h (174mph). The relatively minor enhancements over their immediate predecessors made the model even more desirable than before. Nevertheless, by the time of their launch in October 1993 at the Frankfurt Salon, Ferrari had already determined that a more substantial upgrading would be in order. The 348GTB and GTS thus represented

348GTB.
EDUARDO CARO CABRERO

348GTB engine installation. Note the longer intake plenum chambers of the revised model.
EDUARDO CARO CABRERO

348GTS.

a very short-lived stop-gap, no doubt devised to maintain some market interest in this relatively under-appreciated V8 model ahead of a far more comprehensive and imminent upgrade: the F355. The F355 arrived at the following year's Geneva Show, and attracted significantly more press acclaim and market enthusiasm than its immediate predecessor.

Thus the relatively unloved 348 range gave way to the superficially similar F355, and so a twenty-year tradition of technically unsophisticated, straightforward smaller Ferrari sports-car designs drew to a conclusion. It ushered in an era of complexity, of 5-valve head designs, dynamic suspension arrangements, exotic materials and paddle-shift gearboxes.

348GTB/348GTS (1993–95)

Layout and chassis Two-seat berlinetta or sports with removable roof with steel monocoque body/chassis with tubular steel rear sub-frame

Engine
Type:	F 119 H, mid-mounted longitudinal, 90-degree V8, dry-sump
Block material:	Aluminium alloy with steel liners
Head material:	Aluminium alloy
Cylinders:	8 in vee-configuration
Cooling:	Water
Bore and stroke:	85 × 75mm
Capacity:	3404.70cc
Valves:	Actuation by twin overhead camshafts per bank, 4 valves per cylinder
Compression ratio:	10.8 : 1
Fuelling and Ignition:	Bosch Motronic M2.7 combined fuel injection and ignition
Max. power (din):	320bhp at 7,200rpm
Max. torque (Nm):	324 at 5,000rpm
bhp per tonne:	213 (GTS 212)
bhp per litre:	94
Fuel capacity:	95ltr (20.9gal)

Transmission
Gearbox:	Transverse five speed, plus reverse
Clutch:	Single plate

Ratios
First:	3.214
Second:	2.105
Third:	1.458
Fourth:	1.093
Fifth:	0.861
Reverse:	2.785
Final drive:	3.56:1

Suspension and Steering
Front:	Independent, unequal-length wishbones, coil springs over gas-filled telescopic shock absorbers, anti-rollbar
Rear:	Independent, unequal-length wishbones, coil springs over gas-filled telescopic shock absorbers, anti-rollbar
Steering:	Rack and pinion
Tyres:	215/50 ZR 17 front, 255/45 ZR 17 rear
Wheels:	Alloy, 17in diameter
Rim width:	7.5in front, 9in rear
Turning circle:	12.05m (39.5ft)

Brakes
Type:	Vented discs with ATE anti-skid
Size:	300mm front, 305mm rear

Dimensions
Track:	Front: 1,502mm (59in)
	Rear: 1,578mm (62in)
Wheelbase:	2,450mm (96.5in)
Overall length:	4,230mm (166.5in)
Overall width:	1,894mm (74.6in)
Overall height:	1,170mm (46in)
Unladen weight:	1,500kg (3,308lb), GTS 1,510kg (3,330lb)

Performance
Top speed:	279km/h (173mph)
0–62mph (sec):	5.4
0–400m (sec):	13.5
Standing km (sec):	24.4

■ THE 348

LEFT: **348GTB.**
EDUARDO CARO CABRERO

BELOW: **348 Spider.**
JONATHAN TREMLETT

THE 348

RIGHT: **Too much like a Fiat? The 348 Spider looking suitably exotic at Brooklands, fronting a selection of Fiat hot hatchbacks.**
JONATHAN TREMLETT

BELOW: **348 Spider, tonneau cover in place.**

The 348 Spider

There are some open-air motoring enthusiasts for whom an open-topped car must be fully convertible and not a pseudo-coupé with a lift-out roof panel, however convenient such a feature may be. Just as Porsche experienced with their Targa-topped 911, certain buyers demanded a car in which the entire roof could fold fully flat – though a good deal less than fully flat seemed to be acceptable to Porsche owners, given the rather chunky folded roof that protruded upwards behind the cabin of an early 1990s 911 Cabriolet. In the same way, Ferrari were prevailed upon to develop a full 348 Spider model that would complement – and not replace – the other body styles already available.

There had been no official two-seat spider in Ferrari's range since the demise of the Daytona, but the idea persisted at Ferrari. There had been experimentation with a fully open 328 in the 1980s, though that had come to nothing. However, with the imminent demise of the Mondial Cabriolet, the time was right to revisit the idea of a V8-powered two-seat model, and this time it would be a model that could bear the 'spider' nameplate without apology or excuse.

The 348 Spider remained absolutely true to the 348 aesthetic, and just as the firm had managed with the Mondial, so the soft-top design was an emulation of the lines of the closed car's roofline, replete with flying buttresses. Such similarity between variants reinforced family resemblance and minimized production costs, cleverly reusing many components, including the ts model's door-glasses. The new car would be tested carefully in Pininfarina's wind-tunnel, ensuring that the Spider's aerodynamic as well as aesthetic performance was optimal. Most commentators agreed that the Spider was a visual triumph; a review in *Car and Driver* magazine, December 1993, described its exhibitionist appeal with an unambiguous if curious turn of phrase: 'The eye-frying drop-top 348 attracts attention like a high-rise fire'. Rival US publication *Road and Track* earlier in the year had praised its appearance in more conventional terms, calling it 'low and slinky' and pronouncing it reminiscent of great mid-1960s exotics such as Lamborghini's Miura.

THE 348

Most 348ts bodywork remained barely altered for the fully open car, aside, of course, from the removal of the rear roll structure, and its substitution with a flattened rear deck. Hood stowage was achieved in particularly neat fashion: a well behind the cockpit, which barely encroached on occupant space and only a little on fuel tank capacity, allowed the folded hood to lie almost flush with the rear deck. A vinyl cover was provided to further harmonize the appearance of the stowed hood, though it was rather fiddly to attach.

The hood itself was a manual affair, although it was relatively easy to open: it was released by pulling a handle on the windscreen header rail, then pressing a microswitch caused the door-glasses to drop by 5mm, and then the driver could carefully fold the fabric hood, locking it in stowed position with a bulkhead-mounted lever. While it was a decent enough hood system, it was far from luxurious, and even factory literature acknowledged that it might not be fully watertight in every circumstance, and that 'slight infiltrations from some sealing parts must be considered normal'.

Befitting its status as an extrovertly glamorous automotive conveyance, the 348 Spider was announced with a splash at a high-profile launch event at aspirational Rodeo Drive, Los Angeles, an event that ran concurrently with the Geneva Motor Show in February 1993. This event would become famous as

LEFT: **348 Spider on display at the London Motor Show on the year of its introduction, 1993.**
PHIL HOOPER

BELOW LEFT: **348 Spider.**
JONATHAN TREMLETT

BELOW RIGHT: **348 Spider, Silverstone 2012.**

SPIDER (1993–95)

Layout and chassis Two-seat spider with removable roof with steel monocoque body/chassis with tubular steel rear sub-frame

Engine
Type:	F 119 H, mid-mounted longitudinal, 90-degree V8, dry-sump
Block material:	Aluminium alloy with steel liners
Head material:	Aluminium alloy
Cylinders:	8 in V configuration
Cooling:	Water
Bore and stroke:	85 × 75mm
Capacity:	3404.70cc
Valves:	Actuation by twin overhead camshafts per bank, 4 valves per cylinder
Compression ratio:	10.8:1
Fuelling and Ignition:	Bosch Motronic M2.7 comb ned fuel injection and ignition
Max. power (din):	320bhp at 7,200rpm
Max. torque (Nm):	324 at 5,000rpm
bhp per tonne:	222
bhp per litre:	94
Fuel capacity:	88ltr

Transmission
Gearbox:	Transverse five speed plus reverse
Clutch:	Single plate

Ratios
First:	3.214
Second:	2.105
Third:	1.458
Fourth:	1.093
Fifth:	0.861
Reverse:	2.785
Final drive:	3.56:1

Suspension and Steering
Front:	Independent, unequal-length wishbones, coil springs over gas-filled telescopic shock absorbers, anti-rollbar
Rear:	Independent, unequal-length wishbones, coil springs over gas-filled telescopic shock absorbers, anti-rollbar
Steering:	Rack and pinion
Tyres:	215/50 ZR 17 front, 255/45 ZR 17 rear
Wheels:	Alloy, 17in diameter
Rim width:	7.5in front, 9in rear
Turning circle:	12.05m (39.54ft)

Brakes
Type:	Vented discs with ATE anti-skid
Size:	300mm front, 305mm rear

Dimensions
Track:	Front: 1,502mm (59in)
	Rear: 1,628mm (64in)
Wheelbase:	2,450mm (96.5in)
Overall length:	4,230mm (166.5in)
Overall width:	1,894mm (74.6in)
Overall height:	1,170mm (46in)
Unladen weight:	1,440kg (3,175lb)

Performance
Top speed:	275km/h (171mph)
0–62mph (sec):	5.4
0–400m (sec):	13.5
Standing km (sec):	25.78

---

the 'Rodeo Drive Concours d'Élégance', and in its inaugural year Ferrari's new open car would be presented by Ferrari chairman Luca di Montezemolo and film-star Sharon Stone, who presided over an auction of the first model, selling it to raise more than $1 million for charity.

Despite the glitz of its launch venue, the 348 Spider was far from a boulevard cruiser: rather it was a highly capable addition to the 348 line-up. The fully open bodywork exhibited the same level of torsional rigidity as the ts, and there was little of the typical convertible's defining dynamic weakness of scuttle shake. Strengthening had been applied to the car's windscreen frame and to the side members, to restore the rigidity lost with the amputation of the ts's B-pillar roll structure. Loss of the C pillar meant that the air intakes sited there in its GTB and GTS stablemates were also removed, air instead being drawn from the straked radiator intakes at the bodyside lower flanks.

Arriving in the same year as the updated GTB and GTS models with which it shared showroom space, the Spider's mechanical specification was the same as its siblings, aside from a slight rear track increase – up to 1,628mm (64in) – and with a dry weight naturally a little greater, at 1,440kg (3,175lb). It was a surefooted car with performance barely blunted by its roof conversion, its 320bhp (312bhp in US trim) capable of propelling it to 275km/h (170mph), and despatching the standing kilometre in a very respectable 24.78sec.

Inside, the Spider was configured just like its GTB and GTS siblings, though rear bulkhead treatment naturally differed, and with it the rear portion of the central console moulding: the lockable stowage box of the GTS was replaced with a simpler stowage bin and a wonderfully period audio cassette holder. For the open car the seat designs required amendment in order to carry more substantial seat-belt guides, and the lack of a rear roll-structure meant that the cockpit illumination lamp had to be repositioned between the sun visors.

The Serie Speciale and the 348GT Competizione

The Serie Speciale

In late 1992, in an effort to inject some excitement – if any were truly required – into the 348 line-up, a special edition model arrived in the North American market. There is some debate as to how many were actually produced, though the general consensus is that 115 Serie Speciale cars were built, in two series, the first of 100 cars, the second of fifteen examples; this

ABOVE: **348 Serie Speciale.** Note the splitter beneath the front bumper. PHILIPPE DORIER

LEFT: **348 Serie Speciale;** the exposed rear lights are the most visible amendment on this special edition. PHILIPPE DORIER

desirable 348 variant was available in both berlinetta and ts form. The model ushered in several tweaks conceived to improve road-holding: a wider 1,628mm (64in) rear track, and grippier, asymmetrical Pirelli P-Zero tyres, revised gearing, and the same engine amendments featured on the Spider, liberating an additional 12bhp over the standard car; the Serie Speciale makeover therefore delivered performance benefits as well as aesthetic amendment.

Cosmetic alterations included carbonfibre-shelled F40-style sports seats, rather incongruously but beautifully trimmed in luxurious leather to match the rest of the cabin, and a preview of the scheme that would also appear on incoming GTB, GTS and Spider models whereby lower bodywork extremities were body coloured rather than matt black. The front spoiler had a small splitter extension to so that it protruded further forwards, though it seems this revision did not feature on second series cars delivered through 1994. Most obviously, the rear lights were now exposed with the deletion of the standard car's slatted rear grille, the rear aspect being rather similar to the contemporary French Venturi sports car.

The 348GT Competizione

Introduced in the same year as the Challenge race series was inaugurated, the 348GT Competizione special edition – in berlinetta format only – drew its inspiration directly from the race series. Biased even more strongly towards track capability than the Serie Speciale had been, the GT Competizione was radically lightened. Many creature comforts disappeared: air-conditioning and floor mats were deleted, and carbon and Kevlar composite construction for bumpers and doors made for a seriously lightweight 348. With a dry weight of 1,180kg (2,602lb) – this figure quoted by the factory as being representative of a car complete with all the safety equipment from the 348 Challenge versions – the car was perfectly at home on the race track.

Although the motor was unchanged, transmission was modified, with a lower final drive installed; but the racing clutch that was promised when the cars were announced was dropped from the specification prior to deliveries commencing. Nevertheless the lighter weight and lower gearing imparted greater urge, although no official performance figures were ever released by the factory.

Brakes and suspension were unaltered for road cars, though racy split-rim wheels were unique to the Competizione: the

ABOVE: **348 Serie Speciale interior. Note the numbered plaque on the radio cover above the central console.**
PHILIPPE DORIER

RIGHT: **348GT Competizione.**
SIMON HODSON

THE 348

centre castings— five spokes, naturally – with raised spoke edges were similar in style to those fitted to the 1991 512TR, but at 18in they were bigger than the standard car's rims, and wider too. Pirelli tyres of sizes 225/40/18 and 265/40/18 were installed at the front and rear respectively.

Enamel Scuderia shield badges, previously reserved only for Maranello's racing cars, adorned the front wings to underline the car's sporting potential.

The cabin received a sporty makeover. Changes included Kevlar-covered inner sill panels, and a racy, alcantara steering wheel with crossed flag motif and GT Competizione script emblazoned across its centre, along with the car's series number. Most noticeable were the seats, now a pair of stark racing bucket seats of Kevlar and carbon, with pronounced bolstering and lateral head restraints; these were trimmed in workman-like red fabric, just as those in the 348 Challenge cars.

THE MONDIAL 3.4T

If ever there was an automotive facelift that could be accused of hiding its light under a bushel, it was the upgrading of the Mondial 3.2 to become the Mondial 3.4T. At a casual glance the new car was barely different, and only a keen observer would have spotted the resculpted, more rounded wings and the neater, body-coloured door handles. The new rectangular homofocal headlamp units were invisible in daylight hours, sleekly retracted into the car's nose. More readily apparent – ironically because they were now of a far less obvious design – were the rear wing intake vents, now smaller and tidier rectangular combs. The makeover was smart, and it was definitely a more handsome car, though it could hardly be described as a dramatic improvement over the design it followed.

But its understatement underplayed a remarkable mechanical refactoring, in that the V8 powerplant had been rotated through 90 degrees, to lie longitudinally within the engine bay, and was mounted some 13cm (5in) lower than the outgoing car's engine. It was attached to an innovative new transverse gearbox design that drew influence from Ferrari Formula 1 design experience, and made sense of the 'T' suffix appearing in its model designation. It was also the first Ferrari to be fitted with power-assisted steering.

Other technical novelties included a two-pedal variant that dispensed with the clutch pedal: the French company Valeo had developed an electro-mechanical clutch actuation mechanism controlled by sophisticated software within a

Mondial T Cabriolet.

dedicated ECU, which could interpret various inputs to determine when, and how aggressively, to deploy the clutch. The enlarged V8 motor would subsequently find its way into the two-seat 348.

This powerhouse, pumping out 300bhp, fully laid to rest the four-seat car's reputation as the 'slow Ferrari', the Mondial T sprinting to 62mph (100km/h) in just 6.3sec, and boasting a top speed in excess of 255km/h (158mph). Thus it was fast, with a wider track, lower centre of gravity, and standardized ABS braking: it was also the ultimate Mondial in terms of dynamic capability.

Furthermore it boasted the smartest interior, Ferrari having freshened up the cabin with a curvaceous instrument nacelle, harmoniously integrated centre console and revised seating.

Both open and closed models remained convincing through to the end of production in 1993. This then closed the chapter on Ferrari's foray into two-plus-two seat, mid-engined coupé territory, which had begun with the 308GT4.

CHAPTER NINE

SUCCESSORS

While the 308 and 328 models were always relatively simple in terms of their engineering, the 348 marked a change of direction for Ferrari. The last versions were more complex machines, increasingly dependent on ECU-controlled systems to achieve the seemingly incompatible goals of offering better performance, while sanitizing emissions in the face of more challenging legislation. Certainly this technical sophistication brought benefits in terms of driveability and ease of operation, though such advances began to move the car out of the reach of many otherwise mechanically competent owners, who lacked the confidence and the computer hardware required to maintain and repair such systems. Nevertheless, the 348 remains relatively accessible in comparison to the cars that would follow it down Maranello's production lines. Complex systems and innovative material usage would move Maranello's offerings further forward in dynamic terms, but would also see them move beyond the abilities of most amateur mechanics.

It was not only a growing reliance on technical complexity that would drive succeeding models away from the concept underpinning earlier V8 two-seater designs. Although it was a relatively compact car, because of its side-mounted radiators the 348 was a much wider Ferrari than its immediate predecessors, taking up a good deal more road and therefore presenting a more challenging prospect on the country lanes, on which a 308 or 328 owner could fully exploit their machine. As Ferrari pursued ultimates in terms of road-holding and

Ferrari F355 Spider.
CHAD HORWEDEL

SUCCESSORS

The button-laden steering wheel and paddleshift gearchange are both facts of life for the modern Ferrari driver.
MANGOPULP2008@FLICKR

handling, so each successive V8 design grew wider still. It was a trend that, as far as dimensions were concerned, would see the marque abandon the market sector it had previously contested, leaving Porsche's still compact and nimble 911 to dominate unchallenged. Today, Ferrari's V8 two-seat sports cars, while astonishingly capable and with no shortage of visual drama, have thus moved far from that simple, compact template set by the 308 models, and nowadays share far less in common with their predecessors.

But those early Ferrari V8 two-seaters did exert at least some influence elsewhere in the motor industry, though the inspiration they provided was, of course, limited to firms considering the creation of a mid-engined sports car. Some similarity to the 308/328 was apparent in Toyota's second-generation MR2 of 1989 – indeed, *Modern Motor* magazine even printed an article comparing the two seemingly unconnected cars – and French marque Venturi's coupé and spider designs, following face-lifting through the 1990s, became notably similar in appearance to Ferrari's 348.

Nowadays the cars that most closely resemble the original concepts embodied by Ferrari's earliest V8 cars are not even made at Maranello. Although the motoring press has for three decades or more speculated on the possibility of a new compact Ferrari Dino, the factory has chosen not to pursue this possibility. The would-be owner of such a compact performance car of Italian origin must look instead to stablemate Alfa Romeo, to their lithe and innovative 4C. Or the fast-car enthusiast wanting a little more comfort and additional interior space in a still-compact package might be tempted by Lotus's Evora – surely the spiritual successor to the 308GT4, and seemingly equally under-appreciated in its target market.

The F355

But if Ferrari themselves began to deviate from their earlier recipe of compact dimensions and mechanical simplicity when replacing the 348 range, the alternative approach they pursued would certainly yield most worthy results. In terms of its appearance the F355 was unmistakably an evolution of the 348 design, a cleverly resculpted, curvaceous and classically elegant adaptation of the earlier car, hailed by many as one of Pininfarina's finest works. But to consider the F355 as a simple facelift would drastically undersell the engineering makeover wrought by Ferrari, to arrive at what is perhaps the company's standout product of the 1990s.

Unveiled at the 1994 Geneva Motor Show, the new two-seat Ferrari V8 model ushered in 5-valve head technology in a revised motor design that featured a lofty 11:1 compression ratio and titanium con-rods. Initially featuring Bosch Motronic M2.7, later M5.2 electronic injection, this potent motor generated a massively increased 380bhp, some 109bhp per litre. A six-speed gearbox allowed the driver to make the best of the power available, sufficient to despatch the 0–100km/h dash in just 4.7sec, and to propel the lithe 1,350kg (2,977lb) berlinetta to a 295km/h (183mph) top speed. Clever aerodynamic fettling, including a full body undertray, equalized downforce between the two axles and, partnered with new electronic shock absorbers, ensured the most surefooted handling at any speed.

The F355 addressed many of the criticisms levelled at its predecessor, but the dynamic advantage was won at the cost of the 348's relative unsophistication. F355s, particularly those with the hydraulically operated paddleshift 'F1' gearbox, are complex performance machines. They are significantly less likely to be seen as a DIY maintenance proposition by enthusiast owners than had any previous V8 car. This is not important to many owners, but decisive in terms of ownership demographic – running a F355 can be a costly business!

SUCCESSORS

Visually similar to the 348 series, the F355 was more complex mechanically, with 5-valve cylinder heads and electronic suspension control.

The 360 Modena

If the F355 was a more complex, technical Ferrari than its predecessors, then the 360 Modena represented not just a small step, but a massive leap in that direction. At its core was a brand new aluminium monocoque chassis, offering not only a 28 per cent weight-saving over the outgoing car, but also a 40 per cent improvement in structural rigidity. While the round rear lamps seemed a nod to traditionalism in Ferrari design, it was one of its few aspects that would be familiar.

The central egg-crate grille of the F355 and its predecessors was gone, the 360 Modena instead wearing a McLaren F1-style split grille with a raised section between, which acted as an air inlet for the aerodynamically honed underfloor area. The car's flat bottom led to race-inspired twin rear diffusers for further gains in downforce over the already remarkably efficient F355.

Ferrari F430.

■ SUCCESSORS

The air intakes installed at the upper surfaces of the rear wings were reminiscent of those on the breathtaking Ferrari 250LM V12 race car – but otherwise it was hard to argue that the elegance of this car, or its many other beautiful predecessors, was much in evidence in the brutal, yet undeniably efficient body design that enabled the 360's remarkable performance figures.

An evolution of the 5-valve V8, now 3.6 litres, more than matched the bodywork's excellent aerodynamic performance, offering over 400bhp – a heady 112bhp/litre. Of course, performance was nothing short of exceptional, and this new V8 two-seater, tested in 1999 by journalists from *Autocar* magazine, blasted from 0–60mph in a scant 4.2sec, and from 0–100mph in an even more impressive 8.8sec. Its claimed top speed was 296km/h (184mph). On the basis of its performance and its road-holding – if not necessarily on the basis of its appearance – *Autocar* pronounced it 'the world's best sports car', a judgement with which many enthusiasts and owners concurred.

The F430

The F430, although outwardly similar to its predecessor, proliferated technology into yet more areas of the car's engineering: an electronic differential (E-Diff) appeared, designed with the intention of maximizing deployment of the engine's torque by optimizing traction; carbon ceramic material was adopted for the car's brake discs; and even the traditional steering wheel was reconsidered to accommodate the inrush of electronic systems with a so-called 'manettino' switch that allowed the driver control of the various vehicle dynamics systems now installed.

The Formula 1-inspired paddle-shift gearbox, which had made its debut with the F355, continued to gain in popularity: it was now a serious performance enhancer rather than a technical novelty, promising gearshifts in a brutal 150 milliseconds, contributing to the outstanding performance figures for the 4.3-litre berlinetta – the 0–62mph sprint was despatched in a fearsome 4sec, and its top speed was very close to 322km/h (200mph).

Ferrari's mastery of advanced automotive technology is undeniable. Modern cars feature aluminium-alloy monocoques, carbon ceramic brakes and carbonfibre panelwork, along with such clever technologies as dual-clutch transmission for near-instantaneous gearshifting, magnetic fluid-filled suspension for adaptable ride and road-holding, and naturally intelligent aerodynamics balancing cornering downforce demands with efficiency to allow the highest possible top speeds.

The 458 Italia

While most would agree that Ferrari is now at the forefront of advanced performance car engineering, the same cannot be agreed upon when it comes to aesthetic excellence. The in-house designed 430, while certainly aggressive and purposeful, was rather removed from the elegance of the earlier V8

Ferrari 458 Italia.

Ferraris, lacking much of the delicacy of Pininfarina's original 308. Happily, a return to Pininfarina for the 458 Italia restored much of the beauty that had been surrendered in the interests of efficiency. Performance was no longer the new car's only suit: *Car* magazine reviewing the 458 in May 2012 agreed, considering the 458 Italia '... a shape so relentlessly pretty it just makes you want to burst out cheering.'

But its appearance was by no means at the expense of driving dynamics, and the writer of that review, Anthony ffrench-Constant, eulogized about the incredible experience the 458 offered, and pronounced it 'A Ferrari Enzo would be proud of'! Along with many other enthusiasts, he recognized in it the spirit of the incredibly focused driving machines that had preceded the latest Maranello mid-engined car, an ethos in design and development that offered purity in interaction with the machine, a lack of compromise, and a connection between driver and machine. Most satisfyingly, for the first time since the F355 went out of production, Ferrari could boast in their line-up a mid-engined two-seater that was considered by almost all to be as good to look at as it was to drive.

The Ferrari California

Today Ferrari has a more diverse range than ever, and the mid-engined V8s are not the only cars in the range likely to achieve mass-market popularity. The Ferrari California, for example, is a new departure for the firm in more ways than one. Most obvious is its retractable hardtop, a feature offering comfort and convenience, in particular to owners whom the company seeks to convert from their allegiance to Mercedes. Equally significant is the placement of the latest version of Ferrari's V8 motor ahead of the driver, another first for Ferrari.

While the California offers all the visceral and dynamic excitement of its more focused stablemates, it does demonstrate an acceptance by the factory that the modern Ferrari buyer may be as enthusiastic about comfort and ease of use as they are in outright pace. Is the California a 'dumbing down' of Maranello traditions? Or is it – as Ferrari themselves explain in press materials for the car – a modern reinterpretation of the revered V12 250 California from the late 1950s? Certainly the shortfall in cylinders does somewhat undermine this position, though few could argue that a 490bhp output is insufficient motive power for grand touring duties; a 194mph top speed and 0-62mph dash capability of less than 3.8 seconds underlines its adequacy! Whichever it may be, it is clear that Ferrari enthusiasts can expect even greater levels of flexibility and usability in the future.

Ideal for Purpose

So today's V8 enthusiast can choose where their preferred motor is mounted in the car: mid-ship for absolute dynamic ability, or up front for a more rounded high performance tourer suitable for everyday use. Or as Ferrari puts it in a 2013 brochure for the car '... ideal for those looking for a highly exclusive sports car, who consider driving enjoyment a value to pursue on every occasion: a weekend out of town, a long journey, shopping in the city, or simply getting to the office'.

Ferrari California.
DANIEL F. HUGHES

REPLICA FERRARIS

The Mera

The 'Buyable Alternative': so went the advertising slogan for the Mera, product of specialist vehicle conversion company Corporate Concepts Limited, based in Capac Michigan, as they extolled the virtues of their creation: a combination of 'General Motors reliability, Italian flair and excitement'. Taking a brand new Pontiac Fiero, CCL substituted their own distinctly familiar glassfibre body panels in place of the Fiero's usual skin. These well finished panels bolted directly to the standard body-mounting points on the Fiero's substructure, leaving the car structurally and mechanically unchanged.

Proving the quality of finish inherent in CCL's conversion, the Mera was sold via the US Pontiac Dealer network, as a very expensive approved option, despite the styling being an obvious crib of litigious Ferrari's 308. Although it was offered as an option for both 4- and 6-cylinder Fieros, it seems likely that all orders were for 6-cylinder cars – around 250 were produced between 1987 and 1988, though this was well short of CCL's ambitious plan to produce up to 1,000 cars before the Fiero was phased out by Pontiac. The 2.8-litre V6 car could be had for around $24,995, this price including selected optional equipment such as radio/cassette player, air-conditioning and a $700 leather retrim of the seats, moving them closer in style to the 308s.

Perhaps in an attempt to head off the inevitable, Bob Bracey, head of Corporate Concepts, participated in a November 1986 interview published in US motoring publication *Autoweek*, and did not shirk the delicate subject of potential litigation caused by the extreme similarity to the Italian design. Bracey asserted that the Mera was 'not meant to be a replica or lookalike', claiming the modified Fiero was 'about as close to a Mazda (RX-7) is to a Porsche (944)', sharing not a single line with the Ferrari.

Despite such statements, the intentional similarity was reinforced in unnecessary detailing – although no Ferrari badging or other insignia was fitted to the Mera, plastic wheel trims styled in emulation of Ferrari's famous five-spoke pattern were attached over the standard Fiero wheels. If Pontiac dealers bought Bracey's view, Ferrari certainly disagreed, and by 1988, the Mera received a trademark infringement suit, presented by Ferrari in the Federal District Court in Port Huron. The suit cited the Mera's likeness to the 308

Pontiac Mera. Note the flat rear screen and rear wing-mounted fuel-filler flap.
CHRIS KEATING

and 328 models, and following a settlement between the companies, production was discontinued.

Although CCL never made their conversion available as a DIY kit, the Mera nevertheless represents the progenitor for numerous Fiero conversions that would follow – successive Fiero Conversion bodywork kits are thought to have been moulded from an example of CCL's Mera conversion, or in some cases from panels that had originally been moulded from a Mera – second-generation copies are a most plausible explanation for the ripply panelwork and poor fit displayed by certain examples of such kits! However, not all Fiero rebody kits were of poor quality: glassfibre panelwork offered by Canadian Sports Cars, owned by George Fejer, was reputedly well finished, and the firm even produced a 308-style kit car with spider flat rear-deck bodywork. In the UK, Birmingham-based manufacturer, The Fiero Factory, produced a 308 kit car called the Monza, which seems to be well regarded among enthusiasts; again this was likely to have been based on moulds taken from a Mera.

The 308 Stinger

A rather more faithful replica – still based on the Pontiac Fiero substructure – was sold in the early 1990s by Fiero Plus, based in Ottawa, Canada. The bodywork of the so-called '308 Stinger' differed from the Mera and derivatives, its lines and detailing now moving closer to those of a genuine 308: the luggage compartment lid was narrower, the headlamp pods repositioned, a more authentic door handle design was included, and the engine lid was hinged at roof height, the panel itself now incorporating a lifting section of each buttress. The conversion process was necessarily more involved: no longer a simple bolt-on affair, building a Stinger necessitated modification of the Fiero substructure to permit the details required to increase its similarity to Ferrari's design. Some design compromises remained unaddressed even in the Stinger: the greater width of the Fiero structure, and the different shapes imposed by the Fiero windscreen and flat rear window were two such examples.

The BAS 308 Replica

Perhaps the last word in visual accuracy arrived on the replica scene in the late 1980s, when Banbury Auto Services, previously specialists in crash repairs and turbo installations, decided to venture into the kit-car market with a Ferrari 308GTB replica. Creating accurate moulds from a genuine 308, albeit with rear wheel arches repositioned to allow more space for a longitudinally mounted Rover 3.9-litre V8 and Renault-sourced transaxle, a prototype body on a square-tube space-frame chassis was ready for presentation at Stoneleigh Kit Car Show in 1993. Positive interest in the handsome prototype car bolstered BAS's confidence in ambitious plans to make as many as twenty cars per year.

Unfortunately, by this time the classic car investment bubble had well and truly burst, and the market for a high quality, 308-style kit car at BAS's target build price approaching £30,000 became unrealistic, since values of genuine Ferrari 308s had tumbled, bringing replicas uncomfortably close to the real deal. BAS, now operating under the new name of Prestige Motor Developments, soon ran out of steam, and development ground to a halt: the company managed to produce just three body/chassis combinations before disappearing from the scene. All three would subsequently be completed by enthusiastic and resourceful owners, without access to spares or factory technical support: they had no option but to painstakingly complete the engineering and development of this promising car on their own, adapting and handcrafting innumerable components along the way, but managing to achieve very convincing results.

ABOVE: **Beautifully finished BAS 308GTB replica interior.**

LEFT: **Proportionally accurate BAS 308GTB replica. The one notable dimensional deviation is the relocation of its rear wheel arches to maximize installation space for the longitudinal engine and transmission.**

CHAPTER TEN

MARKETING AND SALES

Incredible as it may seem, even Ferrari salesmen occasionally find themselves having difficulties convincing a would-be buyer to purchase a car that ought to be irresistible. The 308GT4 was just such a car, certainly in the US. Surely a Ferrari sports car designed by Bertone, with crisp contemporary lines, intelligent packaging and impressive practicality would be an easy sell?

Unfortunately its lack of actual Ferrari badging and its starkly different design scheme – in relation to its V6 predecessors, certainly – caused examples of the car to languish unsold in showrooms across the US. Finally the factory relented, understanding the necessity of using the firm's name to increase its appeal, and from mid-1975 the Dino would be peppered with Ferrari badging. But even this did not transform demand and spark a rush to the showrooms. Dealers suffered a similar problem a decade later, as investors abandoned the sports-car investment market in the early 1990s, causing a downturn in sales of the more conventionally attractive 348.

Publicity

But despite such occasional challenges, in the main, Ferraris tend to sell themselves. Rather than relying on billboards, magazine spreads and TV advertisements, Maranello's products are advertised as much by association, as glamorous accessories for the lucky, beautiful people who are enviously observed enjoying their jet-set lifestyles.

Ferrari 308GTS Quattrovalvole on the Ferrari stand, British Motorfair 1983.
WILLIAM MANN

Ferrari Brochures

Aside from sporadic automotive magazine advertisements, about the only publicity materials Ferrari has ever produced are lush and attractive brochures; these are hard to obtain, and are prized by aspiring collectors and schoolboys alike. Strong in layout and design, and often featuring charming artwork or superb photography, they remain eminently collectable, often becoming quite valuable. Early Ferrari V8 brochures were simple, sparse even; the 208GT4 launch brochure, for example, featured quaint, rather impressionist-style artwork at first, though offerings from the 1980s pandered more to those looking for facts and figures. Detailed technical information, comprehensive specifications, and full colour photography were the order of the day through much of the decade's printed marketing features, delighting those lucky to secure such prized publications.

Whether these brochures really generate direct sales is debatable. It seems unlikely that they could ever be persuasive enough to prompt anyone to buy an expensive and uncompromising car they would not otherwise have considered. Perhaps the impression they make on junior enthusiasts might be the inspiration for a future generation of customers.

Celebrity Endorsement

The promise of an implied association of an owner with a world of glamour, luxury and sophistication is more likely to win over potential purchasers – and what could emphasize the point more emphatically than celebrity endorsement? Stars from the music and film business have often been attracted to Ferraris for their own personal transport. Film star Paul Newman, also a notable racer and sports-car enthusiast, visited Maranello to collect an early 308GTB from the factory, press photographs of the visit confirming the patronage of this discerning movie icon; while drummer Cozy Powell and rock and roll legend Elvis Presley were both 308GT4 owners. And a 308GTB bearing the highly appropriate UK registration number 'WHO 308' was reputed to have been owned by lead singer of rock band The Who, Roger Daltrey; it is thought that subsequently the car was raced in the Maranello Challenge Cup in 1996.

V8 Ferraris were highly prized by racing drivers. Mario Andretti celebrated his 1978 World Championship with the purchase of a yellow Ferrari 308GTS, and Nigel Mansell is known to have owned one of the final 328s to be built.

Elvis Presley's 308GT4, on permanent display at Graceland.
PAUL AND KELLY GERRARD

Naturally, Lauda and Villeneuve both enjoyed the use of 308 models provided free by Ferrari, Villeneuve infamously using his to commute between Monaco and Maranello, reputedly covering the 400-plus kilometre route in as little as two and a half hours!

Even race drivers without any direct connection with Ferrari were seduced by the machines from Maranello. Grand Prix driver Martin Brundle treated himself to a 328GTS in classic colour and trim combination of red paintwork and cream leather interior, picking over his ownership experience in a 1986 interview with *Motor* magazine. While critical of some aspects of the interior finish, and bemoaning a slight lack of quality in construction – trim rattles, inoperative central locking and excessive wind noise as a result of a defective A-pillar seal – Brundle nevertheless gave the driving experience a resounding thumbs up, pronouncing the car '...a thrill to drive fast' – from a Grand Prix driver this was positive endorsement indeed!

Appearances in Film and Games

As a low-volume sports-car manufacturer, it is clearly uneconomical for Ferrari to take advertising on the cinema or TV screen. But fortunately for the factory, the inclusion of a Ferrari in a movie or TV production is a frequent occurrence, and Maranello's machines were often used as a visual shorthand

MAGNUM P.I.

Has there ever been a more famous TV car than the 308GTS driven by Hawaii-based private investigator, Thomas Magnum? Vietnam veteran Magnum, played most charismatically by Tom Selleck, spent a proportion of his time overseeing security at 'Robin's Nest', the Hawaiian retreat of wealthy and mysterious novelist, Robin Masters. He enjoyed free accommodation in the comfortable guesthouse, and even better, unfettered use of Masters' cars, including a Ferrari 308 with the licence plate 'ROBIN 1'.

The show's producers had reputedly intended to use a Porsche, but it proved impossible to secure one suitably modified with a larger sunroof to facilitate overhead filming. Second choice was the 308GTS, and because it had a lift-out roof panel it required no such modification, though some changes were still necessary before the car could be used on the show. The seats were modified, set lower and further back, to enable Selleck to fit more comfortably into the cabin.

Given the extended, eight-season run of this successful TV series, it is no surprise to find that not one, but three 308s were used in filming. The car in the pilot and first series was a 1978 308GTS, identifiable by its single exterior mirror and lack of spoiler. This was the car that featured in the opening titles for every show, wearing a licence plate fitted only for the pilot, reading 56E-478. Series two and three featured a 1980 308GTSi, with two mirrors and black grilles adjacent to the headlamp pods.

For the last five series the same 1984 308GTS Quattrovalvole would feature, though as with previous

The 308GTSi used in the filming of *Magnum P.I.*, on display at the Petersen Automotive Museum, Los Angeles.
PAUL AND KELLY GERRARD

series, the genuine cars would be understudied by Fiero-based replicas for certain arduous action sequences. Indeed, the action was often very arduous: in the course of six seasons the 308 was shot, suffered a stolen radio (twice), was forced off the road, subjected to a rear-end shunt, crashed comprehensively on more than one occasion, and even suffered the indignity of being blown up!

When the *Magnum P.I.* TV series came to an end, the cars were sold off. One was purchased by actor Larry Manetti, who had played the character of Rick, one of Magnum's friends in the TV series. Another went on display at Universal Studios, Hollywood; and yet another found its way from Hawaii to Keswick in Cumbria, to become an exhibit at the 'Cars of the Stars' Motor Museum.

Ferrari motor show stands are always a big attraction. Here the 348GTS and 348GTB, the berlinetta in Challenge guise, make their British debut at Earl's Court in 1993.
PHIL HOOPER

MARKETING AND SALES

to demonstrate a character's wealth, taste or glamour. Such appearances often become part of popular culture, even if they are often rather clichéd; many will forever associate the Ferrari 308 with super-model Christie Brinkley, following an appearance driving such a car in National Lampoons Vacation.

It was no surprise that a Ferrari featured in the 1981 movie Cannonball Run, which celebrated the famed 1970s US road race. Its occupants were Dean Martin and Sammy Davis Jr, who attempted to flout the rules of the road by dressing as priests. Dom De Luis's character memorably rationalized the apparent absurdity of their mode of transport by explaining 'They're doing the work of the Lord. In a Ferrari, they can just do it faster'! Even American Express might have helped Ferrari increase the saleability of the 308GTS model, in a French language TV advert in which Scuderia Ferrari driver Gilles Villeneuve drove a 308GTS, as always emphasizing the glamour lifestyle associated with the ownership of such a car.

Ferrari has also enjoyed a healthy representation in more modern modes of entertainment, various V8 models featuring in computer, console and video games; a 328GTS was one of the cars featured in the 2006 version of legendary road-racing game OutRun (Coast 2 Coast), and a 348GTS in the 1997 edition of Grand Theft Auto. It can be argued that such appearances are similar to film and TV appearances in that they inspire a new generation of car enthusiasts at a suitably impressionable age, young people who are probably less likely to be exposed to the aspirational influence of Ferrari in other media.

The Competitors

Over the years Ferrari has pitted its V8 contenders against many illustrious sports-car rivals. Inevitably the fiercest rivalry in the marketplace – as on the racetrack – came from Porsche, with their evergreen 911 series, a potent and practical competitor that evolved in parallel with Ferrari's two-seat range. Through the decades, other competitors have come and gone, challengers to the 308, 328 and 348 arriving from iconic marques including Lotus and Lamborghini, as well as from upstarts and interlopers in the market such as Venturi, and latterly even Honda. Although certain rivals have enjoyed considerable success – Porsche having sold more cars in 1987 alone than Ferrari had constructed through its entire forty-year history – nevertheless the market for Ferrari V8 models has remained consistent and viable, from their introduction in 1973 right up to the present day.

The Porsche 911

All the way through the 1970s and 1980s – and arguably through every other decade in which it has existed – the 911 was the default choice for a buyer wanting a performance car they could use every day. For example, the 911SC, contemporary with the 308GTB between 1978 and 1983, was fast and reliable, fitted with the same Bosch K-Jetronic injection system later adopted by Ferrari to improve the 308's usability. With reasonable space for luggage under its front lid, and with two small rear seats, the 911 offered more practicality than most sports cars, but still enjoyed the reflected glory of an aspirational badge reminding all of the firm's notable Le Mans successes. Huge traction coupled with rather nervous steering appealed to the enthusiastic driver keen to hone their skills in a capable if sometimes unforgiving driver's machine. For those who could live with quirkily floor-hinged pedals and a slightly humdrum saloon-style interior, the 204bhp 911SC was indeed a very tempting prospect.

Porsche continually evolved the 911, upgrading it broadly in line with Ferrari's programme of improvement; later SC models competed with the 308GTB/Si, the more powerful 230bhp 3.2-litre Carrera taking the fight to the Quattrovalvole range, and the 250bhp 3.6-litre range, fast and powerful – and with the option of four-wheel drive – sure-footed competition for the 348. Always sold in far greater numbers than any Ferrari, the 911 has long been the runaway market leader; the SC and visually similar Carrera 3.2 models selling more than 130,000 units, representing a ratio of more than six 911s delivered for every 308 or 328 variant produced by Ferrari.

911SC.

■ MARKETING AND SALES

The Lotus Esprit Turbo

British specialist sports-car manufacturer Norfolk-based Lotus produced many interesting cars through the 1970s and 1980s, such as the Élite and Éclat; but while these were similar to the 308GT4 in their two-plus-two configuration, and even though they were agile and light, they lagged behind Ferrari's cars in outright pace. Arriving in 1980, at first known as the Essex Commemorative Esprit Turbo, Lotus's update of their handsome two-seater was the first of Norfolk's cars to take the performance fight to Ferrari. With 210bhp at its disposal courtesy of a Garrett T3 blower attached to Lotus's familiar 2.2-litre 4-cylinder motor, the Turbo now had the power to match its crisp Giuigaro-designed bodywork.

Not only was it fast, it was also a delight to drive: incisive steering and typically Lotus compliant but accurate suspension provided excellent handling and road-holding to match its undeniable speed. Always cheaper than the 308GTB, the Lotus was hobbled by a rather unconvincing cockpit and certain low-rent fitments including Morris door handles, and perhaps also by its lack of an exotic multi-cylinder motor. Nevertheless Lotus persevered with the Esprit: with a miniscule budget, it extended the model's lifespan with a clever facelift in 1987, devised by Peter Stevens – designer of the Mclaren F1.

Despite selling in ever smaller numbers, the press remained enthusiastic about Lotus's sportiest model, and it is testament to the effectiveness of the clever reworking that the charge-cooled Esprit SE remained a credible competitor to the Ferrari 348tb into the 1990s. Generating an impressive 264bhp from the familiar and efficient twin-cam engine, the Esprit SE could blitz to a 265km/h (165mph) top speed via a punchy 5sec 0–62mph dash.

Lotus Esprit.
PAWEŁ SKRZYPCZYŃSKI

Lamborghini's Urraco, Silhouette and Jalpa

The Ferrari 308GT4 was not Bertone designer Marcello Gandini's first attempt at a two-plus-two seat mid-engined exotic sports car. Before the project for Maranello, Bertone had been commissioned by upstart Ferrari rival, Lamborghini, where he designed the conceptually similar Urraco. Quite similar in overall form, though with some typically Lamborghini detailing, particularly the heavily slatted rear window, the handsome Urraco was launched in 1972, intended as a smaller, more cost-effective and practical sports car, falling beneath the Miura and Espada in Lamborghini's exotic range.

Initially powered by a 2.5-litre transverse V8 pushing out 220bhp, the motor was soon enlarged to 3.0 litres, for a claimed 265bhp. Rather an effort to drive despite its smaller size, and lacking a little in its quality of finish and cabin ergonomics, the Urraco was destined, like all Lamborghinis of the period, to achieve typically tiny sales volumes; by the time it ended production in 1979, just 780 had been produced.

But that was not the end of the line for Lamborghini's aspirations to make inroads into the 308's market. The Silhouette of 1976 was a dramatic visual update of the Urraco, losing the pinched rear seats and gaining a targa-style, lift-out roof panel,

Lamborghini Jalpa.

MARKETING AND SALES

Maserati Merak.

Maserati Shamal.
ADRIAN TURNER

along with boxy wheel arches that became a Lamborghini trademark, as similar items were appended to the outlandish Countach supercar. With 250bhp produced from its 3.0-litre V8, the car was capable of 260kmh (160mph). Just fifty-three Silhouettes would be produced, before in 1981 the visually similar Jalpa became Lamborghini's 308 challenger. Its engine now expanded to 3.5 litres, Lamborghini's intention was to build a more usable, easy-to-drive car, though it would, of course, retain Lamborghini's exotic sense of theatre in its appearance.

Ferrari fought back with ever more user-friendly 308 variants – the GTB/Si, then Quattrovalvole, and finally the 328, at which time Lamborghini's new owner, Chrysler, opted to retire the model. Just 410 examples of the under-rated and under-achieving Jalpa were produced.

Maserati's Merak and Shamal

Incredibly, in the early 1970s a buyer looking for an exotic mid-engined two-plus-two seat sports car from Italy had not one, but three choices. Sharing much of its Giorgetto Giugiaro-designed bodyshell with the incredible Bora, Maserati's Merak vied with Lamborghini's Urraco and Ferrari's 308GT4 as it attempted to bring the glamour and excitement of an Italian supercar within reach of a slightly less well-heeled buyer requiring at least some semblance of practicality. A compact 190bhp V6 devised for the Citroën SM-Maserati project meant that there was enough space in the bodyshell for a second row of seats, cramped but usable for children, or as a perch for luggage.

The car was suffused with influences from Citroen, the French firm having taken over Maserati in 1968, including unusual hydraulic systems used for the braking system, clutch and headlamp pod operation. The Merak even shared its dashboard moulding with the SM-Maserati coupé. Beautiful to look at and very pleasant to drive, the Merak evolved as Maserati changed ownership, falling into Alejandro DeTomaso's hands in 1975, and subsequently shedding many Citroen-derived details. The SM dashboard disappeared as the car was lightened, and a more powerful motor with larger carburettors and higher compression ratio gave 220bhp in the revised 'SS' model.

Despite its glamorous appearance, the car was clearly hard to sell, its cylinder-count shortfall relative to the Ferrari and Lamborghini perhaps a disadvantage in the showroom. Uncertainty about Maserati's continued viability as a manufacturer cannot have helped, undermining confidence that factory support would remain available for this complex and potentially fragile sports car. Construction ended after a decade of production when just 1,817 cars had been built.

Later Maseratis were more saloon-like, and therefore no longer directly comparable to Ferrari's V8 offerings, though the highly evolved and barely Biturbo-based Shamal did have a V8 motor of 3.2 litres boosted by a pair of IHI turbochargers for a strong 326bhp. Similar in performance to Ferrari's 348, this aggressively styled, four-seat coupé may have been on sale at the same time, but the two cars were very different expressions of the modern Italian sports-car constructor's art. With bodywork by Gandini, the Maserati's wild detailing – bulged wings, slashed rear wheel arches, anthracite roll hoop and even a spoiler over the windscreen wipers – could not fully disguise

■ MARKETING AND SALES

Alpine A610.
HEIDI FOSKETT

MVS Venturi.
PASCAL LEHMANN

the original Biturbo bodyshell beneath. Buyers were not convinced, no doubt favouring Maranello's more modern challenger, and just 369 examples of the Shamal were produced.

The Renault Alpine GTA Turbo

Descended from an illustrious line of French competition cars, the Renault Alpine GTA Turbo seemed an unlikely challenger to Ferrari's new 328GTB. Quirky but attractive, and efficient too, its slippery 0.30cD body was constructed from polyester resin for a feather-light kerbweight of just 1,180kg (2,602lb). Sharing its turbocharged PRV V6 engine with the staid Renault 25 saloon, the GTA made more effective use of the 200bhp on offer, being capable of 0–62mph in 7sec and a 249km/h (155mph) top speed. The standing kilometre was achieved in 26.8sec.

With the convenience of two-plus-two seating and modest operating costs, the GTA should have stormed the market, but in the event fewer than 7,500 cars were built, including a non-turbo version, and its A610 successor, an updated rival for the 348 range.

The MVS Venturi

Alpine was not the only Ferrari challenger to emanate from France. The MVS Venturi was the product of three motor enthusiasts: stylist Gerard Godfroy, specialist constructor Heuliez, and production engineer Claude Poiraud, and was a surprise arrival in the sports-car market, an extended period of development coming to fruition around the time the 348 was introduced. Indeed the Venturi has a coincidental resemblance to the Maranello machine. Manufacture de Vehicules Sportifs first presented a prototype to the world at the Paris Show in September 1984. Their ambitions were lofty, as their intention was to build a car to rival Ferrari's mid-engined two-seaters.

With handsome bodywork in composite materials and a powerfully upgraded 260bhp, turbocharged, Renault-derived, 2.8-litreV6, the car was surprisingly well finished, though it was impossible to hide its parts-bin engineering – the Renault Fuego windscreen, BMW rear lamps and Renault 5 door-handles rather gave the game away. But it was fast and drove well. Despite its near parity of performance with the 348, and the factory's overall accomplishment of having produced a car that was as rewarding to drive as it was to look at, like its compatriot the Alpine GTA, it did not sell well enough to keep the company afloat. By the time production was discontinued, barely 600 examples had been built.

The Honda NSX

In the 1990 Grand Prix World Championship, Prost, having defected from McLaren, was Scuderia Ferrari's great hope for World Championship success. Frustratingly, the season would not go Maranello's way and Ayrton Senna, driving a Honda-

MARKETING AND SALES

Honda NSX.

powered McLaren, would take the honours that year. It wasn't the only challenge Ferrari would face from the Japanese carmaker that year, for in 1990 Honda unveiled their NSX sports car. A really intelligent rethinking of the entire sports-car concept, the NSX was the first production car to feature an all-aluminium monocoque, and its 3.0-litre V6 incorporated leading-edge motor technology, including Honda's impressive 'variable valve timing and lift electronic control' (VTEC) system.

Bringing previously unimagined levels of user-friendliness and reliability to the rarefied high performance sports-car market, many NSX coupés were used every day by their owners, some achieving mileages of several hundred thousand miles, which was most uncharacteristic for this type of car. Journalists, too, raved about Honda's addition to the performance car market, *Road and Track*, among others, running an article in 1991 which compared the NSX most favourably with the 348tb, hailing it as 'the ergonomic exotic', before concluding it was a better sports car for everyday use, if giving a rather less exotic experience than Ferrari's berlinetta.

Although the NSX would become something of a benchmark in terms of capabilities – McLaren F1 designer Gordon Murray using it as a benchmark for ride quality and handling – Honda chose not to follow up on their success, perhaps accepting that it was not competence that would turn would-be owners away from their Ferraris, or even from their 911s. So after fifteen years in production and with more than 18,000 examples produced, Honda quietly discontinued the NSX – though the firm does periodically threaten to resurrect the model, unveiling new NSX-concept cars once in a while.

PRODUCTION FIGURES

Model	Years produced	Total
308GT4	1973–1980	2,826
308GTB	1975–1980	2,897
308GTS	1977–1980	3,219
308GTBi	1980–1982	494
308GTSi	1980–1983	1,749
208GT4	1975–1980	840
208GTB	1980–1982	160
208GTS	1980–1982	140
208GTB Turbo	1982–1985	437
208GTS Turbo	1982–1985	250
GTB Turbo	1986–1989	308
GTS Turbo	1986–1989	828
308GTB Quattrovalvole	1982–1985	748
308GTS Quattrovalvole	1982–1985	3,042
328GTB	1985–1989	1,344
328GTS	1985–1989	6,068
348tb	1989–1993	2,894
348ts	1989–1993	4,228
348GTB	1993–1995	222
348GTS	1993–1995	218
348GT Competizione	1993	50
348 Spider	1993–1995	1,090

CHAPTER ELEVEN

ON TRACK

Ferrari's new V8 motor was eminently suited to the race track: strong, relatively straightforward, and of course powerful. It would prove competitive in certain applications, though the car in which it made its debut on track would not achieve successes at the highest level. The 3-litre motor made its competitive debut in a 308GT4 soon after the road car's introduction, and variants of the engine would continue to serve at the forefront of international competition well into the 1990s.

The 308 on Track

The 308GT4/LM

Arriving in 1974, the factory prepared a 308GT4 road car – chassis number 08020 – for owner Bill Schanbacher, the objective being to compete at Le Mans that year in endurance racing's premier race. The 308GT4/LM, as it would be known, received a lightly modified engine, amendments including porting tweaks, high-lift camshafts, bigger Weber 42mm carburettors, and Daytona pistons, which made for a claimed 300bhp at 8,200rpm, and a top speed of 176mph. Additional baffles were added to the sump, to ward off potential reliability issues associated with oil pickup during high-speed cornering. Suspension was re-bushed and anti-rollbars revised, and the brakes also received some attention; Girling four piston callipers fitted and fed cool air by large trunking pipes, making sense of the prominent air intakes at the lower front edge of the boxy wheel arches. The bigger arches covered larger 8 × 15in split-rim wheels at the front, and massive 10.5 × 15in wheels at the rear.

The car's bodywork was further modified: in addition to those wheel arches, the most obvious amendments were a low-mounted, full-width rear wing, a gaping air intake freed from the road-car's obligation to carry a front bumper, and a large front spoiler blending into the front wheel arches. Aluminium replaced steel for all the car's opening panels, and perspex superseded glass for all windows, apart from the windscreen. With a stripped-out interior, the weight saving was substantial, the car estimated to weigh just 1,065kg (2,348lb) fuelled.

Competing in the prototype class due to its lack of FIA homologation, driven by Jean Louis Lafosse and Giancarlo Gagliardi, the 308GT4/LM retired at Le Mans with a failed clutch in 1974 after four hours, while lying in 38th place. Though it returned the following year, again entered by the famed NART équipe, winners of Ferrari's last ever Le Mans, a decent qualifying performance came to nothing. Its lap time should have secured a mid-grid position, but race organizers made a late decision to move the car to the prototype class rather than allow it to compete in the Group 5 GT class for which it had been designed. After a somewhat arbitrary interpretation of the rules by the organizers, the Automobile Club de l'Ouest, the car was deemed to have failed to qualify, and despite NART protests, could not race. In disgust, NART boss Chinetti withdrew all his cars from the race, and the 308's Le Mans career was over.

Although the 308GTB would later prove to be most at home on the rough terrain of rally stages, the model actually made its debut in competition on track, though just like the rally cars they would not be factory entered into competition, but instead campaigned by well established collaborators with independent race teams. Trusted Ecurie Francorchamps took ownership

OPPOSITE PAGE:
The increased width of the rear track on Michelotto's rally 308s is very apparent from this viewpoint.
ALAIN HUGON

■ ON TRACK

Wild 308GT4 LM.
RICHARD DREDGE, MAGIC CAR PICS
(WWW.MAGICCARPICS.CO.UK)

of a glassfibre prototype 308GTB that the factory had experimented with. The car featured such modifications as single one piece front-end moulding incorporating wings, front lid and a very prominent front air-dam, and substantially extended rear wheel arches, amended suspension and a motor delivering outputs around 295bhp at 8,000rpm: plenty of go to match the purposeful appearance. The car – chassis number 22711 – was entered into the Spa 600km race. This would be just the first of a series of sports-car races in which the 308 would participate through the late 1970s, at many illustrious tracks including Zolder and Zandvoort.

The 308GT/M

The race-track 308 concept was further explored in the first half of the 1980s in a rather more extreme form by Michelotto; working against the 'anything goes' Group B regulations, he devised the 308GT/M for clients wanting a more track-focused Ferrari. Michelotto's evolution gave the engine a longitudinal installation, complete with Kugelfischer mechanical injection for a reliable 370bhp. Power was pushed through a Hewland gearbox.

Employing much composite technology for the rather brutal bodywork, which reputedly weighed just 840kg (1,852lb), the compact car looked little like the 308 on which it was based, with a shovel-like front aspect and high-set tail. By the time the car's development was complete, its unquestionable speed was no longer enough for Group B success, where four-wheel drive had become order of the day. The first car produced went to Ecurie Francorchamps, and two further iterations were produced, the last delivered just as Group B cars were banned from competition. Although the 308GT/M never got the opportunity to fulfil its potential, Michelotto's experience in developing the model would prove influential in subsequent work with the 288 Evoluzione; this car was also influential in the development of perhaps the most extreme Ferrari V8 sports car of all time: the Ferrari F40.

The Rally 308s

The 308GTB would see far more competitive action – and significantly greater, if unexpected, success – not on the track but off-road. In emulation of the similarly mid-engined and Ferrari-powered Lancia Stratos, the 308GTB would quickly be adapted to become a potent rally car, initially to Group 4 configuration, though later in more extreme guise, contesting rallies in the legendary Group B class, competing with honour against the class's bespoke rally monsters.

The rally cars were largely prepared by trusted dealership-turned-race preparer, Michelotto. Founded by Giuliano Michelotto in Padua in 1969, Michelotto was soon producing competition cars for rallying, seeing much success in Group 4 with the iconic Lancia Stratos. As the Lancia was retired from the front line, so Michelotto turned instead to Ferrari, constructing a series of specially fettled 308GTBs, each based on used road-car chassis; indeed, one of their GTBs actually bore the chassis number 08380, a 308GT4 chassis number. Favouring glassfibre-bodied GTBs for their weight advantage, Michelotto's production of Group 4 rally specification 308s began in 1978, and finished in 1984, their last car by now a Group B machine.

Michelotto 308GT/M.
JONATHAN TREMLETT

Michelotto's eleven Group 4 cars were given a high compression (10.5:1) dry-sump V8 engine, and the unit was given its own engine-type designation of F 106 A21. With mechanically driven Kugelfischer fuel injection, the 2-valve V8 was good for around 305bhp, making the stripped-out sub-1,000kg cars very rapid rally weapons. Campagnolo 15in light alloy wheels (8in wide fronts and 12in wide rears) were fitted – the same design previously seen on Lancia's Stratos rally cars – and large Lockheed brakes featuring twin-cylinder callipers improved stopping performance.

Success was soon achieved by the rally 308s, the Rallye del Monza being won outright in 1979 by driver 'Lele' Pinto. Further glories quickly accrued; in 1981 respected racer Jean-Claude Andruet was engaged to drive alongside mysterious and glamorous female navigator Michele Petit – known at the

ABOVE: **Michelotto 308GTB/M.**
SIMON WATLING

LEFT: **Michelotto 308GTB/M, very much at home on track.**
MARC LE BELLER

■ ON TRACK

Ferrari 308GTB Group B rally car prepared by Tony Worswick.

time by pseudonym 'Biche' – reuniting a team that had won several major events in a Lancia Stratos, including a win on the 1973 Tour de l'Aisne. Experienced rally-man Andruet, formerly an Alpine A110 pilot, was already very familiar with powerful mid-engined rally racers, and he was something of a Ferrari specialist too, having driven a Daytona Gp4 racer and a BB512 LM on track.

The Michelotto-prepared, glassfibre 308GTB, supplied by French Ferrari distributor CH. Pozzi, won several major rallies in 1981 and 1982, including the Targa Florio and Tour de France. Sponsored by audio company Pioneer for the 1982 season, Andruet's car continued to deliver, winning the Tour de France a second time. Andruet's success with the 308 was not unique; Tonino Tognana also won events in 1982, including securing a second successive Targa Florio victory for Ferrari's berlinetta. But while these privately entered 308s secured significant wins, much to the delight of the many rally fans who adored them, they could not aspire to overall success against the mighty works teams who were contesting the World Rally Championship.

The Group B 30s

It was a situation that would only worsen as ever-more exotic and rapid Group B cars began to appear in the decade's frantic escalation of technology. In the face of bespoke-built Group B cars, usually of exotic and horrendously expensive

Bespoke injection system fitted to Tony Worswick's 308 Group B rally car.

construction, and deploying four-wheel drive and forced induction, the Group 4 Ferraris stood little chance of overall honours. In a noble attempt to level the field, four further 308s were entrusted to Michelotto, to be built to Group B specification: a revised injection system, adjustable suspension, slightly narrower wheels, and the use of new 4-valve heads. Three of the cars were run by Italian team, Promotorsport, winning five events in the Italian International Rallye Championship in 1983, and winning outright the 1984 Spanish International Rallye Championship.

But despite success at national level, glory on the international stage was beyond the 308's capabilities, where it faced audacious contenders such as Peugeot's 205 T16, Ford's RS200 and Lancia's Delta S4. In 1984, Ferrari unveiled its 288GTO supercar, a highly evolved 308 that was initially conceived for Group B, though its lack of four-wheel drive would probably have constrained its chances for rally success. However, a series of tragic accidents meant that all Group B series would be discontinued in 1987 before the GTO could even be considered for competitive action. In any case, the 288GTO would become the darling of late-eighties supercar investors and therefore a vastly appreciating asset, doubtless far too valuable to form the basis of a competition car.

Michelotto's 308 racers would not represent the model's only Group B participation. In response to the discontinuation of Group 4 regulations under which he had previously campaigned a Hart-powered Ford Escort, driver Tony Worswick settled upon a damaged Ferrari 308GTB as a suitable candidate from which a competitive Group B rally car could be developed. With assistance from Colonel Ronnie Hoare at Ferrari UK and Maranello Concessionaires Limited, Worswick Engineering constructed the only right-hand-drive Group B 308 rally car in parallel with on-going Michelotto efforts.

In its bright yellow livery, Worswick's 308 was a most popular sight as it competed in numerous events between 1982 and 1987. It was a most successful competition pairing, particularly so on tarmac-biased events, Worswick garnering many national rally wins before going on to take the inaugural Maranello Challenge Race Series with the car in 1986. Surprisingly, aside from bringing the car closer to the ground surface, the car was raced on track, more or less using the team's tarmac rally settings.

Initially powered by a modified 2-valve motor, the berlinetta was intelligently developed for rally use, most significantly in its bodywork, which featured bespoke panelwork constructed from the extremely lightweight Kevlar/carbon hybrid composite of which Worswick Engineering was an early pioneer. The

Workmanlike interior of a Group B racer.

outcome was a highly impressive weight reduction, the relatively standard-appearing car tipping the scales at less than 1,000kg (2,205lb). Clever features included quick-release composite inner rear wheel arches, allowing a change of drop gears to be made in just eight minutes, thereby permitting alteration of the car's final drive with unfeasible speed between stages.

Continuously developed during the course of Worswick's European campaigns, the bright yellow car's power increased significantly with the installation of a quattrovalvole motor that had been modified for potential use in a Formula 3000 car, producing an estimated 430bhp. Also used in its development between 1981 and 1986, as Worswick competed in the European Rally Championship, were a number of Michelotto parts, such as close-ratio gears, springs and shocks, as well as bespoke items created by the British team – camshafts and slide injection, and also solid suspension bushes and a quick steering rack (both items were subsequently made available by Worswick Engineering to 308 owners in kit form). Always incredibly popular with spectators, Ferrari rally cars were much in demand by rally organizers, keen to secure these rather improbable, handsome and rapid star turns for their event.

Tucked away by Worswick for several years following the demise of Group B racing, the car was refreshed to meet an invitation from Lord March to participate at the 2009 Goodwood Festival of Speed. It has become a popular attraction at Group B car club events, always beautifully presented and excitingly demonstrated by its talented and enthusiastic owner and driver.

ON TRACK

Ferrari 308GTB Group B.

Carma FF Group 5 Sportscar. 1981 Silverstone 6 Hours.
ANTHONY FOSH

Alba Ferrari at Sebring, 1988.
MARK WINDECKER

Endurance Racing

The Carma FF

Perhaps the most famous racing 308 was that campaigned by Carlo Facetti and Martino Finotto's Carma racing team in several endurance events through 1980. Although the 308GTB was homologated by Ferrari for Group 4 racing, the factory had never prepared their own cars for racing, leaving this to private teams. The FF 308, as Carma's car would be known, was a privately developed, extensively modified 308GTB; aside from the doors, glasshouse and roof, it was just about impossible to discern the original Ferrari underpinning this extreme car.

With huge underbody venturi tunnel, heavy front spoiler and elongated tail, the Carma FF was an exciting new mount for Facetti, an experienced driver who had previously driven a Group 5 Lancia Stratos Turbo in a partnership with ex-F1 driver Vittorio Brambilla. The Carma was as fast as it looked, achieving several pole positions through 1980. Reputedly producing 840bhp from its V8, heavily boosted by twin turbochargers, the Carma FF was a popular addition to sports-car grids at events such as the 1980 Daytona 24 – though it managed just six laps of that race, and was one of several retirements that year. Fast but rather temperamental, it was retired after a single season.

Ferrari in IMSA GT Racing

But the Carma team would continue to uphold Maranello's honour in sports-car racing, persevering with Ferrari power in IMSA GT racing. Race-car constructor Alba had produced several race chassis, purchased by teams using diverse power units including engines from Ferrari, Chevrolet and Mazda. Facetti and Finotto installed a Ferrari V8 in their Alba, to compete in the Camel Light class of the IMSA GT Championship. They would use the Alba to decent effect in 1986 and 1987 seasons, leading the Lights class field home twice in 1986.

But the Alba would be less competitive against newer IMSA designs, and the Carma team subsequently switched Ferrari engines to Tiga chassis, finally joining forces with Gaston André Racing, also Ferrari V8 stalwarts in IMSA, to take advantage of the newer, more competitive Spice Lights chassis. Installed in the Spice, the Quattrovalvole powerplant developed a reputed 460bhp, and was coupled via a custom bell-housing to a Hewland DG gearbox. Four wins in 1990 underlined the car's capability, but with the prospect of carrying a further 22.7kg (50lb) of ballast for the 1991 season, Finotto called time on his IMSA adventures.

A further interesting IMSA Ferrari project was started by American automotive engineering company Huffaker, a tube-framed Ferrari 308 designed for racing in IMSA, GTU class. Its extremely stylized body blended 288 features such as bulged wings and 250GTO-style rear wing vents, in a profile that was superficially similar but more rakish than any offering from Maranello. It was light, too, weighing in at just 900kg (1,985lb). It should have been as fast as it looked, with a quoted 390bhp output from a modified and longitudinally mounted Ferrari V8 attached to a Hewland Indycar-style transmission, and featuring single seater-style inboard suspension. Sadly, rule changes for 1991 rendered this interesting car obsolete before it had turned a wheel in anger, and its potential for success will remain forever unknown.

It was just one of several IMSA 308 projects of the period; Ferrari specialists Berlinetta Motorcars ran a highly evolved

Spice Ferrari, Mid-Ohio, 1990.
MARK WINDECKER

■ ON TRACK

glassfibre 308GTB in the IMSA GTS class in 1992, a turbocharged car fitted with a quattrovalvole motor, somewhat improbably running a standard transmission and clutch despite the hike in power over standard. The car gave a very respectable account of itself against the big budget teams, lap times being reportedly broadly comparable to the Rousch Ford Mustangs competing at the same time.

The 348 on Track

Substantially different to the 308/328 line it succeeded, there was much uncertainty as to the 348's race-track potential. In order to find out, during 1991, chassis number 82881 was allocated to famed Belgian racing equipe, Écurie Francorchamps, their brief to assess whether the new berlinetta was fit for competition use.

The 348tb/f

With composite doors and polycarbonate windows, and missing the controversial Testarossa-style door-strakes and tail-lights, the 348tb/f, as it would be known (the 'f' denoting its creator, Francorchamps), was quoted as weighing in at only 1,165kg (2,569lb), a very worthwhile saving over the production car. As well as being significantly lighter, grip was improved with some serious downforce, generated from a revised bumper arrangement featuring a low air dam and ground-effect underbody venturi, their presence indicated by deeper sill mouldings painted in black. Later in its life, the car received a substantial black tail spoiler.

ABOVE: **Pit stop for the Alba Ferrari, Sebring 1988.** MARK WINDECKER

RIGHT: **Ferrari 348tb/f, in the pits at the Spa Classic 2012. The picture on the pit wall shows the unique rear lamp treatment on this one-off car.** ESMPHOTO: ENRIQUE SAMPEDRO MOYANO

158

ON TRACK

Though the car saw some measure of track action, it was not formally entered in major events, most frequently appearing at Spa Ferrari race days, though development work on this car would pave the way for later Ferrari 348GT competition cars. The car was a visual treat, too – two of the more controversial elements of the 348's design were simplified, giving a remarkably prescient hint at the factory F355 restyle to come. Round rear lamps returned, and the air intakes shorn of strakes would lend the would-be racer pure, clean lines.

Michelotto Racers

When the time came for the 348 to be prepared for serious track action, it was Michelotto that would again be entrusted with the task, the firm's collaboration with Ferrari by this time longstanding and very fruitful. Indeed, Michelotto is proud to consider itself the closest Ferrari has to its own racing preparation subcontractor, having assisted the factory in construction of the 288GTO Evoluzione, the F40LM, and in maintenance and development of the open 333SP prototype racer. In 1993, Michelotto prepared eleven examples of the 348CSAI-GT, effectively a ready-to-race GT car eligible for such premier events as the Le Mans and Daytona 24 Hour races. Although most cars were purchased as track toys or investments, a few of these purposeful machines got the opportunity to do what they had been designed for. Michelotto 348s entered in the Italian Supercar GT Series by the Italian Jolly Club team were most successful, winning two titles outright in 1993 and 1994, and a further three category titles.

A further pair of Michelotto racers would be designated as 348GTC-LM models, devised to race at La Sarthe, and other major sports-car races in the course of 1994 by Ferrari clubs from Italy and Spain. At the 1994 Le Mans 24 Hour endurance race, the Ferrari 348GTC-LM entered by Team Repsol Ferrari Espana and piloted by Alfonso de Orleans, Tomas Saldana and Andres Vilarino finished a creditable eleventh overall, completing 277 laps to cross the line as the fourth GT2 car home behind three Porsche 911 GTs. The Ferrari Club Italia's entry managed just twenty-three laps before fuel pump issues halted its race. The eleventh-placed car also managed a decent sixth place at the Vallelunga 4 Hour in the same year, while the Italian car claimed a fifth place finish at the Spa 4 Hour race, and an excellent second at the Vallelunga 6 Hour event.

A further GT2 class 348 competed at 1994's race, though it, too, did not finish: the car entered by the British Simpson Engineering team retired with clutch problems after fifty-seven laps. It was not the car's first outing at the legendary circuit though, the team having brought the 348LM to La Sarthe for the 1993 race, though they did not make the start after suffering an accident during the warm-up. The team persevered with the car through to 1997, competing in various events in various GT classes, with limited success.

A 348 constructed by Michelotto also competed in the IMSA-run, 24 Hour of Daytona race in 1994. A private entry fielded by Florida-based Ferrari dealers Tom and Steve Shelton, the car finished in sixteenth place. Said to generate 360bhp from its Michelotto-modified motor, it had been made lighter by use of composite bumpers and doors, front compartment and engine lids, and a heavily stripped interior; as a result the

Ferrari 348GTC-LM, Le Mans 1994. JERRY LEWIS-EVANS

ON TRACK

car was fast, achieving over 273km/h (170mph) on the Daytona banking. The 348's finish was a most respectable achievement given the serious cost of competing at this level, the attempt arguably paving the way for more specialized Maranello machinery that would compete in later rounds – the breathtaking 333SP racer competed at the highest level in IMSA races through to the end of 1998.

The Ferrari Challenge 348 Race Series

'Win on Sunday, sell on Monday' is an often repeated justification for racing, though many a car firm has discovered that it can, and often does, ring true. On-track prowess can add kudos and credibility to a given marque or model, especially for those selling performance cars. As the 348 suffered the misfortune of arriving just as sports-car sales slumped, so the old mantra was dusted off, and the 348 went racing. Ferrari even devised a racing strategy that was guaranteed to see a 348 take the chequered flag every time: the Challenge 348 race series launched in 1993 was a one make championship, with races held in Italy and Europe for lightly modified 348s, often supporting prominent race events at prestigious racetracks including Magny-Cours, Monza and the Nürburgring. These races represented a strong image-building opportunity for the 348, one that was extended the following year to North America where a further series was convened.

The cars competing in the series were essentially standard road cars, either tb or ts models, with a kit of parts installed to make them ready for the track. A full roll-cage, red-trimmed OMP racing seats with racing harnesses and an alcantara steering wheel were fitted inside the car. A fire extinguisher was also part of the package, along with the race-track mandated battery isolating switch. Fog-lamp covers were first replaced by polycarbonate equivalents, then removed entirely to allow better brake cooling, the vacated voids in the bumper being repurposed as intakes. Stock wheels with slick tyres in the first year were subsequently replaced with larger 18in Speedline wheels, quite similar in style to those that would be fitted to the F355 road cars. The car's standard tail badge was substituted with a more prestigious '348 Challenge' script.

ABOVE: **Ferrari 348tb Challenge series racer.**
DANIEL F. HUGHES

LEFT: **Much modified 308GTB, SCCA National in Gratten, 1988.**
MARK WINDECKER

ON TRACK

RIGHT: **Ferrari 348 Challenge; scenes from race weekend, Mosport Park 1994.**
JASON VANDERHILL

BELOW: **Ferrari 348tb Challenge series racer.**
JONATHAN TREMLETT

An upgraded ECU was provided according to Ferrari press materials, which increased power output to 320bhp, with a higher 7,800rpm redline. Other small modifications were made to fuel pumps, as well as lower gearing for first and second gears, and the fitment of racing brake pads. Suspension was also made lower and stiffer. However, the cars were otherwise largely standard, the restrictive regulations prohibiting changes to most components, so while the ABS could be deactivated the system could not be removed. Similarly the air-compressor drive-belt could be removed, but the compressor had to remain in place. Minimum weight for the competing cars was set at 1,360kg (2,999lb).

The Challenge series certainly made a difference in Maranello's quest to shift cars in the depressed 1990s sports-car market. *Automotive News* ran an article in 1994 about the US-based Challenge series, in which Richard Koppelman, president of Miller Motorcars in Greenwich, explained the effectiveness of the series: 'I was sceptical at first, but we've sold a lot of cars because of racing,' and went on to say: 'A lot of customers who don't want to race, want to know they could. They say, "My God, I didn't know these cars were so good!" They take a pounding, and nothing breaks.'

Taking the promotional value of the Challenge series right back to the road, North American Ferrari customers were even offered the option to purchase a road-or-race variant brand new: this was a limited edition known as the 348 Factory Challenge, which was essentially a car to Challenge specification, though the track-equipment package remained a $14,000 option even on these cars, in acknowledgement that certain owners would choose not to compete in their cars.

The Challenge kit was fully reversible, and many Challenge cars have subsequently been returned to road duty, in some cases their owners totally unaware of their car's competition history.

Since its inauguration in 1993, heavily promoted and supported by Ferrari, the Challenge series has gone on to become a most popular crowd-pleasing race spectacle. The eligible

ON TRACK

model has changed several times since the 348 series began, 1995 being the last year in which 348s could compete – alongside the incoming F355 Challenge racer.

Club and Historic Racing

All variants of Ferrari 308 have been popular for many years in various series' club and historic racing around the world. In the UK, owners of 308s and 328s have enjoyed the excitement of on-track action in many race series, from the Maranello Challenge Race Series that began in 1986, to today's Pirelli Formula Ferrari Classic, in which examples of all models of the 308 and 328 ranges are enthusiastically campaigned on some of the world's finest circuits, including Silverstone and Spa-Francorchamps. Two- and four-seat Ferrari V8s are often entered in Historic Intermarque races, warmly received by spectators who always enjoy the sight and sound of a Ferrari being driven as its maker intended. Requiring comparatively little modification to be suitable for track activity, and with strong and simple mechanicals, the 308 and 328 can be surprisingly cost-effective race cars, their surefooted handling and decent power output offering plenty of driving excitement to go with the glamour of becoming a Ferrari racing driver.

The Ferrari 308GTB also remains a popular addition to any historic rally's entry list. While original Group 4 cars are now considered rather too valuable to race regularly, 308s still compete in these events; several specialist companies such as ASM

308GT4 and 328GTB, Thruxton 2013.

328s on track.
SIMON WATLING

LANCIA LC2 GROUP C

Following Ferrari's withdrawal from sports-car racing in the early 1980s, upholding Fiat Group honour in that arena would fall to Lancia. The firm's turbocharged LC1 racer represented a reasonably successful stop-gap until the Group C regulations came into force, rendering the powerful but thirsty 4-cylinder design uncompetitive. Lancia's legendary competitions manager Cesare Fiorio, the motivating force behind the Lancia Stratos rally car, determined that a different powerplant would be required for the LC1's successor: powerful certainly, but with the more moderate level of fuel consumption necessitated by incoming Group C rules. The most suitable engine available within the Fiat Group was Ferrari's 308 Quattrovalvole V8, augmented by a pair of KKK turbochargers. With a reduced capacity of 2593cc, opening the potential for re-use in American CART single-seater racing cars, this version of Ferrari's V8 received type number 268C. In qualifying tune the motor could develop up to 800bhp, though 560bhp at 8,500rpm was more suited to the races – a perfect compromise between speed and economy.

Dallara was conscripted to create a chassis to underpin the handsome bodywork. The shape of its window line, like that of the Lancia Stratos, was inspired by the opening of a full-face crash helmet. Immediately rapid, the LC2 took pole position for its first race, though it could not convert this promise into a race win. In what would be a familiar story through the 1983 season, reliability was lacking. There were other frustrating problems: Lancia had designed the car's suspension for Pirelli radial tyres, but the company pulled out of endurance racing entirely before the season's end, forcing a switch to Dunlop crossplies. The time taken to recalibrate the car to different rubber, along with reliability issues, meant that Lancia's promising car would win just one race that year, though the LC2 was clearly faster than Porsche's dominant 956. Nevertheless there was much anticipation ahead of the following season.

But the LC2 once again flattered to deceive, and once again there was just one win, despite Lancia's efforts. Part-way through 1984, engine capacity was increased to 3105cc, offering 680bhp at 1.3 bar in race trim. The new engine designation was 268 T/8. But sadly the car fared no better in

Ferrari power for Lancia's LC2 Group C contender.
YANN SEITE

Fabulous Lancia LC2 racer at speed.
YANN SEITE

1985: the refreshed LCs, with resculptured bodywork and revised suspension, were faster than the Porsche 962s as usual, gaining five poles during the season, but once again they were consistent in their failure to convert their pace into results. The LC2s would continue to race into 1986, but persistent reliability issues, along with a distracting gathering of momentum at Lancia's rally team, meant that the manufacturer lost interest in endurance. Privateers persevered with the car right through to 1991, but there were no further wins.

ON TRACK

Glassfibre 308GTB competing in the Pirelli Ferrari Formula Classic series, 2012.
SIMON WATLIN

Michelotto rally car at speed.
SIMON WATLING

Motorsport in Spain, and Finnish ex-rally driver Kari Mäkelä's firm Mäkelä Auto Tuning, can prepare eligible 308s to the appropriate Group 4 specification. Great fun to drive, and often highly competitive, the aged berlinetta remains an attractive proposition to drivers in historic events; in the Tour Auto Rally of 2013, ex-Grand Prix driver Olivier Panis drove a Ferrari 308GTB Group 4 to a very decent second in class.

On the Salt Flats

Texas-based Ferrari restorer and modifier, Bob Norwood, took a damaged Euro specification Ferrari 308GTB Quattrovalvole as the starting point for an audacious attempt in 1985 on the land speed record for 3.0L Class F/GT sports cars, at the time held by a Datsun 240Z. The car featured a highly modified motor, albeit one based on the standard block and crankshaft, with a compression ratio increased to 12:1 through the use of Mahle pistons, and with an aftermarket EFI set-up in place, and was estimated to develop around 300bhp in record-attempt trim. Wearing Volvo wheels fitted with tall and relatively slimline Ferrari 400 rear tyres, and a higher geared differential from an earlier 308GTBi, the relatively standard berlinetta raised the record to a creditable 273.5km/h (170mph) on Bonneville Salt Flats.

Norwood followed up with a successful campaign on further land speed records, using a General Motors small block-powered Ferrari 288GTO replica, built in collaboration with owner John Sullivan. The Norwood Autocraft 388, as the car was known, was based on a 308GTB, and achieved a further record at 320km/h (199mph).

Norwood returned to the salt flats in 1989 with a more extreme challenger: a 308-based NHRA drag racer fitted with a blown flat 12 engine based on a berlinetta Boxer motor. Undeniably rapid – capable of achieving 273km/h (170mph) in less than eight seconds on the drag strip – the 1400bhp car's attempts on the 359km/h (223mph) record for 5.0L and under blown modified sports cars was unfortunately thwarted by rain.

CHAPTER TWELVE

ACCESSORIES AND MODIFICATIONS

Far too beautiful and valuable to be a major target for most customizers, V8 Ferraris have by and large avoided the excessive overstyling inflicted upon many more mainstream cars, and it remains a rarity to see a significantly modified 308, 328 or 348. Indeed in many cases, cars that are modified are often returned to standard configuration by sympathetic owners, or at least to near-standard trim, particularly as older models begin to enjoy significant appreciation of their values. If a modified older car is sighted, it has usually received quite subtle alterations: a stainless-steel custom exhaust system, or replacement wheels, often genuine factory alloys from a newer model Ferrari, or perhaps amended suspension for a lowered stance and better on-track performance. Bodywork modification is relatively rare, and where apparent, again often follows the practice of fitting an alternative factory-standard part – or a near-copy of one – to the car in question: for example, the installation of a rear light panel equipped with a round-lamp – à la F355 – in place of the louvred 348 item.

But this restraint was not always the order of the day where V8 Ferraris were concerned. When they were new, a cottage industry sprang up to modify and personalize Ferrari's 308 range, efforts ranging from discreet wheel upgrades, to full-on, and often outlandishly 'over the top', colour-keyed and excessively spoilered treatments that were in vogue through the earlier part of the 1980s. Such endeavours were particularly popular in the USA, where plenty of new and near-new cars were individualized. Custom front grilles were often designed in part to save weight by discarding the heavyweight US

Modifications are often made to improve the car's track ability.

165

■ ACCESSORIES AND MODIFICATIONS

specification bumpers, and elaborate body-panel resculpturing, especially of wheel arches, allowed space for larger wheel rims and wider tyres.

Also popular were interior retrims in varying degrees of exuberance and flashiness, and chromed split-rim wheels – with centres often finished in gold – were perfectly in tune with the spirit of 1980s excess. Some owners chose to express their individuality by appending Zender-constructed bodykits, these elaborate items supposedly wind-tunnel tested. The same firm offered a four-outlet exhaust system to replace the single outlet fitted to early European cars.

Custom-Specialist Koenig

Also in tune with the times were the more outlandish offerings from famed custom-specialist Koenig. Former racer, Willy Koenig, founded this eponymous tuning house that offered various styling packages for 308 models, and subsequently for 328s and 348s too. Koenig's overblown panelwork often featured additional air inlets and ducts, wide wheel arches – extended by up to 28cm (11in) in some cases – extra deep front spoilers and a high Group C racer-style rear wing. The inevitable lattice-spoked wheels often completed Koenig's fully colour-keyed efforts to improve on Pininfarina's masterpiece.

But with Koenig it was not all show. The firm also offered 308 engine tuning packages to provide power outputs ranging from 270 to 400bhp, courtesy of upgraded engine internals, water intercooling and even water injection for lowering the temperature of turbocharged intake air. Koenig's particularly neat and professional turbocharger installation was well executed, though rather mischievously their twin cast intake plenums bore an italicized 'turbo' script that looked suspiciously like Porsche's 911 Turbo badge. Koenig's efforts included revised engine internals, water injection and twin Rayjay turbochargers applied to the 328, which resulted in a 450bhp monster, alleged to be capable of over 300km/h (190mph), courtesy of a lengthened final drive ratio. A similar makeover was offered for the 348 – again including the option of a powerful modified twin-turbocharged motor – though these appear to be rather rarer than Koenig's 1980s projects.

ABOVE: **Outrageous Koenig 308GTS.**
NILS SCHÖNIG-HILLERT

RIGHT: **Koenig 308GTS. Note the very 1980s BBS-style lattice wheels, a popular option of the period.**
MORTEN ALLERÖD

ACCESSORIES AND MODIFICATIONS

Janspeed's complex 308 Turbo conversion.
PHOTO © FERRARIBYNEILLBRUCE.CO.UK

Turbo Conversions

The turbo conversion was very much in vogue throughout the 1980s, with various offerings available from tuning houses such as Ameritech and BAE. For the UK market, Janspeed devised a turbo installation for the 308GTB on behalf of Maranello Concessionaires, using a Garrett T04 turbocharger to provide modest intake air compression – a light pressure turbo installation – before blowing it through the standard carburettors. It was a highly complex installation involving custom manifolds and intercooling using Freon gas from the air-conditioning system, though the system did allow the standard compression ratio to be retained, the motor thus unaltered from factory specification. Janspeed even fitted an extra oil pump to ensure adequate lubrication of the turbocharger. Despite the Renault-sourced Turbo script badge – seemingly the only dubious aspect of this professional installation – this interesting project appears to have come to nothing.

288GTO Replicas

With the appearance of the breathtaking 288GTO, many 308 owners looked to modifiers to emulate that car's detailing on their own cars. Adopting the gaping grille containing paired driving lamps thus became quite a well established 308 modification, though some owners were motivated to go further still. US-based modifier Jim Carpenter, among others, redeveloped a number of 308s, potentially as many as fifty cars being converted into 288GTO near-replicas, in terms of appearance at least. A handful of cars were given more extreme modifications, whereby they were mechanically altered as well as aesthetically. Some featured longitudinal engine conversions based around a twin-turbocharged 308-based motor using the Getrag G50 gearbox from contemporary Porsche 911s, while others received longitudinal 348 powerpacks. A few GTO replicas contain potent F355 motors.

The 288GTO look, a popular aesthetic for Ferrari 308 modifiers worldwide.

■ ACCESSORIES AND MODIFICATIONS

LEFT: **Sharp-looking modernized 308GT4 on track.** DANIEL F. HUGHES

BELOW: **Ferrari 348tb nicely modified with F355-style wheels and 360 Challenge Stradale racing stripes. Note the Serie Speciale-like front bumper splitter.** SIMON WATLING

Other companies, including Fischer Motorsports, also US-based, continue to offer similar services, and for those interested in DIY makeovers, GTO-style body panels are readily available from Ferrari modifiers and specialists such as 288GTO Heaven in California, or Berlinetta Motorcars based on Long Island.

Nowadays, however, the trend towards 308 and 328 modification is in reverse, and originality is becoming more fashionable now these cars have achieved classic status, though occasionally a modified car will be spotted at club events. The 308GT4, with its rather edgy design scheme, responds surprisingly well to sympathetic updating: de-chromed cars wearing large modern wheel rims can appear handsome and contemporary, if less understated than Bertone originally intended.

Updating the 348

More recently, modifiers' attention has turned somewhat inevitably to the newer cars, and the 348 is more frequently considered for such ministrations. Certain 348 owners have chosen aesthetic updates inspired by the later F355 to modernize the styling of their car's bodywork. The F355's simpler, shapely lower-door intake panel is a straightforward replacement for the rather 1980s-style louvred vent, and the rear lamp panel featuring traditional round rear lamps can also be substituted to further erase stratification from the older car. Indeed, even the front wings and both bumpers can be adapted to fit, though adding the pronounced rear lip would require involved bodywork surgery at the rear wings. Given how close relative values are these days, for the 348 owner who wants all the later car's looks, it would probably be less costly simply to trade in their car for an F355.

Painted targa panels are consistently popular on GTS models; this is a straightforward if rather time-consuming modification, requiring the removal of the panel's texturing before paint can be applied – though the colour-coded roof when in place does give their cars a more harmonious and coupé-like appearance.

Exhaust-system upgrades from such specialists as Larini Quicksilver and Superformance are perennially popular, and a stainless-steel sports system can be a cost-effective upgrade

ACCESSORIES AND MODIFICATIONS

given its potential longevity in comparison to a mild steel equivalent. Interestingly, such systems are rarely terminated in any style other than the Ferrari standard four-exit arrangement, reinforcing the fact that this cue is now an integral part of everyone's view of how a Ferrari should look.

Performance Upgrades

Although most Ferrari owners tend to be satisfied with the level of performance with which their cars left the factory, a few succumb to the temptation of releasing a little more power. Whether for road use or track, there are numerous upgrades available from a myriad of performance tuning specialists, with several such companies dedicated entirely to all things Ferrari. While most owners only go so far as to install high-lift camshafts and high-compression pistons, some more committed upgraders take a more extreme approach to increasing their cars' performance.

The 308 motor can be extensively – and expensively – improved; for example, US specialist Carobu embarked on a project to install larger pistons and an F355 crankshaft into a 308 motor for an increase in displacement to 3.5 litres: this after discovering that the evolutionary nature of Ferrari's development of their V8 meant that crankshafts for successors from 328 to 360 could be adapted to fit. With special forged pistons, larger exhaust valves and altered camshafts, Carobu's conversion yielded over 300bhp from its motor, despite retaining Marelli ignition and K-Jetronic fuel injection.

But such conversions are by no means the only way to provide the older V8 cars with more punch. Several 308s have received F355 powerpack transplants, enthusiasts often dubbing such cars '358s'. Even more audacious was a car offered for sale at the 'Historics' auction at Brooklands in 2013. Reputed to have been converted in the late 1980s at Nigel Mansell's Ferrari Dealership, Emblem Sports Cars in Dorset, this 1985 GTS Quattrovalvole was converted to incorporate a V12 motor from a 400i, incredibly still fitted in the original transverse location.

Where a Ferrari is concerned, engine swaps or even upgrades quite rapidly consume vast sums of cash. Given that Maranello's motors, even in standard trim, already deliver

ABOVE: **Track-focused exhaust arrangement on this 308GT4. Note the all-fibreglass bumper, which the model was sometimes fitted with when it left the factory.**

RIGHT: **Many modified Ferraris draw inspiration from competition models, emulating cars such as this stillborn Huffaker 308 IMSA racer.**
SIMON DAVISON

ACCESSORIES AND MODIFICATIONS

decent levels of power if maintained in good condition, popular modifications to these cars relate to handling and stopping, rather than improving 'go'. Many upgrades available today for the earlier V8 Ferrari models are competition-inspired. Specialists around the world have developed brake upgrades, firmer suspension bushes, lowered suspension kits and all manner of other tweaks to make these older cars more nimble on road or track. QV London, for example, offers road-holding kits, six-pot brake calliper kits, and engine upgrades ranging from mild, for street use, to wild, for the committed track driver only.

Although the standard suspension arrangements are very much capable of offering satisfaction in spirited driving, when replacement time arrives many owners choose to upgrade to even more sporty arrangements. Rather than installing OEM Koni replacement shocks, owners particularly interested in readying their cars for occasional track use might opt for an adjustable alternative. Some choose custom shocks and springs from any number of fast road or racing component specialists, such as Koni Racing or perhaps German Wilbers items – though one cost-effective solution popular in the US is to use aluminium-bodied adjustable shock absorbers produced by QA1 Motorsport, often partnered with Eibach after-market springs. Not only does such an arrangement allow the driver to personalize their car's settings, these efficient components also offer a saving of around 12kg (26lb) over the standard equipment items; furthermore the smaller outer diameter of these after-market springs leaves a little more space for wider tyres.

Equally popular and relatively easy to install are the so-called polybushes. Harder suspension bushing divides opinion, some drivers feeling that the reduction in compliance offers greater accuracy of suspension response, while others feel they have a detrimental impact on the car's ride and have a tendency to skittish handling.

Other Modifications

In the same way that Koenig makeovers fell from fashion after their heyday through the 1980s, so other styles of modification come and go. Modular Gotti wheels were quite popular through the early 1980s, their somewhat showy style arguably rather better suited to such cars as De Tomaso's brutish Pantera. Similarly BBS lattice wheels were all the rage for a time; one *Road and Track* magazine 308 road test by race driver Bob Bondurant featured a car so equipped. More recently, as befits the growing trend toward originality in earlier V8 Ferrari models, more popular wheel upgrades tend to emulate the style of factory standard wheels; Speedline, for example, offers a wheel design that was markedly similar to that fitted to the rare 348 Competizione, and reproductions of the original style penta-star wheels are also now offered in various finishes and sizes by such specialists as UK-based Superformance. This respected specialist can also supply faster-acting steering racks to replace the rather ponderous originals.

In period, perhaps the most desirable accessory was the luxurious Schedoni fitted luggage set, designed to maximize the limited stowage space available in these compact cars. Today a raft of accessories are marketed to the classic Ferrari owner wishing to personalize their car, from elaborately embroidered floor mats to racy steering wheels, and even Ferrari-branded child seats so the younger enthusiast can travel in safety and style.

A pair of modified 308s. Note the significantly enlarged and extended wheel arches on the GTS model in the foreground.
DANIEL F. HUGHES

ACCESSORIES AND MODIFICATIONS

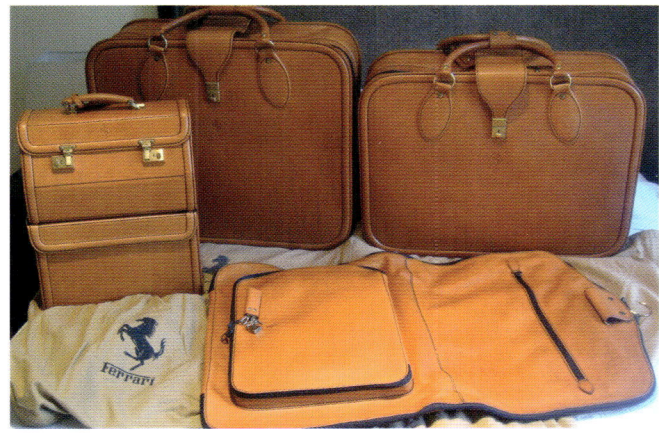

Optional fitted 348 luggage set, beautifully made by Schedoni.
EDUARDO CARO CABRERO

Agostini's Half-Scale 308

If being a passenger offers insufficient excitement for the junior Ferrari enthusiast, they could always pester their parents to track down one of Agostini's delightful half-scale 308s. This Ravenna-based specialist manufacturer of high quality sportscar replicas for children devised more than one design of glassfibre-bodied 308GTS replica, in each case based on a tubular platform chassis. A simpler variant with a rear-mounted two-stroke driving the rear wheels was relatively straightforward in design, without suspension and with a single drum brake on the rear axle. Nevertheless, with charming lines and smart detailing, which included 'penta-star' wheel covers and four round rear lamps, the Agostini 308GTS would surely be a great hit with any junior Ferrari enthusiast. Later versions received a different bodyshell, more accurate in its proportions and with detailing that closely emulated the real car. Leather-trimmed seats, functioning pop-up headlamps, louvred rear quarter windows, opening doors and even genuine alloy wheels made this car a very sophisticated – and very expensive – childhood treat.

Test-Mules

Perhaps the fastest and most extremely modified V8 Ferraris are those used by the factory in testing the engine for the Enzo supercar. Based on 348s that were crudely elongated and widened, and with an engine delivering over 600bhp, the test-mule bore little relation to the production car on which it was based.

Maybe more exotic still was the Ferrari 308 used as a test-mule by upstart supercar manufacturer, Cizeta. Ex-Lamborghini employee Claudio Zampolli's Cizeta V16T featured an audacious bespoke powerplant containing no fewer than 16 cylinders in V formation, in a single block casting a metre wide. Incredibly, this outlandish 560bhp unit would be mid-mounted into the car, not longitudinally, but transversely. A central

Delightful De Agostini child-size 308.
DENIS CARON

■ ACCESSORIES AND MODIFICATIONS

One of the 348-based Enzo Ferrari test prototypes.
STIJN BRAES

power take-off mated to a gearbox that extended back to make an unusual T-shaped powerpack explained the V16T model designation. The bodywork was designed by legend Marcello Gandini, but before it was ready, Zampolli is said to have installed his incredible engine into a heavily modified 308GTS, and reportedly covered 96,500km (60,000 miles) in it.

Perhaps this was the car that gave rise to a long-standing and persistent myth that the Cizeta's engine was in effect a pair of 308 units joined together in a single block casting. However, this was not the case, and the unit was an original design, though it worked in effect as a pair of flat-plane V8 units sharing a block casting – a fact underlined by the use of two sets of Bosch K-Jetronic injection, and two crankshafts either side of the central power take-off that fed drive to the gearbox. The motor's internal dimensions confirm that little of the V16's componentry could never have been Ferrari-sourced – although its car's 86 × 64.5mm bore and stroke measurements are intriguingly shared with those of the Lamborghini Urraco P300.

Perhaps not to all tastes, these chromed alloy wheels certainly make a statement.

ACCESSORIES AND MODIFICATIONS

THE ZAGATO 348TB ELABORAZIONE

Zagato 348 Elaborazione.
HENRIK SOMMER

Although many customizers have tried their hand at improving the lines of the various Pininfarina V8 models, few boasted anywhere near the level of credibility of Milanese coachbuilder Zagato. True, the firm was a shadow of its illustrious former self, the market for bespoke bodywork having gradually evaporated in the face of onerous – and in many markets, mandatory – crash-test legislation. Zagato was throughout the 1930s the carrozzeria of choice for racers, thanks to their prowess in lightweight body construction. With a breathtaking catalogue of highly individual designs, some beautiful, others wilfully quirky, Zagato can claim such gems as Aston Martin's beautiful and effective DB4GT Zagato and the stunning Lancia Integrale-based Hyena coupé.

Expectation must have run high as their take on the Ferrari 348tb was revealed. An enthusiast had commissioned Zagato to make certain amendments to the appearance of their own car, the intention being to change the aesthetic character of the car from Pininfarina's elegant if rather conservative line, to something more individualistic. Their mission was certainly accomplished, though the outcome was by no means to every Ferrari fan's taste. Zagato designer Marco Pedracini, the man behind the firm's desirable and convincing Hyena, was constrained by the need to leave the car sufficiently unaltered from factory guise to avoid prohibitively costly crash-testing, whilst giving the impression of a fully bespoke design.

The result was the Zagato 348tb Elaborazione. Zagato was sufficiently confident in their handiwork to propose a production run of twenty-two further cars. Each would wear the same series of forty amendments to Pininfarina's original work, including of course the trademark double-bubble roof panel, modified luggage lid inset with twinned NACA ducts in place of the standard slot-like vent feeding air into the cabin, and a much larger variation of the NACA duct replacing the louvred vents across the original car's doors. A simple if rather aftermarket appearing front bumper contained deeply recessed round indicators and driving lamps between an oval dummy grille recalling that of the 250GTO, though this feature disappeared from later cars. At the rear, similarly bland round tail-lights were installed, six in total.

Continuing the referencing of 250GTO, reprofiled rear wings carried three vents rather like those Pininfarina had cut into the rear wings of the 288GTO. One interesting detail was the large plexi-glass panel inset into the revised engine cover, perhaps the inspiration for similar viewing panes that would appear on later V8 Ferrari designs. Blocky wing mirrors, set closer to the bodywork, and a pop-up rear spoiler completed the exterior transformation.

The interior was barely altered, aside from some tweaks to the standard seat designs and a retrim of some interior panels such as the lower dashboard in suede. A rear-view camera relayed pictures to a gimmicky, dash-mounted 3in monitor.

While the design was certainly individual, in detailing it was rather uneven and lacked cohesion, leaving many enthusiasts cold. Some details were prescient: that display-case engine lid for one, and the unadorned door-mounted air intakes that hinted at those that would feature on the 348's successor, the F355. But with a price tag around two and a half times that of a standard car, and given its typically Zagato divisive aesthetic, the production run was curtailed after around ten cars were produced, initial estimates for demand having proved rather optimistic.

Seldom spotted today, the Elaborazione makeover has not aged gracefully, though the design works better in certain colour schemes, particularly silver. When they infrequently come up for sale, the price tag reflects their rarity and perhaps the esteem in which coachbuilder Zagato is held in enthusiast circles, despite the inconsistency of their works.

ACCESSORIES AND MODIFICATIONS

The Wazuma V8 F Quad Bike

Even more outlandish than any customization project or factory test-mule, French modifier Lazareth offers arguably the most ridiculous, and ridiculously named, Ferrari 308-based vehicle. The Wazuma V8 F quad bike has at its heart a Ferrari 308 V8 motor, coupled with a BMW M3 SMG sequential manual gearbox. Very smartly presented, and featuring many high-specification components including Brembo brakes and Momo alloy wheel rims, the 650kg (1,433lb) quad bike nevertheless struggles to justify is ambitious 200,000 Euro price tag – though it does look tremendous fun!

In Miniature

There cannot be many model or toy car makers that have not modelled at least one Ferrari. Indeed, the cars from Maranello must be among the most popular – and strong-selling – subjects for them all, and given its instant familiarity to almost everyone who thinks of the marque, surely the Ferrari 308 is among the most modelled of them all. Models arrived pretty quickly following the launch of the 308 series, and the tally continues to rise, most of the major manufacturers having produced at least one version or other over the years.

Corgi offered the 308GTS variant in not one, but two scales – a larger 1:36 model featuring opening engine cover and pop-up headlamps, cleverly activated by a small lever under the front bumper, and a simpler, smaller 1:55 scale variant. Matchbox presented a very similar 1:55 car, albeit in the GTB Berlinetta body style, with nicer proportions, and wheels more accurately sized for the car than those of Corgi's effort. Maisto also produced a 1:55 Ferrari 308GTB, and Majorette a similarly sized 328GTB. Since the early 1980s there have been numerous die-cast 308 and 328 models produced in the popular-for-play 1:55 and slightly smaller 1:64 scale favoured by Hot Wheels.

Such models often originated, and indeed continue to be produced in China; they come in a wide range of colours, often adorned with garish decals. The quality of proportion and detailing is wildly variable, some quite acceptable, others barely recognizable as a Ferrari 308 at all, and often with inaccurate features when compared to the real cars. Many GTB models have been produced featuring the louvred sail-panels of a GTS, and it is common to see a 328 model painted in the two-tone 'Boxer' colour scheme that was an option only on its predecessor.

Not surprisingly, the 308 was well represented in the Italian model market, both Polisitil and Bburago modelling several variants in a range of scales and with different levels of detail. Polistil offered both GTB and GT4 models, the latter a rather crude – and now quite rare – 1:43 model with opening doors, often presented in silver or green paintwork. There were numerous 1:24 Polistil 308s, both GTB and GTS, including a representation of the famous GTS featured in the TV series, *Magnum PI*, a marketing tie-up that Corgi also exploited with an edition of their GTS model. Bburago also made several versions of the GTB, including models of the Michelotto rally cars in scales 1:43, 1:32 and 1:24. Just like the real cars, these models enjoyed an extended production run, Bburago even producing an Italia 1990-liveried 308GTB in celebration of Italy's opportunity to host the FIFA football world cup.

But it was not all rehashing of older models at Bburago: the 348 was also modelled by the Italian maker, in the large 1:18 scale as well as the usual 1:24 and 1:43 scales, produced in several colours and variations, including certain of the Challenge 348 series race cars. Bburago's 348 was even available in easy-build kit format.

Maisto produced 308s and 348s in 1:24 and 1:36 scales, the latter appearing in their so-called 'Supercar collection' series, presented both in Maisto-branded packaging, and in bright

OPPOSITE PAGE:
A fun collection of Ferrari models.

THIS PAGE:
Corgi's popular 1:36 scale 308GTS, Maisto 348 and Majorette 328 to the sides. Behind is a Century model in less common 1:38 scale.

ACCESSORIES AND MODIFICATIONS

LEFT: **Polistil 308GT4 in front of three Bburago model racers, all 1:43 scale.**

BELOW LEFT: **Bburago 348tb Challenge, 1:18 scale.**

BELOW RIGHT: **Excellent 1:24 scale 308 models. Note the representation of Elvis Presley's own car with nicely depicted wire-spoked Borrani wheels.**

HOT WHEELS IMAGES COURTESY MATTEL, INC. © 2013

yellow boxes through Shell as giveaways in a fuel promotion. In more recent years, Maisto also produced a highly popular and nicely detailed large 1:18 scale 348ts, as did Mira, whose range also featured a Spider of similar size. For collectors preferring this larger scale, Anson came up with a version of their own, and so did resin model specialist, Starter, their model also offered in ready-built form. Kyosho's offerings in 1:18 were very popular, and both the 328GTB and 328GTS were represented in their range – featuring the domed-centre wheels of late model cars – alongside their smart representations of the 308GTB and 308GTS. Kyosho was even bigger in smaller models, their 1:64 range featuring the 308GTB Quattrovalvole, 328GTB and 348 Spider, as well as a cute 308GT4 model, presented in tiny 1:100 scale.

US toy giant, Mattel, through their brand Hot Wheels, have achieved the status of official manufacturer of Ferrari models. The Hot Wheels brand – introduced in 1968 – has a long history of producing die-cast toy Ferrari models for play, similar to Lesney's contemporary Matchbox series. Efforts included a 308GTB fitted with outsized wheels, and a rather crude 348tb. Certainly great fun, these slightly cartoonish models have

BARBIE AND THE FERRARI

With the exception of her rather tacky beach-buggy and a monstrous six-wheeled motorhome, Barbie's vehicle choices have generally been quite good. Just three years after the doll made its debut at the International Toy Fair in New York, March 1959, American toy manufacturer Mattel Inc. accessorized Barbie with her first car. An Austin Healey roadster, recognizable despite being unconventionally proportioned (rather like the doll, in fact), was presented in oh-so-sixties shades including pastel orange, light purple and lavender. The British sports car was followed by a Mercedes 300 roadster and a wacky T-bucket hot-rod.

Many more followed: several versions of Corvette's Stingray, usually pink of course, a VW Golf cabriolet, a Jeep or two, and more recently a Porsche 911 and Boxster, several Ford Mustangs, a Jaguar XJS (finished in pink sparkles metal-flake style, no less!), and a cute Fiat 500. Mattel Inc. also provided the world's most famous doll with perhaps the most famous car of all. One of the first toys to benefit from a marketing strategy based extensively on television advertising, Barbie's Ferrari 328GTS was introduced to consumers via a 1987 TV commercial that exclaimed that 'Barbie's Ferrari is a red-hot dream'.

Mattel 328GTS.
JOANNE EGGLETON

The 328GTS produced by Mattel Inc. is really rather accomplished. It is very large at almost 56cm (22in) long, proportioned with reasonable accuracy and generally well detailed, though the chrome-effect wheels are a little ostentatious. The interior is quite basic, seat facings and console detailing being nothing more than stickers, and the seatbelts are ridiculously distended to fit the doll's controversial physique – but overall the large plastic car is really rather presentable.

All Ferraris are always well represented in collectors' 1:43 scale. Clockwise from top left: Herpa 348ts, Vitesse 308GTB, Bang 348 Spider, Vitesse 308GTB Michelotto Group IV.

■ ACCESSORIES AND MODIFICATIONS

Delightfully irreverent Micro Machines 308 monster trucks, tiny at less than 3cm (1in) in length.

been augmented in recent years by more serious attempts to represent Ferrari's cars with a degree of accuracy.

Mattel's offerings nowadays compete with the most respected model makers, and the US company compiled a very comprehensive range that covered all the models featured in this book. Both 308GTB and 308GTS are offered in the excellent 1:18 scale Élite range, including the obligatory *Magnum P.I.* version. There is a superbly detailed 308GT4 model that can be had in several colours, including an interesting black version fitted with Borrani wire-wheels, depicting the very car owned by Elvis Presley. The 328GTB has been represented by Hot Wheels in smaller 1:43 scale in the so-called Élite Series, and various versions of the 348 series are also present in the range, in the smaller and larger scales.

The two-seat Ferraris of the 1980s and 1990s are no less well represented in the collector's favourite 1:43 scale, where most of the bigger names have one or more in their ranges most of the time. Vitesse modelled the 308 extensively, with roadgoing US and European specifications depicted, as well as many race and rally variants, complete with Michelotto-style extended wheel arches and accurate sponsors' liveries. Ixo modelled a 348ts, and Bang offered a series of 348 models most attractively presented in various Challenge race-car liveries, alongside a beautifully detailed 348 Spider. Herpa also offered a delicate 348 model, moulded in plastic rather than die-cast, an excellent representation with crisp, precise detailing; removable targa panel, opening doors, engine and luggage bay lids, and even reflective mirror inserts. The same manufacturer also offered both tb and ts models in smaller 1:87 scale. Best managed an interesting representation of the 208GTB, with generally smart detailing but let down slightly by crooked wing mirrors and a rather crudely reproduced flank-mounted NACA duct. Italian specialist ABC also took part in the smaller car action with a 208GT4 represented in the same 1:43 scale.

Famous resin model kit specialist Provence Moulage featured a 348ts in their illustrious range, and lesser known resin model specialist AIMS replicated both 328GTB and GTS equipped with full Koenig body styling. French manufacturer Record MRF marketed a 308 with chromed wheels, though the model was otherwise faithful to the standard specification. Starter produced resin kits for 348ts and also the 308GTB in Michelotto rally-car form; this popular variant was also selected for production by Italian company Arena. As would be expected, well known maker BBR also offered a selection of 308, 328 and 348 models in their line-up.

For those who prefer their scale Ferraris to be mobile, 308GTB rally slot-car racers are available from Scalextric. Model-making enthusiasts are also well provided for, and plastic kit giant, Revell, has produced several 308 kits in their most popular 1:24 scale, including yet another *Magnum P.I* branded tie-in. A 348 in the same scale is also offered by Fujimi. Hasegawa have modelled in the 1:24 scale, too, the 348tb and ts, and 328GTB and GTS figuring in their line-up. Century also made a plastic kit of the 328GTB, though they chose the relatively unusual 1:38 scale for their version.

CHAPTER THIRTEEN

BUYING AND OWNERSHIP

Surely most sports-car enthusiasts have at one time or another dreamed of a prancing horse in their garage? For anyone determined to make that dream reality, a little time spent in research can save a potentially expensive mistake. Ferrari ownership always comes at a cost, and the purchase of those more affordable models is no barrier to horrendous repair or restoration expenses. Indeed, purchase and running costs do vary significantly between the models. Given their innate desirability, it may come as a surprise to learn that the cars covered by this book represent some of the most cost-effective ways into the rarefied world of Ferrari ownership. Apart from that period in the late 1980s when frenzied buying by individual investors, hedge funds and pensions companies made the purchase of Maranello's more accessible machinery temporarily unattainable, the first series of Ferrari's V8 family – glassfibre berlinettas aside – are even now readily accessible, at prices broadly equivalent to a decent, if not spectacular, sports coupé from premium car makers Audi, BMW or Mercedes.

What To Buy?

So the would-be purchaser, having decided to fulfil the Ferrari ownership dream, will inevitably ask, which of these models is best? Well, unfortunately there is no single answer to that question.

The 308GT4

If a modicum of practicality is required – a decent boot and the requirement to seat more than a single passenger – there

Ferrari 328GTS.
PAWEŁ SKRZYPCZYŃSKI

■ BUYING AND OWNERSHIP

LEFT: **Ferrari 308GT4.**

BELOW: **Ferrari 308GTB Quattrovalvole.**
JOHN DICKENS

is only one choice. Having sat in the doldrums for such a long time, hampered by its divisive and once unloved 1970s silhouette, the 308GT4, while still a relatively affordable Ferrari, is currently enjoying something of a renaissance. However, reappraisal of this period piece means their affordable price tag may not persist much longer: in their October 2013 edition, *Classic Cars* magazine gave fulsome praise to the two-plus-two, pitting Ferrari's one-time underdog against contemporaries including the more powerful DeTomaso Pantera: 'The 308 delivers the kind of complete, coherent experience you'd expect of an Italian racing car in a compact, exciting package. It doesn't just win this test, it deserves re-evaluation alongside some of the genre's greats.'

Its razor-edged styling, once controversial, enjoys a wonderful retro-futuristic appeal now that all things 1970s have returned to the height of fashion. It evokes its period wonderfully; in a nostalgically reminiscent screen role in the 2013 Lauda vs Hunt movie *Rush*, a 308GT4 was used to underline the dashing and sophisticated lifestyle that Grand Prix drivers of the period enjoyed.

308 and 328 GTB/GTS

For the would-be owner attracted to the two-seat 308, the selection process is trickier. Certainly the 308 and then the 328 that evolved from it, are all but universally considered to be just as beautiful and desirable today as they were at launch.

BUYING AND OWNERSHIP

A key giveaway of glassfibre construction: the seam marking the transition from steel A pillar to glassfibre roof panel.
MIKE MOORE

But there are marked differences between the various evolutions of Ferrari's popular two-seaters, and each brings a distinct flavour to the ownership experience. If money is no object, price alone tells us that the original glassfibre berlinetta – especially one built for the European market – is the one to have. Marginally more resistant to the plague of corrosion, and particularly well suited to track work due to its lighter weight and

Belying the reputation for fragility, most Ferraris are more than capable of withstanding the rigours of track use.

dry-sump oil system, there is much to commend the first of the series. However, the premium in purchase price is out of proportion to the car's superiority over later models; the weight-saving is less significant than factory figures suggest, and while the body is certainly immune from rust, that is not to say that the same applies to the car's space-frame chassis. Nevertheless they remain the collector's choice, their perceived superiority coupled with rarity separating them from the steel-bodied cars.

Glassfibre Cars

Those determined to buy a glassfibre car must have their wits about them. Not only should the car be most carefully inspected for condition, there is also the risk of buying a car that was originally steel-bodied. Thanks to Ferrari's rather haphazard chassis-numbering policies of the time, certain unscrupulous individuals have occasionally been tempted to repanel a chassis from that transitional period in which the factory produced cars bodied in both glassfibre and steel, thereafter attempting to pass it off as a genuine and more valuable glassfibre car.

Much risk can be avoided simply by choosing a steel-bodied car in the first place; early steel cars benefit from the same beautiful lines and are similar in their mechanical purity, while offering a most worthwhile reduction in financial outlay over their plastic predecessor for a virtually indistinguishable ownership experience. Even better if you are a convertible motoring enthusiast, and can live with the sacrifice of that dry-sump oiling system; the choice of model here also includes the seductive GTS, a brilliant blend of driver involvement and open air fun.

Injected Cars

Derided due to a relative shortfall in performance, only now are the injected cars coming to be seen for the great ownership prospect they are. Admittedly they are a little down on power, and the intake noise associated with the quadruple carburettors is sadly missed by some, but for an owner intent on enjoying the driving experience without worrying about absolutes in performance – especially in open-topped GTS form – the easier-starting and simpler to maintain Bosch-injected cars are a relative bargain. The Quattrovalvole and 328 models are by far the most usable, blending the lack of mechanical drama – courtesy of Bosch's dependable injection system –

BUYING AND OWNERSHIP

with levels of performance on a par with, or exceeding the earliest, rawest 308s, a most appealing combination.

Even though the oldest 308s are approaching forty years of age, they are eminently usable, and more important readily maintainable. They are simple and robust, with a straightforward frame, easy to repair bodywork and a relatively understressed engine. There is little complexity in any of the car's systems, and as a result ownership of any 308 is unlikely to be more troublesome a prospect than the seemingly more rational purchase of a Porsche 911 of equivalent vintage. Nevertheless, even the most modern 328 still has a wonderful period feel – a real classic Ferrari experience for a most rewarding ownership experience.

Perhaps surprising to new owners will be the low mileage that most cars have covered in their cosseted lifetimes. Around 2,400km (1,500 miles) seems to be the typical annual usage level, and a car that has covered perhaps 5,000km (3,000 miles) per year is well used indeed! On the other hand, such low mileages do give rise to mechanical maladies: like any machine, regular use is important to ensure continued operation of all systems.

The 348

For those seeking a more modern Ferrari, the choice is simple. Unjustly considered by many so-called experts to offer a poorer driving experience than its predecessors, and hampered by the suspicion that Fiat's management was rather too heavily involved for the car truly to embody the spirit of Ferrari, the 348 is also now ripe for reappraisal. Derided unfairly by many commentators as unworthy of the marque, the 348 has been blamed in part for Ferrari's sales shortfall of the early 1990s, a situation that led in 1993 to Ferrari making a trading loss of £3.4m, unthinkable given the desirability and profitability that the firm enjoys today. Even company supremo Luca di Montezemolo has gone on record on more than one occasion deriding the 348. Comments at the 458 launch, to the effect that the 348 he bought himself shortly before assuming control of the company was simply not good enough to wear the badge, were repeated as recently as December 2011; in an interview with *The Daily Telegraph* newspaper he was quoted as saying: 'No, the 348 is not a Ferrari for me.' But this is a rather harsh assessment, particularly given that the successful F355 delivered on his watch was heavily based on what he felt was an underperforming model.

The 348 is by no means the poor car that some would have you believe. Perhaps its build quality was short of its elevated new price tag, or handling and performance were less than exceptional in their contemporary market place, but nowadays the 348 makes a thoroughly convincing classic car choice. Better to drive than many commentators contend – indeed, many who perpetuate the myth have never even driven one – and while by no means devastatingly rapid in the way a current performance car is, a 348 is fast enough to be exciting. And although even the youngest car is now twenty years old,

Note the body-coloured roof panel on this 348, making for a neat, coupé-like appearance.

the 348 offers a much more modern experience altogether than its immediate V8 predecessors. It brings a further step forward in reliability and everyday usability, though at the cost – literally – of typically expensive more modern Ferrari maintenance bills. While running a 348 is not the wallet-draining experience of more recent models, its mechanical complexity is significantly greater than that of the early 308s.

Maintenance and Repair

Despite the twenty-year gap between the production of the first 308 and last example of the 348, there is a good deal of similarity between the models, and prospective owners considering either might expect to see a good deal of similarity in their ownership experiences. All the models covered in this book are endowed with a strong and dependable engine, provided that maintenance has been diligent and comprehensive. Much of the strength springs from the inherent mechanical simplicity of Ferrari's V8 design, and if the engine is in good condition, reliability is readily achievable.

Having said that, even the youngest 348 is an old car, and from time to time components inevitably must fail. All would-be owners of any older Ferrari must accept this possibility, entering into any purchase with their eyes open, and having researched the potential issues they might face.

So just what might they expect?

Rust and Corrosion

Well, it is common knowledge that old Italian cars rust. Nowadays chassis and bodywork corrosion protection applied at Ferrari's factory is state of the art, and today's models are on a par with the best cars made anywhere in terms of rust resistance. But it was not always that way: the earliest 308s were constructed before Ferrari had adopted zinc treatments for panelwork, and each tubular steel chassis wore just a coat of matt black paint to protect it against the elements. Through the course of the 1980s the situation improved dramatically, and the 328 and 348 are much hardier cars, more resilient than their earliest 308 ancestors.

Most 308s have been subject to bodywork refurbishment in their long lives, some cars having been repaired and repainted more than half a dozen times over the years! In many cases, cars no longer wear their original colour scheme, enduringly popular if rather clichéd, so-called 'resale red' frequently applied

Ferraris always attract attention.

Everything Ferrari related – even the charmingly amateur vintage handbooks – are collectable, and often expensive!

as bodywork refurbishment takes place. Many 308GT4s, in particular, suffered neglect as the model endured a period of under-appreciation through the 1980s and 1990s, their perceived un-Ferrari-like styling rather depressing their prices.

While these low prices certainly democratized Ferrari ownership, some cars fell into the hands of owners without the means to maintain them in the best of condition, and perhaps

183

twenty years ago it was entirely possible to find rather sad and rusty GT4s languishing in classified advertisements, the cost of restoration outweighing their post-repair value. But happily this situation has largely been addressed as the market has reappraised Bertone's cars, and most these days are found to be in generally reasonable condition.

Nevertheless, the onset of bodywork (and occasionally chassis) corrosion will be a continual fact of life for the 308 owner, and for those of succeeding cars, too. While the 328 and 348 models, like the last 308s, were better protected, that does not mean they are entirely impermeable, and they, too, will fall victim to rust. When assessing a potential purchase chassis tubes should be inspected carefully: the replacement of rusty sections of chassis outrigger is a very occasional but essential repair necessary to maintain safe and roadworthy condition. As much of the chassis should be viewed as possible, to check that potentially expensive repairs are not urgently required, and also that the chassis has not been subjected to botched or inappropriate amendment. For example, a 308 or 328 poorly converted to right-hand drive can be spotted easily, betrayed by incorrect location of the central tube – it is offset away from the driver in a correct car – which was rarely addressed, leaving the gearlever an uncomfortable stretch away on the wrong side of the car.

On all cars – even glassfibre 308s – side sills are prone to rust. Front wings on 308 and 328 models corrode, usually the area directly behind the wheel arch and in the area adjoining the sill. Door bottoms are also susceptible, though this can be minimized by ensuring door drain holes are kept clear from blockage. Headlamp wells retain water and will inevitably begin to rot, as do the lower corners of the rear wings just ahead of each wheel arch.

The bodyside groove featured on the 308 and 328 can also be an area in which deterioration takes place. Similar outbreaks can be found on 348 rear wings, the area of the body-side groove representing a join between two distinct panels making up the whole. And all models – 348 Spider aside – suffer at the intersection between roof buttress and rear wing: this join can flex over time, promoting the onset of rust around the area.

Even the cleanest car will develop some localized corrosion from time to time. Use of a Carcoon dehumidifier or similar can extend the periods between repaints – but every car, unless maintained in climate-controlled museum conditions, will eventually require tidying.

Maintaining the Engine

In mechanical terms, there is nothing to be afraid of. All cars are quite robust, and the V8 is a dependable motor, relatively understressed and untemperamental in all its capacities and guises. Unlike many Italian designs, Ferrari's powerplant does not seem to consume much oil, though naturally the level must be checked regularly and diligently to ward off potential mechanical disasters – not least because the unit can develop small oil leaks around the various seals. The diligent owner will address such issues quickly, the more laid-back will monitor oil level, recognizing a positive in the situation, in that the leaking oil will coat and protect the car's chassis tubes!

The rubber belts that drive the camshafts in Ferrari's V8s are one of the few areas of weakness. While it is undeniable that routine replacement is vital to guard against the possibility of significant engine damage caused by belt failure, annual or biennial changes are overkill for all but the very few cars that rack up large mileages. Specialists usually suggest a three-year interval for their replacement, and always with high-quality belts. Though not a difficult mechanical task on 308 and 328 models – part of the wheel-arch liner is removable to facilitate access – care is required to ensure the job is done accurately. The same job is a much bigger challenge on the 348 models, requiring the engine and transmission to be removed from the car to allow room to work on the very inaccessible single cambelt.

Idler bearings that tension the belts are often changed at the same time as the belts themselves, and Ferrari specialist

Corrosion is an inescapable fact of life for the classic Ferrari owner.

Club events are well organized and well attended.

Fibreglass 308GTB. Note the convenient tubular hinges within the buttresses, allowing quick and easy removal of the engine lid.

Hill Engineering offers a cost-effective upgraded component that is favoured by most Ferrari-literate engineers.

Given their advancing years, engine ancillaries do have a tendency to fail, though replacement water pumps, starter motors and alternators are easy to source and install. Minor niggles can occur within the engine bay: the heat shields over a 308's exhaust manifolding can rot, and manifold nuts can become rusted solid, though the Ferrari V8 is no worse than any other forty-year-old design in that respect.

There is a good deal of collective knowledge about the quirks and foibles associated with each model, and tapping into this wealth by joining an owners' club or participating on model-specific internet forums, for example, will allow a novice owner to sidestep inconveniences, irritations and frustrations. For example, the 308 and 328 engine cover is rather unfortunately designed in that it dumps any rainwater pooled on its surface on to the engine when opened. The 'savvy' owner will never open the engine cover while it is wet, to avoid the

BUYING AND OWNERSHIP

possibility of water ingress into the engine's deep plug wells. Also a long, sleeve-style cap affair on the HT lead, no doubt designed to keep water out, can actually help retain moisture and can cause a seemingly mysterious misfire. Owners laying up a car for an extended period often leave the leads disconnected to allow any moisture within to evaporate.

Like any other classic car, a sporadically used Ferrari will get through mild-steel exhausts quickly. Unless the intention is to compete in concours events, where originality is essential, it makes sense to view a high quality stainless replacement system as a welcome fitment. Indeed, many an owner feels that such a system – constructed perhaps by a renowned specialist such as Larini or QuickSilver – significantly improves the already tuneful engine note emitted by their car, though some do consider the more intense acoustics of certain systems rather overbearing and intrusive.

Maintaining the Transmission

An engine in less than optimal health will often betray itself by emitting blue smoke, a good indicator that the motor has been treated unsympathetically and over-extended before the oil has had a chance to warm. The transmission is no less sensitive to heavy-handed use before being warmed through, a process that might typically take as far as 16km (10 miles) of restrained travel. A Ferrari gearbox full of cold oil can be difficult to shift into second gear, emphasizing the risk of damaging that gear's already hard-worked synchromesh. Indeed the whole car has a rather unyielding character all round until fully warmed, at which point the driving experience will smooth significantly.

Most owners become used to the routine of shifting from first straight to third until the temperatures rise, treating the box with kid gloves until thoroughly warm. This is eminently sensible, since the transmission is second only to the engine itself as the assembly most likely to lead to a swingeing repair bill in failure. It can be a false economy to purchase a car that has a recalcitrant gearbox, even if it is a little cheaper, though a lucky buyer may discover that the symptoms are simply those of maladjustment of the shift mechanism.

Maintaining the Running Gear

The rest of the running gear on all models is quite hard-wearing, though naturally braking consumables – discs and pads – don't last forever and require periodic replacement. Similarly, suspension components such as shock absorbers, springs and bushes, as on any old car, have to be replaced from time to time. Many owners take the opportunity to upgrade the suspension components, installing more track-focused springs and shock absorber units, or perhaps polybushes – the resulting firmer feel can make great sense on track, though the reduction in ride compliance will not be to all tastes. Whenever the suspension is taken apart, it makes sense to refurbish, paint or powder-coat components such as the wishbones before reassembly, especially for the 348, which featured pressed-steel wishbones; it is by no means unknown for these items to suffer the ravages of corrosion, so very careful inspection and subsequent protection is recommended.

Maintaining Bodywork Trim

Glass and bodywork trim can be difficult and expensive to source. Replacing bumpers can be a very costly business on earlier cars, though glassfibre reproduction GT4 bumpers – just like those fitted to certain cars at the factory – can sometimes be tracked down as a more cost-effective alternative. There are lots of specialists making front and rear valances, usually in glassfibre, but occasionally also in carbonfibre. Indeed, just about all 308 panelwork, from front wings to engine lids, can be sourced new or second-hand via the specialist network, and with a little diligent research alternatives constructed in

Ferrari 328 interior detail.
MANGOPULP2008 @FLICKR

By no means a Ferrari's typical work environment: 348ts in the snow.
JONATHAN TREMLETT

glassfibre or even lighter composite materials can be found. Lamp clusters can be hard to find for certain models – rear lamps for the GT4 and 348 models in particular are expensive replacements – though the round units featured on other models are plentiful and comparatively cheap.

Maintaining the Cabin

An enthusiast unfamiliar with older Ferraris may be surprised by an inspection of the cabin of an early car, not in terms of aesthetic appeal, which is consistent in its period charm – all these cars have attractive cabins – but in terms of fit and finish. There is a noticeable unevenness in construction, interior panels often adjoining with an approximate fit, and carpets sometimes stopping a little short in the space they were designed to cover. It may come as a surprise also that their handmade interiors betray evidence of their means of construction – carpets taped to the floors, and haphazardly bunched wiring can often be seen peeking out from under the dashboard.

It must be borne in mind that all cars have seen decades of use, and a little sympathetic tidying can work wonders, though many enthusiasts prefer the lived-in look, especially in a car that gets used regularly and hard. Connolly leather trim does seem to wear quite quickly, and 'reconnolization' or re-trimming becomes the only resolution to excessively worn seat facings – a substantial expense, particularly for cars featuring the option of an extensively leather-trimmed cabin. Indeed, not only in the cabin, but across the entire car, there is little that is beyond an amateur's grasp in terms of dismantling and refitting components, though a few jobs are certainly best left to the experienced specialist. Window-winding mechanisms on the 308, for example, are complicated and convoluted cable-operated affairs, to which the side-glass is clamped by nut and bolt. Solidified grease within the motor slows window elevation to a frustrating crawl – a long-winded rectification chore, after which care is required to avoid breaking the window by over-tightening the bolts holding the side-glass in place.

Convenient roof panel storage area behind the seats.

■ BUYING AND OWNERSHIP

The 348, by contrast, is a much more refined car than its ancestors, though many in period decried its interior design as unfitting of a Ferrari. The use of certain Fiat Group switchgear, and certainly the plastic squares that pepper the central console, lack the delicacy and charm of a 308's chromed slider controls, but they are harmonious and modern, and in keeping with the usability and efficiency of the newer model. Sound and heat insulation took a significant step forwards in 348 cabin design, not least because the coolant pipes running beneath the cabins of earlier cars were no longer required given its side-mounted water radiators.

Support

Although there are a few foolish owners for whom horrendous maintenance bills are treated almost gleefully as a badge of ownership honour, the costs associated with driving a Ferrari V8 need not be exorbitant in every case. Many maintenance activities can be achieved by the competent and confident owner with reference to the freely available factory workshop manuals. The early 308GT4, 308GTB and GTS models share a charmingly amateur effort, typewritten and with hand-drawn diagrams and schematics that nevertheless facilitate many a job that would otherwise need entrusting to a professional.

Also there is a wealth of information readily available via the internet: Ferrari has made available all relevant handbooks in ubiquitous PDF format. Forums and chat-rooms have accumulated reams of enormously useful technical guides for the amateur spanner-man, and some community-spirited owners have even published 'how-to' videos covering more common repairs. For those less technically minded it is a good idea to establish a rapport with one of the many excellent specialist companies; having that wealth of expertise to lend a hand can make all the difference should the dream purchase prove troublesome.

Parts support from the Ferrari factory is very good; Maranello Parts Centre, based in Surrey, England, now has exclusive global distribution rights for all factory parts for any pre-1995 Ferrari road car. And a huge network of specialists has built up over time, respected companies providing reproduction or replacement parts often at lower prices than those of Ferrari dealers, easing the expense of maintenance, repair and restoration. From the smallest components to the largest, all the cars covered in this book are extremely well supported and almost any part can be sourced with a little homework, from the hard-to-find tiny rubber grommets that seal 308 exterior door handles to an entire replacement chassis and body unit. Some previously unobtainable parts have been returned to production; reproduction 308 alloy road wheels,

308GT4 belonging to event organizer, Richard Davis, in exalted company at the grid, Brands Hatch 2013, attending the laudable Not Forgotten Association, offering injured soldiers high speed rides around this famous race track.
RICHARD DAVIS

BUYING AND OWNERSHIP

Many owners choose to exercise their cars on track, and newcomers are most welcome to join the friendly and colourful grids of various Ferrari race series.

for example, now permit the upgrading of 14in or metric wheels to the more contemporary 16in size offered optionally when cars were new. For the purist, the Ferrari factory offers a service to authenticate classic models, this exacting inspection usually necessitates a series of corrections before the car can be certified original by the company that created it.

Enjoy Your Ferrari!

But ownership is not only about restoration, maintenance and repair: there is also the opportunity to socialize with fellow Ferrari enthusiasts, and drive the car! Ferrari clubs for like-minded Maranello fans convene events at which owners can enjoy their cars, either on the road, at shows or on track. Owners' Club regional groups can also be quite active, arranging get-togethers on a smaller, though no less ambitious scale, from local meetings and driving excursions, to Ferrari holidays centred around a visit to Maranello. Classic Ferrari ownership need not be a selfish pleasure: several events have sprung up at which enthusiasts may purchase rides to enjoy an on-track Ferrari experience whilst raising funds for various charities. Amongst them is 'The Supercar Event' held at the Dunsfold Top Gear track each June, with The Children's Trust the beneficiary. Brands Hatch also hosts an event that offers injured soldiers from the Not Forgotten Association high speed rides round the famous Kent circuit.

So, whether your preference is for touring or racing, and whether or not you choose to embrace the social opportunities associated with ownership, any one of the Ferrari V8 cars covered in this book would make a great entry into Ferrari ownership. They are deeply satisfying to drive, the earliest cars blending a raw, visceral character in performance with a surprising degree of practicality, later cars a perfectly judged blend of easily accessible performance with a surprising degree of refinement. As the 308 evolved and evolved again into a friendlier, even more easy-to-use package, it retained much of its essential character and aesthetic appeal. Performance, never a poor suit for any of the cars covered in this book, improved as the cars were developed and refined, and the later 348 remains a seriously fast car, requiring commitment and alertness to drive quickly – though of course it cannot compare with the astounding performance of the latest of Maranello's output.

Driving a Ferrari is always an event. Many bystanders will react positively on seeing one of the older cars, and an owner will soon become used to strangers taking photographs of their pride and joy, or becoming engaged in car-park chats with interested observers. But it should not be the reaction from others that motivates a would-be owner to possess any

BUYING AND OWNERSHIP

one of these cars: each is a superb driving machine that can turn any drive into an exhilarating adventure. Tenacious road-holding and sublime engine sounds inspire confidence and egg on the lucky driver. And like so many of the cars from Maranello, they are gorgeous to look at, like rolling sculpture, their breathtaking lines penned by artists of the highest order, and still attractive today despite the passing of decades since they were first sketched.

Any car that combines such beauty and style with this dynamic driving experience deserves a place among the best classic sports cars. And each deserves the name almost denied the cars by Enzo Ferrari himself in favour of a name given in commemoration of his beloved son Dino. The once rather unloved Dino 308GT4, along with the rest of the 308 range, and the 328 and 348 models, are all without doubt or question those most magical of machines. They are thoroughbred Ferraris.

Every drive an adventure!
PAWEŁ SKRZYPCZYŃSKI

Ferrari 308GTB Quattrovalvole on a pilgrimage to Maranello.
JOHN DICKENS

INDEX

Agostini 308 171
Alba 157
Alfa Corse 10
Alfa Romeo 9
Alfa Romeo Carabo 25
Andretti, Mario 143
Andruet, Claude 153
ANFIA 57
Artz Gunther 68
Auto Avio Costruzione 815 10
Auto Becker 68
Autocar magazine 41, 48, 99, 112, 138
Automotive News 161
Autosport magazine 48, 51
Autoweek 140

Banbury Auto Services 141
BAS 141
Bellei, Angelo 21–22
Bertone
Carrozzeria 20, 21, 25, 29
Rainbow 42
Spider 68
Bondurant, Bob 47, 170
Bosch K-Jetronic 64, 80, 145
Bosch Motronic 118, 126
Boxer paintwork 34
Brambilla, Vittorio 157
Brundle, Martin 143

Car and Driver magazine 48, 74, 129

Car magazine 30, 31, 50, 74, 114, 139
Carobu 169
CCL 140
Centro Stile 57
Chiti, Carlo 21
Cisitalia 202 64
Cizeta V16T 171–172
Classic and Sportscar magazine 57
Classic Cars magazine 180
CMN 9
Colombo 13
Cooper 13
Corporate Concepts Limited 140
Cosworth 89

Daltrey, Roger 143
DeTomaso 147, 180
Dino badging 30, 48
DP Designs 68
Dry-sump lubrication system 49, 117
Ecurie Francorchamp 151, 158
Emissions equipment 32

Fast Lane magazine 114
Ferrari
Alfredo (Dino) 9, 14
Brochures 143
Challenge Series 114–115, 133, 160

Enzo 9
Numbering 12
Scuderia 9
308, 328, 348 Road Models
308GT4 25–42
308GTB 43–58
308GTS 58–62
308GTBi 63–73
308GTSi 63–73
308 Spiders 68, 100
208GT4 76–78
208GTB 78–79
208GTB Turbo 79–82
GTB Turbo 82–87
GTS Turbo 82–87
308GTBi Quattrovalvole 88–96
308GTSi Quattrovalvole 88–96
328GTB 96–107
328GTS 96–107
348tb 109–125
348ts 109–125
348GTB 126–128
348GTS 126–128
348 Spider 129–131
348 Serie Speciale 131–133
348GT Competizione 133
308, 328, 348 Competition Models
308GT4/LM 151
308GT/M 152
308GTB Group IV 152–154

308 GTB Group B 154–156
Carma FF 156–157
348tb/f 158–159
348GTC-LM 159
348LM 159
Other road models
125 11
166 11
206GT 17
246GT 18
250GT SWB 12
288GTO 57, 84–85
365P 17
458 Italia 65, 138–139
California 139
Daytona 57
Dino Berlinetta Speciale 16, 57
F40 57
F355 113, 127, 136
F430 138
Mondial 3.2 98
Mondial 8 63, 74
Mondial Quattrovalvole 97
Mondial T 119, 120, 134
Testarossa 98, 109
Other competition models,
126 C2 79
248SP 21
250GT LM 14, 57, 138
250GT Tour de France 60
288GTO Evoluzione 159
312T 120

191

INDEX

360 Modena 137–138
365 California Spider 44
365GT4 Berlinetta Boxer 18
Grand Prix Dino 15
IMSA Ferraris 157–158
Tipo 158 21
Fiat
  Dino 19–20
  X1/9 42
Fioravanti, Leonardo 57, 111
Fiori, Cesare 163
Firing order 23
Forghieri, Mauro 79, 120
Frere, Paul 31, 47
Fuel injection benefits 69

Gandini, Marcello 16, 20, 25, 147
Giugiaro, Giorgetto 147
Glassfibre bodywork 46–47, 52–53, 181
Group B 50, 84,

Honda NSX 148
Huffaker 157

IHI Turbochargers 83, 147
IVA tax 75

Janspeed 167

KKK Turbochargers 79–80, 163
Koenig 82, 166
Kugelfischer 69, 152

Lamborghini
  Countach 29
  Jalpa 147
  Miura 14, 129
  Silhouette 146–147
  Urraco 30, 34, 78, 146, 172

Lancia
  8.32 108
  Aurelia B20 64
  Florida II 64
  Lancia-Ferrari D50 14,21, 108
  LC2 163
  Stratos 20, 34, 154
Lauda, Niki 45, 85, 143
Lorenz and Rankl 68
Lotus
  Cars 46, 50
  Esprit Turbo 88, 100, 146
Lucas fuel injection 69

Magnum P.I. 144, 175, 178
Mansell, Nigel 100, 143
Maranello 11
Marelli electronic ignition 67
Maserati
  Biturbo 89
  Merak 78, 147
  Shamal 147–148
Mera 140
Michelotto 152, 159
Monocoque construction 109, 115
Montezemolo, Luca di 131, 182
Motor magazine 62, 92, 100, 143
Motorsport magazine 36
Movies
  Against All Odds 96
  Dirty Rotten Scoundrels 97
  National Lampoon's Vacation 145
  To Live and Die in LA 96
Multi-valve engine technology 89–91
MVS Venturi 148
Nader, Ralph 56

NART 151
Newman, Paul 143
Norwood, Bob 164

Octane magazine 57
Ownership 183–190

Petit, Michele 153
Pininfarina
  Carrozzeria 64, 139
  Millechiodi 70, 84
  Modulo 44
Pinto, Lele 153
Pironi, Didier 79,80
Platini, Michel 74
Pontiac Fiero 140, 144
Porsche
  911 series 145
  911 Targa 58
  911SC 62, 88
  911 Cabriolet 129
  911 Carrera 100
Powell Cozy 143
Pozzi, CH 154
Presley, Elvis 143, 178
Production figures 149

Renault Alpine GTA 148
Road and Track magazine 31, 45, 47, 51, 62, 67, 71, 129, 149
Rocchi, Franco 22
Rodeo Drive 130

Scaglietti 33, 115
Scale models 175–178
Selleck, Tom, 144
Sharknose 15
Specification tables
  308GT4 41
  308GTB 58
  308GTS 62
  308GTBi 73

308GTSi 73
208GT4 77
208GTB 79
208GTB Turbo 83
GTB Turbo 86
GTS Turbo 86
308GTBi Quattrovalvole 96
308GTSi Quattrovalvole 96
328GTB 107
328GTS 107
348tb 125
348ts 125
348GTB 128
348GTS 128
348 Spider 131
Spiders 68, 100
Stinger 140
Surtees, John 21

Test Mules 171–172
Teves Mk2 ABS braking system 104, 121
Tiga 157
Tognana, Tonino 154
Trasversale gearbox 119–120
TRX road wheels 70, 71, 94
Turbo conversions 167

US speedometer 37, 73

Villeneuve, Gilles 79,143
Vitaloni 42

Worswick, Tony 155

Zagato 348tb Elaborazione 173
Zender 166
Zimmermann, Ekkehard 68
Zincrox 93